VOICE OVER MAN

PETER DICKSON

Published by

© September 2020

VOICE
OVER
MAN

PETER DICKSON

Published by

PROVOX

MIC 1

REVIEWS FOR VOICEOVER MAN

A WONDERFUL READ, PETER'S WIT AND
HEART ARE AS BIG AS HIS VOICE

· DERMOT O'LEARY ·
TV PRESENTER

GREAT YARNS AND EXCELLENT STORIES FROM
THE MAN WITH THE VOICE OF GRAVEL AND GRAVY

· VIC REEVES ·
COMEDIAN & SURREALIST PAINTER

THE WEIRD THING IS, I READ THE ENTIRE BOOK IN HIS VOICE

· JAMES MAY ·
MOTORING JOURNALIST & TV PRESENTER

THERE ARE JUST TWO GREAT VOICES FOR ME – TOM WAITS
AND THIS GUY. PETER HAS A LEGENDARY VOICE. COME ON,
YOU'VE TRIED TO SOUND LIKE HIM. YOU HAVE. DON'T DENY
IT! WELL, THIS IS THE STORY OF HOW HE DID IT... FOR REAL

· RICHARD HAMMOND ·
MOTORING JOURNALIST & TV PRESENTER

NOT ONLY ONE OF THE MOST RECOGNISED AND
LOVED VOICES IN THE ENGLISH–SPEAKING WORLD,
BUT A SUBLIME WIT, A THOUGHTFUL CONTEMPLATOR
OF HUMANITY AND, ABOVE ALL, A TOTAL GENT

· ALEXANDER ARMSTRONG ·
TV PRESENTER, COMEDIAN & SINGER

THEY SAY A GOOD WRITER NEEDS TO FIND HIS VOICE.
PETER DICKSON CERTAINLY HAS NO TROUBLE FINDING HIS!

· DANNY WALLACE ·
AUTHOR

PETER DICKSON? OUR SURVEY SAYS... THE BEST IN THE BUSINESS!

· LES DENNIS ·
ACTOR & TV PRESENTER

A UNIQUE VOICE HAS WRITTEN A UNIQUE STORY
PACKED WITH HUMOUR AND HEART

· GYLES BRANDRETH ·
AUTHOR, PUBLIC SPEAKER & BROADCASTER

THE SHOWBIZ STORIES PETER HAS SHARED WITH ME OVER
A GLASS OF CHATEAUNEUF–DU–PAPE ARE EXTRAORDINARY.
UNFORTUNATELY, NONE OF THEM ARE HERE FOR LEGAL
REASONS BUT IT'S STILL A THRILLING READ!

· JOE LYCETT ·
COMEDIAN & BROADCASTER

AT LAST, THE MASTER OF VOICEOVERS PUTS HIS MEMORY
WHERE HIS MOUTH IS AND THE RESULT IS A HILARIOUS READ!

· RORY BREMNER ·
COMEDIAN & SATIRIST

HE'S THE MOST INSPIRATIONAL PERFORMER I KNOW

· PATRICK KIELTY ·
COMEDIAN

A WONDERFUL READ FROM A TRUE GENIUS
OF THE VOICEOVER WORLD

· THE EARL OF ERNE ·
CROM CASTLE. NORTHERN IRELAND

PETER IS ONE OF THE BEST VOICES IN ENTERTAINMENT,
HE'S NOW ONE OF THE BEST WRITERS. A TOP READ
FROM A FELLOW NORTHERN IRISHMAN

· EAMMON HOLMES ·
JOURNALIST & TV PRESENTER

ON THE PRICE IS RIGHT, THE BIGGEST LAUGHS WERE IN
MY DRESSING ROOM, AS HE RECOUNTED MANY OF THE
TALES YOU ARE ABOUT TO READ IN THIS BOOK

· JOE PASQUALE ·
COMEDIAN & TV PRESENTER

IF ANYONE HAS THE X FACTOR, IT'S PETER DICKSON.
'VOICEOVER MAN' IS NOT ONLY A WONDERFUL READ BUT IS
YOUR PRIVATE INVITATION SIT BACK AND SHARE A VIRTUAL
PINT WITH ONE OF THE WORLD'S GREAT STORY TELLERS

· JOE CIPRIANO ·
VOICE OF 'AMERICA'S GOT TALENT'

PETER'S STORY PRESENTS AN AMAZING INSIGHT INTO SO MANY
CONNECTED BUT DIFFERENT WORLDS — SIMPLY FASCINATING

· MARCUS BENTLEY ·
VOICE OF 'BIG BROTHER'

PROOF THAT BEING A VOICEOVER REQUIRES REAL TALENT.
PETER'S YEARS OF EXPERIENCE AS THE MOST RECOGNISABLE
VOICE IN BRITAIN, COME WITH SOME OF THE BEST
SHOWBIZ STORIES I'VE EVER HEARD!

· SCOTT MILLS ·
BBC RADIO 1 DJ

A CLEVERLY WRITTEN, WRY OBSERVATION THAT GENTLY LIFTS THE LID ON THE WORLD OF VOICEOVER, WHERE FOLK SHOUT ABOUT EVERYTHING AND NOTHING, IN DARK CLAUSTROPHOBIC ROOMS, WITHOUT ANY AIR-CONDITIONING. IT'S QUITE BRILLIANT!

· ALAN DEDICOAT ·
VOICE OF THE UK LOTTERY, 'STRICTLY COME DANCING'

I ONCE ASKED PETER DICKSON WHAT IT'S LIKE TO BE THE VOICE OF GOD. HE REPLIED AS THE VOICE OF GOD. THIS IS A FABULOUS INSIGHT INTO NOT ONLY PETER'S CAREER BUT ALSO A WORLD WHERE THE VOICE IS THE STAR

· MAXINE MAWHINNEY ·
BROADCASTER & JOURNALIST

PETER DICKSON IS THE GOLD STANDARD OF BRITISH VOICE ACTORS, A LEGEND OF THE INDUSTRY. HIS BOOK OFFERS THE ACCUMULATED INSIGHTS, GOOD HUMOUR, AND BRILLIANT WIT THAT HAVE PROPELLED PETER TO THE TOP OF THE BUSINESS

· J.MICHAEL COLLINS ·
VOICE ACTOR & VOICEOVER COACH

'VOICEOVER MAN' IS A GLORIOUS ROMP THROUGH THE WORLD OF VOICEOVER FROM ONE OF THE BEST. IT'S A LAUGH A MINUTE. I LOVED IT

· LEWIS MACLEOD ·
VOICE ACTOR & SATIRIST

PETER TAKES YOU BEHIND THE SCENES OF ICONIC SHOWS AND STUDIOS TO MEET EQUALLY ICONIC CHARACTERS. IT'S A RIB-TICKLING PAGE-TURNER BY ONE OF THE FUNNIEST, MOST GENEROUS AND ACCOMPLISHED MEN IN VOICEOVER. JUST BUY IT, FOR PETE'S SAKE!

· PAUL STRIKWERDA ·
VOICE ACTOR & AUTHOR

VOICEOVER MAN

The extraordinary story of a professional voice actor

Peter Dickson

Provox Publishing

First Published in Great Britain by Provox
Copyright © Peter Dickson 2020

Cover & interior design — *Connor Dickson – dcksn.com*
Typesetting & image design — *Predra6 Markovic*
Publishing manager — *Sam Pearce – SWATT Books Ltd*

A CIP catalogue record for this title is available from The British Library

Trade Paperback ISBN — 978-1-8381597-0-2
Trade Hardback ISBN — 978-1-8381597-1-9
eBook ISBN — 978-1-8381597-2-6

This book is dedicated to my wife Barbara, without whom not a single scintilla of this would have been possible and with apologies to my sons Connor and Ryan, who had to endure their father talking to himself, for years on end.

CONTENTS

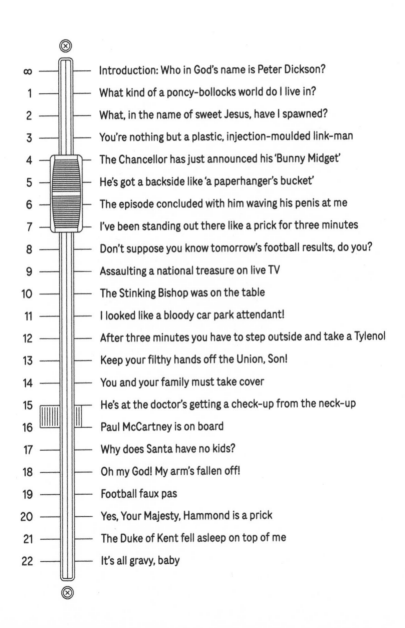

INTRODUCTION

⊢————————————⊣

U nlike, *Kleenex* or *Clorox*, Peter Dickson is not a household name so while he may not be very effective at or indeed remotely interested in cleaning under your rim or around your U-Bend, his voice is heard in every household in the United Kingdom and beyond; every hour of every day, of every year. From selflessly lending his vocal talent to: radio and TV commercials, video games, documentaries, radio programmes, interactive telephone systems, corporate audio and video productions, game shows and family-friendly TV broadcast entertainment behemoths, he is quite literally all over the ruddy place!

'*Voiceover Man*', is a fascinating insight into the life of one of the world's most prolific voiceover artists. From barking like a dog on pet food commercials and shouting about pizzas and furniture, to his universally recognised work on the world's biggest talent shows – '*The X Factor*' and '*Britain's Got Talent*', to yelling "Come On Down!" as Bruce Forsyth's sidekick on '*The Price Is Right*' on TV in the UK and putting the spring, into Jerry Springer – to the whacky world of '*Mr Mad*', '*Voiceover Man*', and other characters on BBC Radio 1, he recounts the highs and lows of his deeply unconventional career.

This is a book which will appeal to anyone who has ever wondered what actually goes on behind the scenes on TV and radio. It's a frank and very personal account of a life lived in the media. Not in the full glare of the spotlight on the shiny floor in front of the camera, but in the dark spaces the public never gets to see; the voice booths, control rooms, offices, dressing rooms and dimly lit corridors backstage. If you liked; *'The Larry Sanders Show'*, *'W1A'*, *'Curb Your Enthusiasm'* and *'Toast of London'* – you'll love this!

Peter Dickson has been a professional voiceover artist for forty-five years. He has worked in all sectors of the entertainment industry and alongside many of its biggest stars. He is the voice of over 200 TV series – many of them multi-award winning, the promo voice for over 60 TV channels, he has acted on over 30 of the world's top-selling AAA game titles and has voiced over 30,000 TV and radio commercials. He founded and co-owns *'GravyfortheBrain.com'* – the world's biggest online voiceover training school and mentoring resource for established and aspiring voice talent, founded and co-owns *'ReAttendance.com'* – the global virtual events platform, he has an honours degree in psychology, is a member of *'British Actors Equity'* and the *'Chartered Institute of Journalists'* and is understandably, ever so slightly knackered.

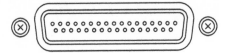

PREFACE

├──────────────────┤

I have wanted to write the story of my professional life for quite some time but kept putting it off. I was just too busy. Friends and colleagues, however, urged me to write it and so over a period of about four years, I completed what you now hold in your hand. An account of the amazing career I've enjoyed, in the incredibly niche world of voice acting.

It's a love story in many respects, because it's a career I adore and one that has afforded me so many wonderful opportunities, many of which are chronicled in these pages.

Writing it has also given me the chance to recognise the help and encouragement I have received on my journey, from those who went before me and I hope it will act as a guiding light for those who come behind.

So, this book is dedicated to the one million professional voice actors in the world today, who sit in small airless rooms day in, day out, reading aloud the carefully crafted words of others. Their names and faces you will never recognise or indeed know – but their familiar, comforting voices will continue to inform, entertain and move you throughout your whole life.

PREFACE

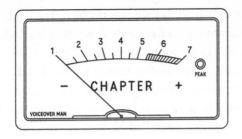

WHAT KIND OF A
PONCY-BOLLOCKS WORLD
DO I LIVE IN?

⊢——————————⊣

S he reached for the small, red talkback switch on the producer's desk.

"Could you be a little more, you know... dog-like?"

The request was spoken with barely disguised contempt.

"Yes, I could," I replied. "If you could be a bit more like a fucking human being. I mean – Jesus wept – how difficult can this be?"

I didn't actually say that of course, but I distinctly heard myself utter the words inside my head as I nonchalantly gazed around the three-metre square airtight, padded cell, in which I was currently imprisoned.

This session's going nowhere fast, I thought.

Steve, the sound engineer, visibly winced and looked at the floor. The producer from the agency looked on impassively while the two creative copywriters just looked embarrassed. Fresh out of media college, and an internship at some Shoreditch boutique brand agency, she was no more than twenty-five years old – platinum blonde hair, blue eyes and a Gen Z attitude to match. She was glaring at me through the quadruple glazing of the soundproof window, separating the sound booth in which I was sitting, from the control room. This was the twenty-third take in a voiceover session that should have finished almost twenty minutes ago and would have, had she approved take three, which was the best. The talkback microphone clicked off and slammed into the slowly developing headache caused by the increasing airlessness in the room. Through the glass, I could see her mouthing, like a fish out of water. Unfortunately for her, I had learnt to lip read. All those years spent in acoustically isolated voice booths had seen to that. The obscenities were pouring from her now. Steve, the sound engineer, with his back to her but facing me rolled his eyes to the ceiling. He'd seen and heard it all before, probably many times already that week, and then slowly dropped his chin resignedly onto his chest. She paused, mid-rant to sip her barista-style – skinny-white-latte-flat-almond-mocha-ristretto and gave her equally complicated keto-centric lunch order to the pre-pubescent studio runner, who was all of sixteen years old and greener behind the ears than an avocado salad – which coincidentally, is what she just ordered for lunch. Although she could just as easily have been calling him a fucking idiot, it was hard to tell as her articulation wasn't that great.

"Take twenty-four!" It was Steve on the talkback.

I cleared my throat, took a deep breath, and barked like a bitch on heat for the twenty-fourth time that morning.

Dog food commercials never were my favourite. Campaigns for breakfast cereal or soap powder were the main prize for every voiceover artist worth his or her salt. The tasty residuals that rolled in via one's agent, less the obligatory 16.5% plus VAT, more than made up for the ritual humiliation and there was plenty of it – humiliation, that is.

Ah yes! I forgot to explain. No, I'll do better than that – let me introduce myself. My name is Peter. Peter Dickson: Voice artist, voice talent, voiceover, voice-over, voiceover-talent, voice actor, voiceover actor, voiceover artist, voiceover man, MVO1, announcer guy, voice of God, gob on a stick, vocal prostitute. Call me what you will, all the above apply. I answer to Peter, Pete, Dicko, Dickers, Dickson, Pedro, Rachael Adedeji and occasionally "Hey you asshole!" Contrary to my loud public persona, I am somewhat reserved but always optimistic, especially when there is the possibility of a grand to be trousered before lunch. My glass is always half full, often quite literally. Don't ask me to tell you who I really am, I lost myself years ago.

I looked through the glass. She was caressing her expensive, blonde Toni & Guy tresses and smiling like an alligator who had just spotted baby duckling on the happy hour menu at the 'cranky-creek' buffet. Nanoseconds later, static in my headphones as the talkback flicked back into life.

"Yeah, Yeah. Thanks for coming in Peter. I think we have it! Good job. Yeah. Anyway… err… umm… you are free to go… and like… have a great day."

I gently placed the DT-100 headphones on the blue Hessian topped coffee-stained desk, on the side of which was crudely carved: "Enn Rules" – a reference to veteran UK voice actor Enn Reitel, who had carved his name on every available surface, in every voice booth in the city before he buggered off to Los Angeles. As I got up to leave, I glanced at the spit spattered Neumann U47 vintage microphone, one of a priceless matched pair and a veteran of a million sessions. The Neumann U47 is the granddaddy of large diaphragm condenser microphones and features a legendary sound that has captured the voices of the greatest singers of the modern era. The Beatles used it to great effect, as did Frank Sinatra. From Ella to Adele, the vocal sounds of jazz, rock, folk and pop would not be the same without a U47 in the studio. It's finely tuned gold diaphragm accurately captures the frequencies of the human voice and has made it the undisputed, all-time king of vocal microphones. Everyone should have one, if you have a spare £10,000 that is.

Emerging from the cramped booth into the narrow blue-carpeted corridor outside, I was hit by the intense scent of freshly brewed Arabica coffee and oriental lilies in full bloom. I said goodbye to the cheery, tattooed girl with the pierced nose and black lipstick on reception and popped a grape from a large bowl on the desk into my mouth. This is my life I thought. This is the way it has been… and always will be. Still, what was it Churchill used to say? *Onwards and upwards. K.B.O – Keep buggering on.* That was it. There was always L'Oréal, Dominos, MoneySuperMarket, Walkers or British Gas… or maybe a nice Toilet Duck to look forward to – heck, I'd even voice Tenna Lady!

The good folks at McCann's Advertising Agency in Herbrand Street, in London WC1, were a nice, cheerful, happy bunch – especially after their smoking breaks. They were always terribly grateful and usually paid on time. The pay was the reward – and pay they did, I made sure of that. We had an understanding ever since I threatened to take an oxyacetylene blow-torch to a gold-ormolu table belonging to Howard, the former chairman, back in '97. I was only joking of course, but in the brutally unhinged, booze and sometimes drug-fuelled world of advertising, it's best not to take any chances. So, they paid plus interest, every damn penny. I swore the cheque was smeared with blood, but then again, it could have been soup. Howard had a penchant for a lunchtime bowl of Borscht at Smollensky's on the Strand.

Back out in a sun-drenched Greek Street, the world was going about its business as normal, or as normal as things ever are around these parts. The pavement cafes, on the corner of Old Compton Street, were awash with chorus boys from the Prince Edward Theatre, pouring over 'The Stage'. Ah yes, Old Compton Street, an exotic thoroughfare. It's a busy street, smack bang in the middle of Soho, constantly bustling with tourists and those who work in the district. Then, there are the barrow boys from the nearby Berwick Street market, whose cries of "Come on ladies! BIG bananas, four for a pound!" ring through the narrow Walkers Court leading to Brewer Street a block away. Old Compton Street is at the very centre of Soho life. It's a vibrant, cosmopolitan artery and is rude, crude and brimming with opportunity. It's the gateway to the many infamous streets that run north to Oxford Street and south to Shaftsbury Avenue – Dean, Wardour, Greek and Frith; the spiritual home of London's media folk who live, work and drink (mostly drink, to be honest) in this most bohemian of districts. The late Jeffrey Barnard described Soho as: 'His Disney World. A place full of poets, painters, prostitutes, bookmakers, runners, bohemians, bums, café philosophers, crooks and cranks.' For a young man about town, it was about as exotic a place you could conceivably wish for. The tables and chairs of the legendary Bar Italia, just around the corner in Frith, spill out into the street. It's nicotine-stained interior and old brass mechanical cash register, with its authentic green patina, haven't changed since the '50s. And above it all, rising into a cerulean haze, the pungent aroma of freshly ground Arabica coffee, Turkish cigarettes and softly baked croissants, mingling with the less appealing scent of diesel fumes, vomit, dropped kebabs, rotting fruit, dog shit, drains blocked by fatbergs and stale urine. Good grief – it's enough to lift my spirits just thinking about it. I bloody love this place! Always have, ever since I first snuck into the Windmill Theatre in Great Windmill Street with my pal Noel Ardis, to see a static strip show while on a Belfast Royal Academy school trip to London in 1973. Those were the days where, if it moved – it was rude! The Corporation of London had granted the theatre a licence to permit naked ladies to appear on stage, on the condition that they struck a pose before the curtain went up and stayed totally immobile for their ten minute performance, oogled them from the fetid, sticky darkness of an inky black, flea-ridden auditorium.

I headed for the Dog and Duck, alias 'Normans', which was Barnard's second home and ordered a coffee. I have studiously avoided alcohol during the working day, ever since I met Bill. Ah yes, Bill – Big Bill Mitchell. God rest his soul. Let me tell you about Bill – the man, the myth, the legend. Bill and I had been booked to voice a commercial together at the lovely Silk Sound studios in London's Berwick Street, back in 1993. Bill had turned up early and was waiting in the reception, perched on the arm a blood-red Chesterfield leather sofa. I think some of the blood might have been mine, it was mixed with sweat and tears; some of which were his. There he was wearing his signature black portmanteau, black shirt, black tie with a single black rhinestone, black jacket, black sunglasses, black gloves, oversized black fedora hat, black trousers, black socks, black belt, black braces and black leather silver-tipped boots with black Cuban heels. He carried a black Malacca silver-topped cane for beating off undesirables, and I use that phrase advisedly. He was a colourful character – in monochrome, a real-life oxymoron and at the time, he owned one of the most famous voices in the UK. Bill looked like the sort of guy who would quite cheerfully gouge out your eyes with an Apache knife while whistling Lieutenant Ricketts well-known marching tune, 'Colonel Bogey'. His reputation quite literally preceded him and as a young impressionable chap, I was in total awe of this towering man with an equally towering reputation. Bill was Canadian by birth but following an inability to find his way back to Heathrow Airport in the 1970s, he was adopted by an adoring British public, as the deep brown voice that launched a thousand products, all of them bad for you.

The creative director on the session had, as is customary, asked us if we would like a drink before we began.

"Oh, just a glass of water please," was my Pavlovian response. The creative turned to Bill.

"And you Bill… err… what would you like?"

There was a palpable pause as the question penetrated his hazy consciousness. He hadn't been to bed for forty-eight hours, judging by the 6 o'clock shadow on his not so finely chiselled 'Desperate Dan' chin.

"Beer!"

Was the impossibly deep and resonant monosyllabic reply.

Fabulous. It was 10.02am! An eager-faced runner was despatched to obtain the refreshments from the kitchen two floors below. Dear Bill must have consumed four litres of industrial-strength Carlsberg lager during that session – What else? He also chain-smoked nearly two packs of full fat, Marlborough Reds for the entire two hours, filling an oversized cut glass ashtray until it was almost brimming over with ash and butts. The health police would have had a coronary if they'd seen it. In fact, I'm surprised Bill didn't. Though it did get him in the end. This was self-medication, dispensed on the scale of an inner-city NHS pharmacy. The booth we both occupied was no more than eight feet by six. It stank like an East End pub in the '60s and visibility was down to zero feet with headlights dipped and wipers on max. But he delivered his line to perfection in the way he had always done – *"Carlsberg. Probably the best lager in the world"* – refused to do retakes and breathed like an Indian Railways 4-6-2 Pacific steam locomotive ascending a 1:10 gradient. They don't make them like him anymore. If I'm not mistaken, I think that they've now thrown away the mould – and shot the mould maker – twenty-seven times in the head. And two more times for good measure. Bill was unique, a one-off, a maverick. He never worked after lunch and only a fool tried to book him.

My pocket began to vibrate. I whipped out my mobile. It was my agent. She was the one voice I was ever truly pleased to hear, apart from my accountant calling to tell me that I have far too much money. Since that has yet to happen, I'll stick with my agent. Her call always heralded another crack of the whip. On days when she didn't call, I would call her to check that she was still alive.

"I thought you had died," I said.

"What? Yes, never mind. Look, Peter are you free between two o'clock and four?" She said.

I knew I was but always liked to give the impression I was in demand, even to my agent. Pathetic, I know, I can't help myself.

"One moment," I said.

I pretended to flick through my diary by flicking a copy of 'Sporting Life' which I found on the bar counter.

"Err, yes. I can squeeze in whatever it is… if I shuffle something else around."

Why did I perform this ridiculous charade every time she called?

"So, err... What's up?" I enquired.

"Look. I've had Martin on the phone, from Ogilvy. He's doing a radio spot for Range Rover. He'd like to pencil you in to play the part of an Eskimo. Interested?"

I paused for effect, yet my heart was racing. Car commercials were notorious for their longevity and could run and run for months, even years. This meant lots of lovely residuals if the spot ran on multiple national stations... well, you can imagine the frisson!

"Err... yes, I could be persuaded" I said, feigning indifference.

"Yes. Well, you know what Martin's like," she said. "He's a bit of a stickler for detail when it comes to performance."

"Oh no! Not that method shit," I said.

There was a pause on the other end of the line.

"Yes, I'm afraid so. They want you to eat ice cubes before you read the lines."

"Oh! I see." What kind of a poncy bollocks world do I live in? "OK," I said, when and where!" There was a slight hesitation.

"Don't get too excited," she said. "At this stage, it's only a test."

A test was ad-speak for an audition. I would be *trying out* for the part. No residuals guaranteed, just a lousy session fee, if I was lucky. The shadows that were being cast across the street by the hulking façade of Soho House opposite, seemed to lengthen. The world was turning all right, but my luck certainly wasn't.

As I swallowed a mouthful of ice for the eighteenth time that morning, I began to wonder how my life had come to this. How did I end up here, in this most ridiculous of all professions? Most of my contemporaries had moved, with apparent ease from school to university and then on to do something sensible with their lives. A quick trawl of LinkedIn proved that. Professors, entrepreneurs, high court judges, fast jet pilots, army officers, actuaries, hedge fund managers, bankers even a very successful cat burglar called Peter Scott. Scott had made a name for himself on the French Riviera, as one of the most successful and celebrated 'gentleman' thieves of his generation – stealing jewels, furs and artwork from the likes of Sophia Loren and Elizabeth Taylor worth over £30M! The very definition of success in most people's eyes. But I for some reason had never taken the easy route.

The road less travelled had always been more alluring and in some ways, it had its compensation. You were a free man, a *freelance* living each day as it came and not sworn to the service of any lord or master. In many ways, it was a life I was destined to live from an early age. You see, I was different from the other boys. Very different. Unlike them, conformity was not in my nature. I was a rebel.

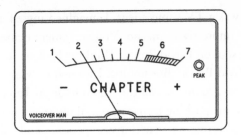

CHAPTER

WHAT, IN THE NAME OF
SWEET JESUS, HAVE I SPAWNED?

I can remember quite clearly, the defining moment when I decided on the career path I was going to take. My father had one of those wonderful old wooden encased ECKO U109 radiograms, that glowed orange from the illumination of the exotic German valves within it. I recall as a child, being completely transfixed by the wonderful fruity voices that emanated from it while listening to what was then called The BBC Light Programme and The BBC Home Service. Ever since those early days, I knew I wanted to be on the radio or TV. Years later, while I was at secondary school, I went to the Ravenhill Rugby ground in Belfast in Northern Ireland, in March 1972 to see the school's Rugby cup final. My school The Belfast Royal Academy was playing against Ballymena Academy. The event was being recorded by BBC TV Northern Ireland, for broadcast later in the day. Rugby is almost a national sport in Ireland and each year thousands of old boys would eagerly anticipate the school final to re-live their youth. Like radio, I was fascinated by TV. I had once longed to be a TV cameraman. Like a sad Billy-no-friends, I used to fantasise about being a cameraman on 'Top of The Pops'. I would cavort around my impossibly small bedroom in Knock, East Belfast as a child, with an empty toilet roll clamped to one eye

– pretending it was a TV camera lens. I imagined myself as a cameraman on one of those impressively macho 'Vinten' camera cranes, performing a perfect tracking shot on David Bowie. Thinking back on it, most of my pals wanted to be David Bowie. But not me. I wanted to wear a hard hat and a high-viz tabard and zoom around the studio floor on Top of the Pops with a man in front of me pushing teenagers out of my way. I really *was* weird! It seemed such a glamorous and exciting occupation – and still does, in many respects. Though sadly, the Vinten crane has now been replaced by the altogether more hi-tech 'Techno Crane' which for safety reasons no longer requires a man to ride on it. I really should seek professional help for this!

The camaraderie and esprit de corps amongst those camera crews is extraordinary. Anyhow, following the Rugby match I got chatting to one of the hairy arsed, Woodbine smoking, tattooed rigger drivers from one of the big outside broadcast trucks and persuaded him to show me around the inside of the rig. A request that nowadays would involve, triplicate form filling, a chaperone service and background 'Captain Paedo' checks, but this was the '70s and as we all know, paedos didn't exist back then – especially in Northern Ireland.

Inside, it was an impressive control room on wheels. Tardis-like and with big banks of monitors, showing pictures from all the cameras dotted around the ground. Later, I hitched a lift back into town. Riding high above the traffic in the cab of that huge green liveried truck with its hand-painted gold BBC crest emblazoned on the door, under which were inscribed the words: **'BBC. Nation shall speak peace onto Nation'.** Now there's a noble sentiment and corporate mission statement! I remember thinking that this was the life for me. Not driving a truck, of course, but working for the BBC, doing... well, anything. It was curious, as I was only fourteen or fifteen at the time but I had definitely found my calling. I was obsessed. I was a rebel who now had a cause!

On passing my eleven-plus Grammar School entrance exam on the second attempt, which was known as 'the review', my parents had bought me a brand spanking new National Panasonic cassette recorder, which was cutting edge technology back then, can you believe it? I would spend hours on that, recording little programmes, performing on the fly drop-in edits, and reading aloud in the privacy of my bedroom where no one could see or hear me, or so I thought. My father was probably listening at the door thinking

"What in the name of sweet Jesus have I spawned?" I was a strange kid. Outwardly normal in every respect but with this weird compulsion to talk out loud in rooms on my own. I am laughing now because you could say I haven't changed one bit! I have since discovered that all broadcasters are weird, some more than others, and then some! Some manage to make me look normal. Don't worry, we'll talk about them later.

On another school trip in 1973, we had ventured into town for a guided tour of the BBC studios. I recall to this day being struck by the almost indescribably unique smell of the place. All studios have a very similar type of aroma. It has nothing whatsoever to do with the people who inhabit them, although that is sometimes true, especially in hospital radio. It has more to do with the smell of the equipment! I know it sounds ridiculous but bear with me for a moment! I've tried to figure it out and have concluded that it's something to do with the odour given off by warm electrical circuits and valves. It's an enticing aroma of ozone, burning dust, old socks, warm wood, valves and toasty circuit boards and its one I still relish to this day. Oddly, BBC and Independent Local Radio stations smell differently as do TV and radio studios. Film studios have an odour all of their own! I should really seek some professional help with this but blindfold me and I can tell the difference between: Broadcasting House, ITV's London Studios, Pinewood, Elstree, Fountain Studios and the BBC TV Centre on London's Wood Lane.

I had joined the BBC straight out of school – as a boy announcer. Truthfully, I was still attending school and squeezing the pubescent spots on my face when I got my first big break. On the recommendation of a chap I had met at the Queen's University Film Society called Bryan Drysdale, who was a BBC cameraman, I wrote to the Presentation Dept at the BBC in Belfast to enquire if any part-time jobs were going. To my utter amazement, I was called in to audition. Serendipity has played a huge part in my life, although I don't for one moment believe that observation is unique to me. At that audition, I was asked to read a news bulletin and some continuity announcements. A week later, shortly after I had returned home from school and still in my school uniform, I took a phone call from the personal assistant to the head of presentation at the BBC in Northern Ireland and was asked if I could start work on the following Monday at 6pm! My mother, once she had got over the initial shock, agreed to drive me there. Consequently, I hold the dubious distinction of being the youngest ever newsreader in the BBC's history. Something I was slightly embarrassed about at the time but now am inordinately proud of. When I think back, I must have had one hell of a brass neck! I was all of seventeen years old and barely out of short trousers, marching confidently into the British Broadcasting Corporation like I owned the ruddy place! I had lied about my age of course, in just the same way I lied to you just now about the trousers. See? I can't help myself. Back then, the employment regulations were somewhat laxer than they are now. 'Money laundering' was something you did if you carelessly left a £5 note in the back pocket of your jeans. Those were the days when the Sunday joint didn't make you dizzy, when spit roasting was something that was strictly confined to a butcher's shop front window and when the phrase 'doggy fashion' referred to knitwear for poodles. Anyhow, I digress.

My first live broadcast was reading the Ulster farming fat stock prices at 6am on BBC Radio Ulster, to a small audience of grubby fingered, ruddy-cheeked provincial farmers. The prices for hoggets and steers had seemed so terribly important then. It probably would have been easier and cheaper to record it and post a cassette in a Jiffy bag to every single farmer in the province. Nonetheless, I can vividly remember walking on air down Royal Avenue, in Belfast after that first broadcast, literally bursting with pride and excitement and thinking the whole world was my lobster. I will never forget that feeling. I was seventeen years old and had reached the very pinnacle of my career. I'd made it! I was a media celebrity. I was famous. I *spoke to the people and for the people…* or so I naively thought. The 'nation unto nation" bit would have to wait. I was a really impatient weirdo. Anyway, I am getting ahead of myself.

In 1975, I went on to read Psychology at Queen's University in Belfast. I say read, I actually lounged around in my pyjamas for three and a half years drinking beer, staying up all night listening to music, trying to chat up girls, making short films and flying planes at the University Air Squadron. Then there followed six months of sheer terror, when I realised that my final exams were imminent and I was caught in the headlights like Basil Fawlty's Manuel, 'I know nothing!' During my four years there, I continued my happy association with the BBC. In 1977, my second year at Queen's, I moved over to TV and progressed to reading the news on the main current affairs show, the imaginatively titled: "Scene around Six" with anchor Barry Cow-

BBC

BRITISH BROADCASTING CORPORATION

BROADCASTING HOUSE LONDON W1A 1AA

TELEPHONE 01-580 4468   TELEX: 265781

TELEGRAMS AND CABLES: BROADCASTS LONDON TELEX

PERSONAL   5th September, 1980

Dear Mr. Dickson,

    80.G.2327: ANNOUNCERS, NORTHERN IRELAND

    Thank you for attending the Appointment Board held in connection with the above advertisement.

    I am pleased to be able to tell you that you have been selected for one of the 2-year contracts.

    Your appointment will be effected by Mr. D. Hill, S.Pers.O.N.I.

                Yours sincerely,

                (Barbara Todd)
          Senior Appointments Officer

Mr. P. Dickson
through
S.Pers.O.N.I.

My first full-time offer from the BBC – 1980 – Belfast.

an, who sadly died in 2004. Barry was a real Cock O' the North. He was a diminutive man, around five feet seven inches tall with a larger than life personality and a ruddy complexion, which was hidden by a neatly clipped ginger beard. Barry was what they used to call, 'a ladies' man'. As opposed to 'a lady-man'... of which there were several at the BBC in Belfast. If he were alive today, he would tell you that he taught me everything I know. So, I must be grateful. The trouble is I have forgotten most of it but in my eyes, Barry was 'it' and I totally idolised him.

So, there I was enjoying a strange double life. Attending lectures on psychology in the morning and afternoon, following which my doppelganger would amble down to BBC Broadcasting House on Ormeau Avenue in Belfast, dodging the occasional burning bus, rubber or actual bullet or angry mob, to slap on some pan stick and a dab of Leichner powder number two and read the news on TV, in those hideously clipped anglicised Ulster-Scots tones I had adopted back then. My friends at the University faculty and in the Halls of residence where I lived, took great delight in trying to get me pissed in the union bar before I skipped off to the Beeb to start a shift. On many occasions, I must confess to telling them I was due on air in a couple of hours, when of course I wasn't. On a student's meagre income though, free drinks were not to be sniffed at – though we tried that too! I don't recommend it, by the way – well not with Appleton one hundred percent proof Jamaican rum anyway!

By the general standards of the day, I was relatively well off. I collected a small grant each year to help with living expenses but am still proud to this day that I never asked my parents for a financial contribution. The BBC saw to that. I collected my wages each week from the head of news, a genial, six-foot-tall Ulsterman called Robin Walsh, who later became the Controller of the BBC in Northern Ireland. Robin was the archetypal alpha male. He had the appearance and demeanour of an erudite, sharp-suited '60s ad man but he was this hard-bitten, hard as nails nut-bag mentalist of a former newspaper editor, with dark, deep-set eyes and a mono-brow – who took no prisoners and remains the most direct talking, in your face, scariest person I have ever met in my entire life. If anyone put a foot out of line, they got the full turbo-hot hairdryer treatment from him. A Robin Walsh rebuke was the meteorological equivalent the hurricane saying to the palm tree, hang onto your nuts, this is no ordinary blow job! My weekly meeting with Robin was a somewhat tawdry affair. I would amble into his office on the first floor of Broadcasting House in Belfast on a Friday around 7pm after the broadcast, ostensibly for a drink and he would push a small brown envelope with his stubby nicotine-stained fingers, containing the used notes across his leather topped desk. It seemed like a lot to me then, but £23 per week was woeful remuneration for what I did. It wouldn't have even covered Barry's lunch-time bar tab at the BBC Club. I was grateful though, and they knew it. It was mutual exploitation of a type that continues in broadcasting to this day. Hundreds of broadcast media interns who fight for places on productions are woefully treated and poorly paid. If Indeed they are paid at all.

When I graduated from Queens University with my shiny new Bachelor of Arts Honours degree in Psychology, (no idea how that happened as I spent most of my time flying Bulldogs at the University Air Squadron and drinking beer – these two activities always occurred in that order thankfully), I made the transition to working for the BBC full time, initially as a radio announcer in the presentation department in Belfast. Heading up this department was a man called Michael Baguley. 'Buggerley' as he was un-affectionately known, was a fearsome man with a beard which wouldn't have looked out of place on Brian Blessed. In fact, I think they had some sort of unofficial time-sharing arrangement. Come to think of it, I never saw them together in the same room. Baguley looked just like that ruddy-faced matelot who graced the front of a packet of Players 'Old Navy' cigarettes, if you are old enough to remember them. For all his blustering affectation though, he had the air about him of a man who had been pissed on and passed over, one too many times. I can picture him to this day. Suited and booted and squeezed into the smallest office you could possibly imagine with Sylvia, his personal assistant. If you went to central casting and asked for a spinster who looked like a '50s librarian, you'd get Sylvia. Powder blue tweed twin set perfection complete with horn-rimmed spectacles and a row of faux pearls, perched at her vintage Remington. She was long-suffering. Baguley would sit at his desk opposite her day in, day out sharpening his pencils and bawling like a lunatic, at the small Bakelite valve radio perched precariously on the ludicrously high windowsill, in his tiny office without a view.

The stentorian tones of his cultivated Ulster accent would echo through the red linoleum floored corridors of the fourth floor in Broadcasting

House, Belfast. Frequently, and especially after a broadcast, I would get the call from Sylvia. "Mr Baguley would like to see you." It wasn't so much a request or even a suggestion, it was a summons. It generally meant one thing – you were in for a bollocking. I can recall standing in that small office, just him and me. Sylvia had to retire to the outer office with Eileen – the chain-smoking departmental secretary, as there just wasn't physically enough room for three people to be in there simultaneously. He would rant and rave about some mispronunciation or fluff you had made. His face, or what you could see of it behind his glistening dark beard, turning a distinct shade of beetroot. All that adrenaline pumping around his narrowing veins, with nowhere to go. He retired to a bungalow by the sea near Carnelea, five miles to the east of Belfast and left us for that big studio in the sky in 2019. I owe him a huge debt of gratitude, but sadly never got to express it to him personally.

Two of the great characters in the presentation department at the BBC in Northern Ireland were Mike Nunan and David Gamble. These two were the 'Hinge and Bracket' of BBC TV continuity. Like Dame Edna and Dr Evadne, they were a redoubtable double act, the senior announcers and as such had carved out a comfortable little niche for themselves. In reality, they ran the show and often told Baguley where he could stick his pencils. Not for them, the stress of live news or boring Fat Stock prices or getting up at Jesus Christ o'clock to open up Radio Ulster. No. They worked shifts of four days on and four days off in the heady world of regional TV continuity. This was in the early days when the regions, Northern Ireland, Scotland and Wales opted out of the network and blanket covered each programme junction, with a local sounding announcer and regional branding. The bosses thought it gave the channel a local identity, which it undoubtedly did but in essence, it was a crude, difficult and often clumsy technical process. Anyway, after I'd been there a year Baguley decided my time had come to rotate into TV continuity. Needless to say, fearing a hostile takeover Nunan and Gamble weren't too happy about this incursion by a young whippersnapper onto their well-guarded turf. The training began on a Monday morning. I turned up for a familiarisation visit of the continuity suite with Mike Nunan, at the appointed time.

"Hi," he said. Without even glancing up. "You're just in time for the Network Conference."

The network conference was nothing more than a four-way, hands-free telephone call between network presentation personnel in London and the announcers of the three main UK regions; Northern Ireland, Wales and Scotland. The thirty-minute mid-morning hook-up was London's chance to run through their intentions for the afternoon and evenings viewing. It was tedious in the extreme and mind-numbing in its excruciating, split-second detail. Nunan sat there at the big continuity desk, in front of a bank of monitors and flashing lights and transcribed the details of each junction's duration and content on the margin of that week's Radio Times! These days, it's all done electronically and run by computers, but in the late '70s, it was all done by hand using an old-fashioned analogue pencil. Imagine that, kids! Another shock was in store. After the hook-up, I was given a guided tour around the suite. It was all pretty standard stuff. Audio and video quadrant faders on a standard broadcast desk, lots of flashing lights, bells, whistles, switches, monitors showing telecine and VT sources, network output, OB sources, other studio sources, sick bowl, ashtray, bicycle clips, toilet roll, hip flask and last but not least the famous BBC1 TV revolving world... which was... nowhere to be seen.

"Where exactly is that?" I asked.

"Out there in the racks room," said Mike pointing at a door that led into another room.

Grunting and cursing his arthritic hips, he levered his not inconsiderable frame out of his chair and led me out to a technical area and there, in a corner was a wooden box with a hinged lid about the size of a Dansette record player. It was so unprepossessing that you could walk past it and hardly notice it there. "Voila!" Mike had lifted the lid to reveal the contents. It *was* a Dansette record player, but with several astonishing modifications. The silver spindle which would have held the record had been shortened, by someone who evidently specialised in shortening the barrels of shotguns – this was Belfast in the '70s after all. Perched on top of the spindle was a ping pong ball (I'm not kidding), on which had been drawn, in black felt tip pen, a map of the world rather like a globe. To the rear of the Dansette, was a concave mirror and in front, a small black and white camera pointing at it. The picture from this camera was fed into another box of tricks that coloured the landmasses yellow and made the oceans blue. It was an incredible bit of '70s Heath Robinson botched engineering – which actually worked.

It must have cost all of ten shillings and sixpence, (Kids, that's around 56p or 0.000001% of a Bitcoin). Today, interstitial video graphics, imaging and network branding cost the broadcast networks millions of pounds. The contrast with 1975, couldn't be more dazzlingly stark.

Several months later, I am ashamed to say, when I was let loose on TV continuity on my own, I maliciously took a black felt tip pen to the ping pong ball globe and added my very own island to the West of Galway, in mid-Atlantic. Amazingly, no one noticed. I dined out on that one for years. I also took delight in phoning friends at home and telling them to watch BBC1, while I switched the Dansette from 33 to 45 RPM! That's how I rolled back then.

The training progressed. I was as nervous as hell and must have sounded bloody terrified. Running a regional TV continuity suite was, and I'm sure still is a pretty hair-raising experience. Opting out of the network and blanketing programme junctions, sounds like a piece of piss but was actually much more taxing than working at the source in London. For a start, you had to fade down the end of a programme that was ending just nanoseconds before the network did. This involved split-second timing. Next, you had to fade up the Dansette ping pong ball. In one ear you had to monitor what the continuity announcer in London was saying and at the same time listen to yourself in the other ear. Working with split feed headphones is a skill that has stood me in good stead to this day. If the junction involved a couple of trails, you had to run those as well. It went like this, and remember, all of this took place in under sixty seconds.

"This is BBC1 Northern Ireland. In a moment, the news."

You then had to quickly slam the microphone fader shut, press a key and shout "Run VT!" into a talkback microphone, which was connected to the VT operator, three floors above you. With any luck, if the operator was still awake and sober, you were now into a ten second clock counting down to the start of the trailer. The monitor showing the VT source clock would flash to life and the countdown had begun. These days, VT run-up times are practically instant, not back then. It took a good ten seconds for the video to stabilise. Quickly, you had to fade up your microphone and begin your script for whatever programme trailer you were introducing. All the while throughout this, you had to keep an eye on the main output monitor, watch the VT countdown clock, listen to the network announcer in your left ear and try to make sense of what you were reading! Spinning plates in the circus while being chased by a pair of clowns with active chainsaws would have been an easier career choice. With any luck, the VT countdown clock would reach zero, just as you finished speaking. At this point, you had to slam the microphone shut again, lead with the sound fader on the VT machine, fade down the globe and fade up the VT source. Lead with sound followed by vision. I was one-third octopus, one-third man, one-third Reginald Dixon – all feet and fingers, on the Blackpool Tower Ballroom Wurlitzer. You now had about twenty-seven seconds to set up the next item, a live trail from the TV studio four floors upstairs. *"Standby, studio! Coming to you in twenty seconds!" A blur of fingers and faders and bells and whistles and buzzers from distant studios and unseen technicians. Lights flashing here, there and everywhere.*

The VT ended and you had to fade that down, fade up a projected still slide, remember to fade up the microphone, introduce the next trail and again lead with sound then vision and close the microphone again. Now there began the countdown from the Network PA in London, in your left ear.

"OK Regions. Counting out… in 30 seconds. 29, 28, 27…"

This signalled the end of the network junction. Split-second timing. It was like a busy Monday morning at Air Traffic Control at Heathrow. Would the live studio you had just put on the air, finish in time? My talkback to their gallery was now open and active. I could hear the network PA in London continue her countdown. "15, 14, 13, 12, 11, 10, 9, 8…" I began to count out loud with her, so the local studio gallery upstairs could hear me through the open talkback microphone. They, in turn, began to count down in time with me so their presenter, who was live on air, and talking, could hear the countdown in his ear. "3, 2, 1". I stopped my countdown there. My heart was in my mouth and my microphone was now open and live. The presenter had stopped right on cue. Christ knows what he had said. There is only so much information a human brain can absorb into consciousness at any one time.

This really was multi-tasking, my head hurt, and I was flying by the seat of what was left of my pants. I now knew why Nunan kept a set of bicycle clips and a hip flask on the desk. In my ear, I could hear the London announcer begin his introduction to the next programme. Eight seconds left.

"…7, 6, 5, 4…"

I had to get a move on. There was no time to hang around. Mentally I pruned the script, so I could catch up. Editing copy in your head as you read it out loud is a skill I have developed over the years. It's a necessity of the job and has certainly helped pull me out of trouble in many a hair-raising live situation. A quick fade down, fade up to our old friend the Dansette and a few seconds later bang on time, lead with sound, being careful not to re-enter too early and catch the London announcer's dying words. Fade down the globe, fade up BBC1 network vision and opt back into the network nano-seconds later using a specially guarded key, rather like the ones you see on nuclear submarines. Phew! By this stage, I was a sweaty mess. It was mentally draining. On one memorable occasion, I was covering a junction into the children's programme 'Playschool'. As I opted back, I must have faded the network up too early. The viewer heard me say "Playschool," followed by the Network announcer saying; "ool'. Annoyed by my basic error, I uttered the words "Bollocks." The second error I had committed, was forgetting to fade out my microphone! Those poor kids. You can imagine the scenario. "Mum! Mum! What's bollocks?"

From that day on I swore (no pun intended) to never again use bad language in a broadcast studio, and I never have. Non-broadcast studios are another matter altogether and some of the funniest outtakes I have heard, involve well-known celebrities cursing like troopers, at their inability to read a few basic lines of copy. I cherish a recording I have of the lovely former Dr Who actor Tom Baker, during a session for a furniture manufacturer called 'Symphony'. On the tape, Tom can be heard becoming increasingly irritated at the poor grammar and syntax of the script. After about three minutes, Tom loses it, and begins his rant towards the producer with the line;

"They might have lots of furniture at Symphony, but they're woefully short of fucking commas and full stops!"

Another wonderful outtake recording I have features the legendary Orson Welles who was booked to record a TV commercial for Findus frozen peas. You may have heard it yourself, as it has passed into broadcasting folklore. It begins with Orson uttering the immortal line,

"We know a remote farm in Lincolnshire where Mrs Buckley lives."

Ten minutes into the session, which was being directed by a committee of unfortunate young creative types, Orson erupts:

"This script is unrewarding and unpleasant to read. This is a load of shit and you know that. Come on fellas you're losing your heads, it's impossible. I would not direct any living actor like this. The right reading for this is the one I am giving you. Now, what is it that you want, in the depths of your ignorance?"

On the tape, the creative team can be heard, whispering conspiratorially. One of them, rather bravely eventually pipes up.

"That's fine Orson, it really is. We have all we need."

Orson's riposte is classic. "No money is worth this shit!"

This is Orson Welles remember, one of the greatest voices of the twentieth century. I know I have been tempted many times to behave like that in countless sessions but, not being Orson Welles, I have now got a perfect impression of my upper incisors on my bottom lip as proof, if proof were needed, of the number of times I have bitten it! "Never forget," I once overheard the late Mike Hurley a fellow voiceover artist once say; *You are nothing more than a vocal prostitute!*" How true and to this day I have never forgotten it. I have been giving aural pleasure to my clients ever since, and always dancing limply, to their often slightly out of tempo, off-key tune.

Duncan Hearle was the senior announcer at BBC Radio Ulster, or 'Drunken Hole' as we younger disrespectful pups affectionately named him. Though I never saw him touch a drop of the hard stuff, the moniker seemed to fit. He was like everyone's favourite uncle. A big lumpy, lolloping man in his late sixties and an inveterate wearer of the deeply unfashionable bottle green V-neck tank top, (that's a sleeveless cardigan if you are under forty), round NHS glasses and comfy, lambskin lined fleecy slippers. His rounded Ulster vowels had emanated from my father's valve powered radio during the '60s when I was growing up, and to me, he was a huge star who had one of those slightly old fashioned but deeply comforting voices. During my first days at the BBC in Northern Ireland, he took me under his wing and showed me the ropes. Then he showed me the studio and where the canteen was. To this day I have no idea why he was showing me ropes, which he kept in his locker. He did it to every newcomer apparently, he was quite an odd man.

The old radio continuity desk at Radio Ulster was built like a Rolls Royce and probably cost as much. It was virtually bombproof, which was just as well because there were loads of them exploding on a nightly basis outside. Completed and installed back in the days when budgets were only for Chancellors and Aunty BBC had never heard of a bottom line. All black shiny Bakelite and Formica, with gleaming silver-plated knobs and dials illuminated from behind by impossibly exotic looking German valves with names like Telefunken EL84, which cast a comforting orange glow through the ventilation grill onto the wall behind. It must have cost fifty thousand licence fees. In the centre of the desk were the huge, doorknob sized orange handled 'pot' faders. These were the days before the horizontal sliding faders, which are now commonplace on today's mixing desks. I remember Duncan spending hours with me, instructing me on the perfect pot cut. A pot cut was basically a quick fade down of an audio source. A deft flick of the wrist with the hand firmly wrapped around the large knob. Ooh, Err Missus! They were happy days. I would spend hours in there off-air, practising and pretending to present my little music shows with nothing but a box of old and badly scratched vinyl albums for company. It was like heaven to me.

Duncan had his peculiar habits. He would never sit at a microphone without his own five-inch deep foam filled cushion, which he carried everywhere. "A man can't read the news with a numb bum," he would say. I suspect he had piles but was too ashamed to admit it. His right leg would bounce up and down when he was broadcasting, one restless leg unconsciously releasing the nervous tension he obviously felt when he was at the microphone. I learned a lot from him, and I am thankful for his early mentorship. Some years later, I got the guys in graphics to knock up a little sign, which I fixed to the door to the announcer's green room. I had re-christened it, "The Duncan Hearle Suite." For all I know, it is still there to this day. Mind you, after a subsequent Director-General called John Birt pillaged and virtually privatised every part of every building in the BBC's empire, it's probably a cappuccino bar now or a hair salon.

Walter Love was, and still is the Ulster housewives' favourite. Walter was on the announcing team on Radio Ulster, but because of his seniority, he was allowed to present programmes during the day. He was a real smooth operator, with a mane of golden blonde hair studiously combed to cover a nascent bald patch and he had a wardrobe of expensive silk 'Liberty' ties and 'Donegal Tweed' jackets. To me, he seemed fantastically outré. He has an encyclopaedic knowledge of wine and wrote a food and wine column for a local magazine. He is still broadcasting as I write and in 2014, he was inducted into the Irish Radio Hall of Fame. I used to sit behind Walter during his shows and learn how to put together a record show. He was an old-fashioned presenter. He never called himself a DJ. DJ's were flash Harrys who drove soft top coupes, hung around nightclubs and dated dubious women. It just wasn't Walter's style. He too taught me much, and I am grateful. But to progress in this business, one has to adapt and be prepared to change. Change is after all the only constant, as Heraclitus once told me over a pint. The cadences and rhythms of speech modify over time, often subtly but always irreversibly. The cultural zeitgeist moves continually and inexorably through us. Just listen to the speech patterns on any piece of archive footage from forty years ago, and you'll appreciate what I mean. Walter though, for years has continued to plough his formal furrow. Some things and some people never change. God bless him and as I write this, it's good to know he's out there, like the dude he is.

Back in those pioneering days, the late-night duty announcer would work a split shift. Ending at midnight and picking up again at 6 o'clock in the morning. You were expected to stay in the building but oddly, no accommodation arrangements were in place. Thinking about it now, I wonder what on earth we and the broadcast unions were thinking about but amazingly, we were left to our own devices and no one ever complained. The best one could do, was to traipse down to see whichever bronchitic security guard was on duty that evening and sign out an ancient camp bed! This was neither a luxury item nor was it even remotely comfortable nor indeed camp! It was however supremely uncomfortable and almost impossible to erect. It was a self-assembly remnant, salvaged from someone's Anderson Shelter in 1945 and made from green Hessian backed canvas with steel interlocking rods. Constructing the ruddy thing at the end of a tiring day was even more of a nightmare than the real one that was to follow, once you had got to sleep! The bed and a brown horsehair blanket were taken to studio five and assembled. It was then shoved under the studio desk and voila! A place to kip for the night! If you were lucky and managed to ignore the incessant ticking of the studio clock and the faint rumble of the nightly explosions, helicopters, shouting and automatic gunfire, you got a few hours shut eye.

The following morning, you were rudely awakened by the studio manager, flicking on the fluorescent lights at 5am to begin the next day's early news programme! A quick undignified wash and brush up in the rudimentary and always cold toilets at the end of the corridor, and you were set for the day. It was uncomfortable, yet at the time, strangely alluring for all its bohemian qualities and I've no idea at all why we put up with it. It was the '70s, and Belfast was well and truly on the world map – for all the wrong reasons. 'The Troubles', as they are quaintly known were in full swing and it was big business for some. The city's glaziers all drove around in brand new Bentleys, giving everyone the two-fingered salute with one hand while toting a fat Cohiba in the other. City centre bombings, shootings and the daily ritual of tit for tat violence were the order of the day. It was terrorism on an almost industrial scale. Being a news hotspot, the newsroom at the BBC in Belfast was a hive of seemingly never-ending activity. Camera crews, reporters, sound engineers and journalists from around the world were constantly on the move, in and out of Broadcasting House in Belfast. Visiting news gatherers from all around the planet sniffing out the province for whatever discord their journalistic noses could find. Fishing for stories to feed the always voracious, rarely sated news monster, whose appetite we all know never diminishes.

Towards the end of the '70s, I moved to the newsroom to the position of sub-editor. My job was to collate and edit the news bulletins for TV. I would sit at my desk next to the TV news editor and prepare the bulletin for that evening's news show, 'Scene around Six'. It was during this time that I met and got to know many of the well-known and respected broadcast journalists on TV today. People like Jeremy Paxman, Kate Adie, Gavin Esler, James Robbins, Nicholas Witchell, Brian Barron, Bill Neeley and Martin Bell were all there, cutting their early teeth at the coalface of hard-nosed journalism. James actually married a local girl from the village of Comber in County Down where my mother in law lives, and we shared many great times together. Bill Neeley and I started in journalism together as junior overnight reporters on 'Good Morning Ulster'. Laughingly, neither of us knew what the hell we were doing but we had a thirst to learn. Bill it seems, was thirstier than I was, much thirstier. He ended up as ITN's Washington correspondent and later as ITN News at Ten anchor-man. He reached the very pinnacle of his profession. Not only was he tall and blessed with chiselled good looks, but also, I suspect, he had printers' ink in his veins from the start. Journalists, like salesmen, are born not made. I just wasn't born to be one. I didn't have the necessary fire in my belly to make it, and so gently lowered my journalistic ambitions. *"To thine own self be true,"* said Polonius in Hamlet. If something doesn't feel quite right in your gut, then it's not for you. If we all trusted our gut feelings, the world would be a much happier place. Too often people find themselves in jobs, marriages or careers, with no real idea how they got there and hating every second. Honest, objective introspection is difficult, but those who trade in its currency, reap the rewards.

I first realised journalism wasn't for me when I was dispatched one day to interview the Minister for Education at the Department of Education's HQ in Bangor, County Down – about fifteen miles from Belfast. It was a press call to announce some new initiative or other. I wasn't interested then and I'm still not now. The whole pack was there, TV, radio, print media, the lot. As I pressed forward to get my interview, I spotted my old friend James Robbins in the throng.

"Hi, James" I shouted. "It's a bit busy here, isn't it? Have you read the briefing notes from the press office?"

"Yes," he replied. "Have you?"

"Err… No" was my rather sheepish response.

The truth is, I really couldn't be arsed. I asked James to give me a few pointers on what I should be asking, which to my shame and his credit, he dutifully did. He is such a decent bloke. I can't imagine any other journalist doing the same but then again, looking back, he probably just took pity on me. I selected a few of his suggestions and committed them to memory. I should have written them down. My memory isn't what it used to be, and it wasn't up to much then either. The queue of patiently waiting hacks was whittling down nicely. Each one, given four minutes with the Minister. James was two or three in front of me, so I didn't have the luxury of hearing his line of questioning. Directly in front of me was Eammon Malley, from the local independent commercial radio station, Downtown Radio. Eammon is a lovely bloke, but 'diction' is not his middle name. If you've ever heard him on National Radio or TV giving interviews, you'll appreciate my observation. He makes Paisley sound like Joyce Grenfell. Anyhow, Eammon sat down with the 'Grand Fromage' and launched into his first question. The minister looked up and then across to his Civil Service handler and with a commendable measure of insouciance, shrugged his shoulders. It was obvious that his finely tuned English ears hadn't understood a bloody word poor old Eammon had said. The civil servant who was a local chap *had* understood Eammon's question perfectly and took it upon himself to interpret for the hapless politician. By the end of Eammon's allotted four minutes, I was so engrossed in this rich comedic pantomime unfolding in front of my eyes that I completely forgot my reason for being there.

"Who's next?" The civil servant called out.

"Err... Me" I meekly said and stumbled forward to take my seat beside the great man. In doing so, tripping over the trailing lead from Eammon's microphone and nearly ending up in the Ministers lap! It was an inauspicious start and it was only to get worse.

I had only been a journalist for all of three weeks. I could barely get the bloody tape recorder to start. It was one of those quarter-inch tape machines manufactured by a company called Uher, with big clunky push button switches and made in Germany stamped all over it, no doubt as part of their war reparations. The fucking thing weighed a ton and was notoriously unreliable, well in my technically incompetent hands, anything was. I shoved the microphone under his nose and then realised it was me to start. It was a very basic error. I can remember looking at the man, and seeing him thinking, "who is this fool?" I retracted the microphone and held it under my chin, as we had been taught.

I began; "I'm here with the Secretary of state for Health"...

The words had barely left my mouth when he stopped me mid-flow.

"Actually, for the record," he said, "I am the Minister for Education."

Oh, dear. Any credibility I had, had just departed the station and taken the Eurostar to Disneyland. It's hard to recover from an error as basic as that and indeed it was predictably all downhill from there. I can remember staring at the man's expensively patterned silk Hermes tie and admiring his brightly polished New and Lingwood leather shoes, rather than listening to his replies. All I heard was "Blah, blah, fucking blah." It was an utter shambles and to this day, I feel a distinct sense of shame for bringing the BBC's good journalistic name into disrepute.

News reporting in the '70s in Northern Ireland revolved around the quaintly named 'Troubles' – which in linguistic terms is just one step up from a 'kerfuffle'. I have never understood the Ulster capacity for understatement but adore it nonetheless. Atrocities on a grand and shocking scale were an almost daily occurrence and disturbingly, while living in the midst of it one almost became inured to the relentless flow of daily violence. Life though, like show business had to go on and I was amazed at the ability of many ordinary people, who were on the front line of this tsunami of hatred and vitriol to continue to conduct their lives with any semblance of normality. I recall the time in August 1979 when I was on duty, on a beautiful sunny Saturday in the newsroom in Belfast on the first floor of Broadcasting House, when word reached us that Lord Louis Mountbatten had been attacked by the Provisional IRA while fishing in County Sligo. The word on the Press Association wires was that he had been – 'killed by a bomb'. The details were sketchy, to say the least, and we didn't want to go to air with such momentous news until further confirmation had been received. Lord Louis Mountbatten, the former Viceroy of India, World War Two veteran, cousin to the Queen and Uncle to Prince Charles, would have been high on the Provisional IRA's hit list. He owned Classybawn Castle in the village of Mullaghmore, Co Sligo in the Republic and visited every year. Mullaghmore is only twelve miles from the border from Northern Ireland and is an infamous republican stronghold that was euphemistically dubbed 'Bandit Country'. Quite what he was thinking by holidaying there is anyone's guess. He was either foolish or mad. Given his eccentric war record, he was quite possibly both. It was now 11.50am. Half an hour went by and during this time, frantic phone calls were being made by reporters in the Belfast newsroom to firm up the story with their local stringers or contacts in the area. Within half an hour our worst fears were realised. At 12.20pm, we got the confirmation we were hoping wouldn't come. Lord Mountbatten had indeed been murdered by the Provisional IRA. Blown up by a Semtex bomb, which had been placed on his boat overnight. His legs had been blown clean off by the tremendous force of the blast and he had died shortly after being rescued. Sadly, there were other fatalities. One of the Earl's twin grandsons, Nicholas and Paul Maxwell, a fifteen-year-old local lad who was helping that day were also killed. Four others survived. The boat, Shadow V, had been moored at the public dock in the village for the past eleven months. The Provisional IRA would have had ample opportunity to plan and carry out their deadly attack. We went to air; I was the first to break the bad news. The enormity of the event, a major political coup for the IRA sent shockwaves around a war-weary province and around the planet.

Understandably, the daily grind of reporting news such as this got to me in the end. I had interviewed too many policemen's widows, visited one too many households devastated by the news of the murder of a Father, Mother or child. I had spoken to paramilitaries on both sides of the struggle. My heart simply wasn't in it anymore. I'd had enough and resignedly, chucked in the towel.

Belfast in the 1970s was an extremely dangerous place. The hotel where most of the news crews and journalists stayed when they were in the city was 'The Europa' on Great Victoria Street and indeed incredibly, it still stands today. At one time, it held the dubious distinction of being the most bombed hotel in the world! I somehow can't imagine that statistic making it onto their glossy in-room welcome pack – 'Welcome to the Europa Hotel, the world's favourite terrorist target. The management would like to take this opportunity to wish you a pleasant stay and remind you that before retiring at night, you are advised to put your head between your legs and kiss your arse goodbye!' But it was true. It seemed that a week never passed without the Europa's windows or Windees, as they are colloquially known, being blown out. The glaziers of Belfast must have thought that every day was like their birthday, anniversary, and Christmas day rolled into one. Working in Belfast at this time was a surreal experience, yet one somehow got used to the sight of armed soldiers and police on the streets in huge numbers. There was a ring of steel around the city and control zones established, where cars could be parked provided someone remained inside. Above the dull roar of city traffic, one could often hear the equally dull thud of explosions and gunfire. Life though went on, as it does in almost any city torn apart by either ethnic or sectarian violence. The searches, the frisking, the ring of steel around the commercial district and the suspicious glances and air of fear, all became part of the daily routine. The reports of unspeakable violence, kneecapping and the visceral practise of tarring and feathering – was sadly normalised for many. As humans, we are remarkably adaptable to whatever life throws at us and it never ceases to amaze me how people cope, even in the most adverse circumstances but remarkably, we do.

Life in the leafy suburbs of Belfast, however, was as normal as in any part of mainland Britain. Perhaps even more so. The gin-drinking, Jag driving, fur coat wearing no knickers golf club professional classes led the good life, far enough away from the troubles to enjoy a relatively peaceful and it has to be said, civilised existence. It is ironic, that having lived through almost twenty years of what amounted to a civil war on my doorstep and having moved to England in the '80s, the threat, of international terrorism, in the shape of Al Qaeda, ISIS and other radicalised terrorists, now plagues Western cities like London where I now live and work.

Live broadcasting always has an element of unpredictability about it, in that things may not work out the way you planned them, no matter how meticulous your preparation. Sooner or later, events will conspire against you and there is often little you can do about it. I had been working at the BBC in Belfast for several years, and apart from the odd trivial cock-up or fluff, nothing really disastrous had happened to me. The trouble is that this feeling of invulnerability can easily lead one into a false sense of security. What could possibly go wrong? At that age, I had the invincibility of youth on my side, a feeling that one can overcome anything; or so I believed.

On a rare sultry July evening back in 1979, it went wrong, horribly so. Before I recount this sorry tale, you have to bear in mind that this occurred in the days when BBC1 TV closed down for the night. The evening ended with a local news bulletin read on this particularly memorable evening by yours truly. At around 11pm, I was in the BBC club, enjoying a small sherry with the lads from the camera department, when I looked at my watch and said: "Well I had better be going back, I've got to get ready for the midnight news." I turned to Andy who was to be my cameraman for the broadcast and said, "OK I'll see you in a bit." Off I wandered, back to the newsroom to get the script ready. At about 11.30pm, I got the lift up to the fourth floor and made my way to the unattended studio next to the continuity suite. I stuck my head around the door and exchanged pleasantries with David Olver the continuity announcer, who was on shift that night. The small TV studio was no bigger than a broom cupboard. In truth, I think it doubled as an actual broom cupboard during the day. It had one door in, off the main corridor outside. There was a red light on the door to indicate that the studio was live, but the bulb had blown weeks ago, and it was no longer functioning properly. I thought nothing of it. At about 11.45pm, I was expecting Andy the cameraman to turn up, to perform his pre-transmission routine. This involved the lining up of the camera, checking the studio lights and so on. He hadn't appeared by 11.50pm, so I switched everything on and asked David to check if the picture and sound were OK. He gave me the thumbs-up through the glass. Unusual, I thought. Andy was normally pretty reliable. I gave it no further thought and carried on with my last-minute checks on the script. The News editor stuck his head around the door to check if everything was OK. "All systems Go," I said. I was on top of this thing, easy-peasy. At midnight, the continuity announcer handed over to me and I could see my face flash up on the transmission monitor strategically placed to the side of the camera, out of shot. I was live on air. I began to read the news. The lead and the subsequent stories were a further catalogue of senseless brutal violence and mayhem; of who had done what and to whom. It was a grim, depressing daily litany. Suddenly the door behind the camera burst open, slamming into the wall with a force so great, I heard the lighting above my head rattling. Then, in stumbled an obviously very drunk cameraman and an equally inebriated journalist. I hasten to add that the BBC is not like this now, but this was the '70s in 'bomb-tastic' Belfast. Andy, not realising I was live on air, grabbed the panhandle on the camera and depressing the zoom control, instantly produced an unflattering, tight close up of my face. I must have looked horrified. As if that was bad enough, without warning the journo immediately dropped to his hands and knees and began a slow sloth-like crawl towards me, grunting and dribbling as he went. It was like being an extra in a Monty Python sketch. Worryingly, he disappeared from sight. Then out of the corner of my (rather large) eye on the screen, I spotted a small, crumpled note being proffered in my direction, in his nicotine-stained hand. I could hear his laboured breathing and smell the whisky and cigarettes on his breath. Clumsily, he slid it across the desk in my direction and disappeared beneath it with a grunt. I finished the story I was reading and nervously glanced down. Normally, newsreaders scripts are neatly typed affairs, and as such are a joy to read with their double spacing and twelve-point font. But this effort took some beating. I was staring at a sheet of A4 paper, torn in half, on which were clumsily scrawled, in thick HB pencil, the ramblings of either a drunk or a madman or in this case, both. Foolishly, I attempted to read this piece of late-breaking news. I began,

"This evening an army patrol was attacked in the small border village of…"

I paused, not for effect, but because I simply couldn't read this illegible garbage. "Hack… Hack ba… What *was it?*"

I realised I was stumbling and stumbling badly.

"Hack hack… Hack ball, ball, hack… Hack bollocks, ballacks…" The words swam into view and registered. "Hackballs cross," too late.

The damage was done. I had uttered the words Bollocks and the more colloquial version "ballacks" on her Majesty's BBC TV service. Surely, this was the end? The journo on the floor, who reeked so much of Jameson whiskey, that he constituted an immediate fire risk, was rolling around, wheezing at my feet trying to suppress the audible evidence of his mirth but failing badly. The phlegm and the guttural wafts and ripples of gentle farting was something else. I meanwhile had turned a distinct shade of red or dark grey, if you were watching in black and white, as most people were in those days. The incident went by almost unnoticed by the world, or so I thought. An article in the Belfast Telegraph the following day confirmed that my faux pas had been enjoyed by at least one sleep-deprived viewer. The author appeared more amused than appalled. It set the tone for an eventual rebuke from Baguley and it has since passed into local broadcast legend. A tape of the whole farrago still exists in someone's filing cabinet to this day. Such is the thrill of live broadcasting and since that fateful day, I have never taken it for granted although as the years go by, I find myself doing much less of it. Before each live broadcast or event, I now mentally run through the 'what ifs' and 'what to dos'. It was a useful lesson learnt and never forgotten.

BBC Northern Ireland's live current affairs programme 'Spotlight' had invited both the Reverend Doctor Ian Paisley and Gerry Adams on the show, the producers didn't want these two political behemoths to inadvertently meet up in the corridor outside the studio as tensions were high and sparks would inevitably fly. Unfortunately, there was only one way in and one way out of the studio, up a narrow flight of stairs on the eighth floor of Broadcasting House. They took Paisley into the studio through a little door from the Apparatus room, while they ushered Adams, who had already given his interview, out through the main door and down the stairs. It worked a treat in terms of timing and strategy but was given away by John Ardrey the floor manager who, replying on his talkback to the gallery, said in a loud voice:

"Yes Don, Mr Adams has now safely left the studio."

Unfortunately, this was said just as the huge, hulking, lolloping frame of Dr Paisley lumbered round the back of the set and clumped his way onto the studio floor in his size twelve boots. To put it mildly, he went berserk, the bull in the china shop didn't come close – ranting that he'd been tricked.

Under no circumstances, would he appear on any TV programme with Gerry Adams. All twenty-two stone of him made straight for the main studio door and the stairs to the exit, with John Ardrey, the hapless floor manager running down the corridor after him. The producer now had two things to worry about. The first was that Paisley wasn't going to take part in the programme, which left them with about fifteen minutes to fill. The second was that Paisley might storm down the stairs and reach the lift before Gerry Adams had got into it. What actually happened was that a red-faced Paisley turned around and came back, thundering loud admonishments to everyone in his wake. His coarse, ear-shattering, stentorian mid-Antrim rebukes, ricocheting around the un-carpeted vestibule outside the studio could easily have been heard through the open window in the street below. Eventually, after some diplomacy and coaxing and the promise of a hot buttered scone and a cup of BBC tea, he gave the interview, but he gave Barry Cowan, the presenter a comprehensive roasting for the deceptive tactics of the BBC!

His lack of tact aside, John Ardrey the floor manager, was also rather famous for his incessant farting. He claimed he had a medical condition and that there was something wrong with his bowels... too bloody right there was! He used to drop 'em all over the place with no regard for circumstance or context. During a live 'Scene Around Six' programme he dropped the 'mother of all farts', while Barry was interviewing Bishop Robin Eames, the Archbishop of Armagh and Primate of All Ireland. It was silent but very, very deadly. Barry and the hapless Archbishop stuttered momentarily mid-interview but kept going, without as much as a trace of a smirk or hint of a retch on their faces. At the other end of the studio the sports reporter, John Bennett was shaking from the shoulders and struggling for breath. Within seconds we were all struggling for breath because this monstrous gaseous methane emanation from Ardrey, had filled the room like a green mist from Hell itself. Margaret Percy, the duty announcer and newsreader on the show, left the studio holding a hand-embroidered lace hankie to her nose. Joe Barr, the soft shoed, cardigan-wearing studio manager, ran out of the same door. The cameramen were still at their posts but only just. They were collectively tracking their cameras away from the crime scene and zooming in to compensate. There was this quiet pandemonium around the whole studio, people were really flapping. Don Keating the director, who was Gloria Hunniford's husband, was going apoplectic on the talkback asking why Margaret had left the studio and why John Bennett was lying on the desk and gasping for breath. Ardrey meanwhile, remained oblivious to the jeopardy he'd put the programme in. The moment that Bishop Eames left the studio and the show had cut to a VT, Barry said to John:

"John you are one truly sick wee fucker. Why don't you pull down your trousers and we'll all shit in them!"

God bless Barry, he survived regular gas attacks but passed away in 2004, possibly from the long-term effects of inhaling methane.

Bob Crookes, one of the producers at the BBC in Belfast is an honorary Ulsterman. He is an Englishman born and bred, but he adopted Northern Ireland as his new country and loves living there. He was married to a Welshwoman and lived in Hillsborough, Co Down. You can imagine the jokes in his house. There was this Englishman, Ulsterman and Welshwoman... Bob was a big man in every sense of the word. From his square-cut jaw to his forty-inch diameter thighs he had the build and appearance of – a South African Rugby prop forward on steroids. A gentler man though, you couldn't hope to meet. He is generous to a fault and some of his stories about life in the BBC in the '70s and '80s would make your hair stand on end. When I asked him for two of the highlights, he was swift to respond.

Bob was producing 'Talk Back' – the main morning current affairs programme, which was presented by David Dunseath. It was at the time when South Africa was starting to head inexorably towards the Nelson Mandela Presidency. Eugène Terre'Blanche, the leader of the white supremacists the AWB, became famous during South Africa's era of transition, in 1994 from a white minority to a black majority rule. He established the AWB, the Boer dominated party: Afrikaner Weerstandsbeweging. It was a party, which radically opposed the handover of power to the ANC and President Nelson Mandela. Bob recalled, how in an interview on a national TV programme, Terre'Blanche had made some side reference to Northern Ireland so he chased him down via a friend in SAB, The South African Broadcasting Corporation, and got a phone number. Bob rang him at home, explained who he was and Terre'Blanche said he'd be pleased to talk. This was about 11am. The live show began at 12am. As old Eugene agreed to the interview, Bob dashed down to the studio and rang him back from there. Bob then briefed David Dunseath the presenter, told the engineer on duty what he was going to do and then rang Terre'Blanche from one of the four external studio phones, which were all colour coded. Bob got through once again, as David was settling in the studio. He just confirmed a couple of angles, which Terre'Blanche he was happy with, confirmed the name of the interviewer to him and then said to the engineer

"Mr Terre'Blanche on Red."

And to his horror, the engineer leaned over the desk to his talkback button and said, in a fine South African accent:

"G'day Eugène, a bit of a blick day we're heving … eh, shit face?"

Poor Bob. I think his heart momentarily stopped. As he turned and looked at the engineer in horror, the engineer stared blankly back at him apparently waiting for

Terre'Blanche's reply. Then, casually, and without saying anything, moved his hand almost imperceptibly from the inactive green phone channel to the adjacent live channel, the red one, hit the correct 'red' button and said:

"Good morning Mr Terre'Blanche this is the BBC engineer speaking, may I have a few words for level please?"

As a studio practical joke, Bob says he has never encountered one better and I don't think he wants to. The only better one I ever saw was at Radio 2 and it was all the more pleasurable as it involved Jimmy Young. More on that, later.

Bob's other favourite studio story goes something like this. One evening, while Bob was producing the nightly radio current affairs 'PM Programme' out of studio four, a reporter mentioned an item being run on national radio that was stronger than some of their second line stuff so, as was their right, they recorded it off air to rebroadcast it on their own programme. The turnround though was tight – sixty seconds or less. The reporter hand wrote the introduction, rushed into the studio and gave it to the presenter, whose name was Paddy O'Flaherty, a man with a more than a fleeting resemblance to Sinbad the Sailor. As the item ended, the engineer recording it stopped the tape, spliced the end with a razor blade, stuck on a red tail, spooled it back to the beginning, put a green leader on it and handed it to the operator who was playing the tapes into the programme. This poor man, who had been momentarily distracted by another matter, thought he'd been handed a reel that was for disposal. He immediately stuck his pencil through the hole at the centre of the reel and spun the tape wildly onto the floor. Bob and the production team looked on in total horror. Bob stammered out the words; "Arrgh... that's the next tape." Just as Paddy the presenter started to deliver the link live on air, the hapless engineer dived into the heap of tape on the floor, grabbed the green leader, flashed it through the heads on the big Studer A-820 tape machine, and as he hadn't enough time to lace it to the reels, pressed play and began manually guiding the tape through the playback heads! This he did for a full three and a half minutes, the length of the whole report at a perfect nineteen centimetres per second – anyone listening would not have noticed anything unusual. Tension to this already fraught scenario was added by the fact that recording tape, like string, has a habit of entangling itself. Consequently, knots of tape were climbing their way up towards the machine's playback heads through the engineers' hands. A small crowd had now gathered to watch and each time the operator – with a skill he never knew he possessed – flicked the knots with his finger, they magically fell apart to gasps of 'oohs' and 'ahhs' from the assembled onlookers. It was a very hairy moment indeed, but live broadcasting is full of them and it's what makes it so addictive.

Marty Johnston, a good friend and a cameraman at the BBC in those days, was a member of the crew on a live network broadcast of a concert from the Ulster Hall in Belfast at which I was the live announcer. This particular concert was a fairly posh affair – all dinner jackets and ball gowns. The hall was rammed to the rafters with all the usual Ulster culture vultures, who regularly attend such events. It was common practice in those days, to try to disguise the large EMI 2001 cameras they used, though as Marty rightfully argued at the time, you might as well try to hide a NASA rocket! They were big, heavy, obtrusive pieces of kit. The camera crews were instructed to cover them with black cloth so that they were less visible both to the audience and to other cameras, so they were less likely to be seen in-shot. Marty, to his credit, had always expressed concern that covering the cameras with a black drape was not such a great idea, as it left no room for ventilation. Bear in mind that these cameras were by no means like the smaller solid-state digital cameras of today. They contained transformers, valves and six big electric motors to drive the lenses. They generated enough heat to warm an average house on a winter's day. So, there they were, on a blisteringly hot summer evening in the Ulster Hall in downtown Belfast. Some hugely talented soloist was on stage with her legs apart hugging her instrument, giving her all to the Elgar Cello Concerto – and the audience was in raptures. Up in the stage-left gallery, Marty was going from shot to shot and began to notice that the zoom lens was getting sticky and not up to those long imperceptible slow-zooms. Marty told the director, of his problem over the talkback and it was agreed that he would provide only static shots for the rest of the concert. This was not an unusual event as the zoom motors on the cameras were notoriously unreliable and frequently overheated. A little while later, he heard another cameraman mentioning to the racks guys in the back of the control room that his camera appeared to be producing rather lurid colours and asked if they might tweak it. Around about the same time Marty became aware of a burning smell, which appeared to be coming from his camera. He describes it as the sort of smell you used to get from your train set or your Scalextric set when it was too warm... Ozone!

Marty thought he should let the racks engineers know and pressed the buzzer to alert them that he wanted to talk, or rather, whisper. After a few presses, he heard the guy at the other end putting on his cans and he said:

"This better be important – we're doing our fucking timesheets in here!"

Marty whispered that his camera was overheating and that he could distinctly smell burning. Helpfully, the engineer in Racks said,

"Your nose is too close to your fucking arse." And then hung up.

Marty was now on his own. Men made of lesser stuff would have been out of there, but Marty was made of stronger stuff. Like the captain of the Titanic, he was going down with his ship. He began to think how he could best re-arrange the deckchairs – but whichever way he looked at it – his trusty camera was doomed. I don't know if you are familiar with the Elgar Cello Concerto, but it has many quiet passages. During these, appreciative audiences sit with their eyes closed in aural ecstasy. It was during such a section that Marty heard the camera making a noise like an Ulster fry being enthusiastically cooked on an open griddle: eggs, bacon, sausage, soda bread, potato bread, tomatoes, mushrooms; the full nine yards. This was not good. In a state of mild panic, he slowly lifted the ill-advised black cloth, unscrewed the butterfly bolts of the thin metal trapdoor on the side of the camera and gingerly opened it. To his horror, a pall of thick grey smoke billowed out and wafted up to the ceiling. At the same moment, his viewfinder went black and he knew he in trouble – like a WW2 fighter pilot, he reluctantly had to accept the disappointing fact that he'd been shot down by a

Messerschmitt 109. The game was up. As the smoke turned to flames which were now licking up the side of the camera, the smell of burning wires, melting circuit board and painted metal, aided by Brownian motion reached the nearby audience, it became apparent that the poor soloist on stage wasn't getting as much attention as he was. He frantically buzzed the racks boys, but they were too immersed in their timesheets and expenses claims to be bothered answering. He then did the unthinkable. He unplugged the cable to the camera. This was something that had been drummed into every camera trainee at the BBC's technical training school in Evesham, that you did not do. Cameras had to be shut down in a prescribed sequence. Simply cutting the power to them could cause major damage to the expensive colour tubes inside. Balls to that, Marty's tubes were already burning, and fast! He had no option but to pull the plug. As luck would have it, at that moment, the Orchestra went into one of the quieter passages of the concerto and the Cellist was pouring her heart out. Suddenly and without warning, the camera reacted to this unorthodox procedure and erupted violently. Bang! Flash! BOOM!! The audience instantly and visibly recoiled. This was Belfast in the late '70s after all. A millisecond later, Marty emptied the full contents of a six-litre dry powder Chubb fire extinguisher up the arse end of his £200,000 but now worthless TV camera. It sounded like the Flying Scotsman on a full head of steam leaving St Pancras station, as the hissing and spluttering and soft popping sound of expensive valves exploding, echoed around the now silent hall. The embarrassment for Marty was beyond description. The incident made it into the newspaper the next day. Some smart-arse Telegraph music critic described the concert as, "The Elgar concerto for Cello – and Fire extinguisher."

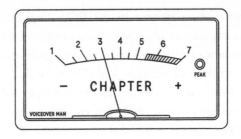

CHAPTER

YOU'RE NOTHING BUT A PLASTIC, INJECTION-MOULDED LINK-MAN

S everal weeks into the new year of 1978, I was excited to discover that BBC Radio 1, the national pop music station was coming to town. The entire week's broadcasting was to come from Belfast. They took over a small studio on the fourth floor and all the presenters and DJ's were flown over from London – at the licence payers' expense. *But who cares?* As I often say, *it's my BBC and I want a part of it!*

One evening, late at night, as I was finishing my duties, I popped into the studio. Radio 1 had closed down for the day and the team had de-camped to their hotel for more of the legendary local hospitality. I don't think they realised quite how generous the hospitality in Belfast can be! I flicked on the studio lights, and there in the middle of the room, was the Radio 1 broadcast desk, complete with logos and signage; in all its red, white and blue glory. Wow! No one was around, so I thought, what an opportunity. I sat down at the controls and marvelled at the thing. Built around the DJ position on three sides were the latest EMT turntables, with slip-mats, Sonifex Cart machines, and what must have been the European Union audio cartridge Mountain. If I'd had a stick, I'd have shaken it at them. Carts, or cartridges, were rather like the old 8 track packs that were popular on domestic hi-fi systems in the 1970s. Big, blue clunky plastic cassettes, containing quarter-inch tape wound inside in a figure of 8 loop. These were the broadcast DJ's stock in trade. You could record anything on to them. Station jingles and idents, sound effects, music beds, you name it. To play one, you slotted it into the cart machine and pressed play. You could even line up four or five in a row and play them in sequence. The possibilities with these machines were endless and they accounted for the dynamic, fast-paced sound that was the hallmark of not only BBC Radio 1 but virtually every single radio station on the planet. I decided to give it a go. I fired up the console slammed a selection of carts into the machines, put a couple of singles on the turntables and for the next two hours, I was a Radio 1 DJ! If anyone had been listening, I must have sounded mad. It was an exhilarating experience, yet I could never imagine how close I would get to the real thing, ten years later.

One Afternoon in June 1980, I was summoned to Baguley's office and given the good news that I was to be the Jury Foreman on that year's "Eurovision Song Contest" pre-selection show. This onerous responsibility required me to sit in front of a camera in a studio in Belfast and deliver the Northern Ireland jury's verdict on who we considered were the best entrants into that year's contest. The eventual winner would then go through to represent the UK, in the main event some weeks later. I was all of twenty-three years old and this was to be my first exposure on live National TV on BBC1. The big day came around and I was naturally apprehensive. I watched the studio monitor as the voting began, the other regional presenters ahead of me doing a fine job. Then it came to my turn. Terry Wogan, the host who I had admired for years, handed over to me and I began to announce the results of the Belfast jury. I looked up at the monitor to the side of my camera and saw myself, picture in picture in a small box to the right of Terry's head. This was it, my big moment on national TV with an audience of 12 million on BBC1! I got through it OK, and as we were wrapping up, Terry threw an unexpected question. I don't know quite what happened, but I must have misheard him and my response was at odds with the question. Howls of laughter rang into my earpiece from the gallery and the audience in Television Centre London. I squirmed with embarrassment, not quite knowing what to do or say next. That was it, I was off and the next results from some hapless presenter in Wales were on screen. I remember John Ardrey, the farting floor manager giving us the all-clear, which given his condition was, to say the least ironic. He was still laughing while at the same time trying hard not to let one go. He did try to console me as best he could, but I knew I had blown it, which is indeed what he did shortly afterwards – several huge gaseous egg-filled guffs, in the space of sixty seconds. He kindly offered to share a cab home with me, but I declined on account that I didn't have my gas mask with me. The next day in one of the national broadsheets, a TV reviewer had written a piece about the show. He singled me out for some pretty damning criticism. The words he used about me were particularly stinging. I was described as nothing but, "a plastic, injection-moulded link man." From that day on, I resolved to be less predictable and a great deal truer to myself. It was the right decision but a decision that was to land me in even more trouble later in my career.

By the early 1980s, I had started to branch out and take on other work. I was commissioned by the BBC's World service to make a short series of radio programmes about life in Northern Ireland. The first was to cover the remarkable history of the famous Belfast shipbuilders Harland & Wolff, where my father had toiled for his entire working life. I set about my task with all the enthusiasm of a poker player with a fistful of aces. When I had conducted all the interviews, recorded my links and cut the whole thing together, feeling rather pleased with myself, I handed the finished programme over to the producer. Several days later, I had an irate call from her, inviting me over to discuss the show. What I hadn't considered, was the target audience for this programme. Intended for transmission on The World Service, naturally, the listeners would not have had English as their first language. On listening back to the recording, I was horrified to hear my links peppered with idiom and colloquial analogy. Phrases like, "Lame duck" and "Dead in the water" cropped up with alarming regularity. The exasperated producer explained to me that non-English speaking listeners, would be completely bemused by such phrases and as such, the programme as it stood, would be un-transmittable! It was a salutary lesson. I had to remake the entire thing from scratch. I have never since forgotten that radio is an intensely personal experience. Unlike TV, it is essentially a one to one medium. I scream at the radio even today when I hear presenters saying things like, "Hello everyone" when a simple "Hello" would do and the lesson about knowing your audience is one that is even more relevant in the world of voiceover.

In 1980 I was commissioned, by the BBC's arts and entertainment department to read the 'Morning Story' on National BBC Radio 4. It was a short story, written by a local Irish author. This was my first experience of voice acting and an experience that would shape the rest of my career. I took to it like 'a duck to water'. (BBC World service listeners please see the explanation on page 523!). Long-form projects like this allow you to get your teeth into a subject. To give full rein to all the emotion and expression contained in the text. Light and shade, variation in intensity, prosody, pitch and volume, accents for direct speech, and the all-important *emphaaaasis*, dear boy! Most people can read, that's a given. But reading text out loud and holding a listener's attention, is another matter altogether. Actors such as Benedict Cumberbatch, Johnny Heller, Scott Brick, Peter Kenny, Morgan Freeman, Bryan Cranston, Martin Jarvis, Michael Gambon, James Faulkner and Sean Pertwee are all masters of the art. I studied them keenly and learnt much from their individual styles. This kind of work is now the thing I love doing best. Documentary narration is another favourite and a form of voiceover that I would get to know well later in my career.

Paul Muldoon, the celebrated poet and contemporary of Seamus Heaney, was a producer in the arts and entertainment department at the BBC at that time. He held the post of Oxford Professor of Poetry from 1999 to 2004. He then went to Princeton University and was both the Howard G. B. Clark '21 Professor in the Humanities and chair of the Lewis Centre for the Arts Professor Emeritus. Along with Judith Elliot, they ran the arts department at BBC Northern Ireland. I got to know Paul fairly well and found him to be thoroughly likeable. He had a typical poet's demeanour and was a fan of the crushed corduroy, tweed jacket with leather elbow patches, suede shoe look. One always got the impression, when talking to Paul that his mind was on other things – which it probably was. Indeed, so vague was his approach it was often hard to tell if he was speaking to you or merely thinking to himself, out loud! I ran into him recently in London's Greek Street, and we caught up with each other's lives over coffee in the Bar Italia. Paul has now moved permanently to the USA, taking up residency as Emeritus Professor of Poetry at the University of Princeton in New Jersey. I have no doubt the Yanks adore his dreamy Celtic charm. Several weeks after this chance encounter, I received the sad news that a good friend of mine, a commercials producer had died in tragic circumstances. I don't know why, but I wrote a short poem about him and emailed it to Paul in the USA. Now, I haven't written a poem since I was seventeen years old, but he wrote back thanking me for it and saying how moved he was. I wasn't sure if he was being kind or sympathetic, but I appreciated his reply. I like Poetry. Someone once wrote: It's simply the right words in the right order, easier said than done but when done well, it can start a revolution.

Towards the end of my time at the BBC in Northern Ireland, in 1980 I found myself in Dublin, or more precisely, Bray, a small-town south of the City in County Wicklow. I had gone with a small independent film company to make a documentary about the film studios there. Ireland's Ardmore Studios were experiencing something of a revival. The Irish government had relaxed the taxation rules for foreign artists and film production companies, giving them valuable tax breaks. Many American and British stars had based themselves in Ireland for this very reason. It was, to all intents and purposes an artistic tax haven. In production at the studios were two films. One was 'Purple Taxi' and the other was 'Excalibur', directed by the great John Boorman. One afternoon, I found myself alone, wandering down a corridor trying to find the sound stage where Purple Taxi was being shot, when a slightly built man wearing a beautifully tailored suit, stepped out of a room in front of me. There was no one else around and he proceeded to walk in front of me towards a large set of double doors. He stopped, turned 90°, opened the door, motioned with his hand and said, "After you!" Impressed by the stranger's good manners I turned to him as I walked through and thanked him for his kindness. It was only when I looked at his face, I realised that I was looking at one of the biggest movie stars of all time, and I mean *all* time. They don't come much bigger. I was face to face with none other than Mr Fred Astaire! I didn't know what to do. When something like that happens so unexpectedly, it kind of takes your breath away. I must have appeared somewhat ham-fisted, but I breezed on through as if it was an everyday occurrence! Looking back on it now, it was a wasted opportunity, and I am quite sorry that I didn't at least engage him in polite conversation, though God knows what I would have said. I mean, where on earth would you start? Several doors further on, a woman appeared out of a dressing room. She was heading in the same direction. As she reached for her keys to lock her door, I walked past and held the next doors open for her. By this time, Fred had caught up. "Hi, Charl," he said. I realised this was Charlotte Rampling and the two of them breezed past on their way to the set, thanking me for my courtesy. What a day, this was turning out to be. Later I secured an interview with the great Peter Ustinov, who was also starring in the film. He was a terrific sport and answered all the questions I put to him with his usual acerbic wit. The interview was broadcast the next day on BBC Radio Ulster's morning news programme and was well-received, by all accounts. I was surprised, therefore, to get a phone call the next day from a somewhat irate Frank Delaney, the BBC's Southern Ireland correspondent. He berated me on my insolence and disrespect by complaining in no uncertain terms, that I was encroaching on his exclusive patch! Can you believe the cheek of the man? I had stolen an interview with one of the great raconteurs of the 20th century from under his nose. Unlike Ustinov, I didn't know what to say. Frank had a reputation for being forthright and he certainly left me in no doubt about his attitude to my foray into his territory. All's fair in love and war, I thought.

"Frank," I said, "You'll just have to get up earlier in the mornings." I was a cocky bastard back then.

That was it. Brrrr. The phone went dead. I have since met up with Frank and he feigned ignorance of the episode, which I suppose was generous of him. He's not a bad bloke and is actually great company. That trip to Ardmore also saw me secure an interview with the then-unknown Liam Neeson, who was playing the part of Sir Gawain in Excalibur. I had worked with Liam several years before in a play I was in at Belfast's Lyric theatre. I say, worked with… in essence, I was a spear-carrier on the back row of a Roman legion in St Joan of Arc but share a stage with him, I did! Several years earlier, my Auntie Dorothy, who was the stage manager at the Lyric Theatre had a conversation with Liam that ran like this:

"Dorothy, I'm thinking of heading to London to work."

"Don't be daft, Liam, you are too tall, you'll never get any work there."

It was the career advice equivalent of Dick Rowe's infamous turning down a recording contract for 'The Beatles!"

Later in the same week, on my return to Belfast, I was asked by newsroom colleague and fellow BBC presenter, Sean Rafferty to deliver a birthday present to the home of a friend of his. Sean is one of the original 'Ulster culture vultures' and as such has cultivated friendships with the (mostly) titled great and good of Ireland. From Dowager Duchesses to minor European royalty, Sean it seemed knew them all. Some of them intimately. The address Sean had given me was in one of the swankier areas of Dublin. I was driving a clapped out, rusting Triumph Herald convertible at the time, so I felt a little apprehensive when I arrived at the gates to the property to discover that the driveway was over a mile long! The recipient of the gift was a girl called Sabrina, and that was as much as I knew, as I had glanced at the silver tag attached to the carefully wrapped box on the front seat. The house itself was an imposing, ivy-clad Georgian mansion, typical of many of the homes built and lived in by the English nobility during the 18th and 19th Century in pre-partition Ireland. I rang the bell and some moments later I was greeted by a fresh-faced, woman – all rosy-cheeked and ever so slightly dishevelled in that way the true English aristocracy often are.

"I have a present for Sabrina," I said.

"Oh! How lovely," she said. "That's me!"

She motioned for me to come in. I entered a large hall with a black and white checkerboard marble tile floor which was strewn with expensive-looking Persian rugs. There were the usual age-of-empire artefacts; antiques and trophies strewn around, antelope antlers on the walls, old masters in impossibly ornate gilded frames, Georgian monochrome family images framed in silver, groaning on top of ancient and no doubt priceless, antique mahogany tables. I stepped into the centre of the vast hall. The large oak door behind me ground to a close with a satisfying clunk.

"I'm Sabrina," she said, extending her hand, "lovely to meet you."

"And you too," I stammered.

"I have a gift for you from Sean Rafferty," I said.

A look of delight spread across her slightly flushed cheeks and she took the package from me and placed gently it on the hall table.

"How kind of you to take the time to deliver it," she said. "Have you come far?"

"From Belfast," I said. "But I was passing anyhow" I lied, to ease any embarrassment she might have felt at someone having to make a one hundred mile long journey on her behalf.

By this time, I was putting two and two together. Various items on display in the hall had led me to the conclusion that this was the home of James Guinness, of the famous brewing family. Sabrina was one of his daughters, who at the time was not only the most eligible women in Britain but was dating HRH Prince Charles. She allegedly also dated Rod Stewart, Bryan Ferry, Michael Douglas, Mick Jagger, Dai 'Seducer of the Valleys' Llewellyn and Tory politician Jonathan Aitken. She was dubbed the 'It Girl' of her generation as she also courted Hollywood's, Jack Nicholson... and survived! She is now safely and happily married to playwright Sir Tom Stoppard. How she found the time to start Youth Cable TV with Greg Dyke and be a PA to David Sterling, the founder of the SAS is anyone's guess. The silence was broken by the sound of a bell tinkling in a distant room. A soft, pink rose petal from an arrangement near the front door wafted silently from its bud and landed on the floor.

"Would you like a drink?" she said.

"Oh! Yes please, that would be nice" was my reply.

"OK. Now, umm... what would you like? Tea, coffee, water... or maybe you'd like..." There was a tantalising and possibly carefully crafted pause. "A Guinness?"

A coy smile played across her lips. I imagined that old James must have the bloody stuff on a private tap connected to the brewery, a few miles down the road.

"Yes, a Guinness would be nice," I said, not wishing to appear rude.

"Alright then, a Guinness it is."

It must be odd to have an eponymous drink as famous as that bearing your name. It would be the equivalent of me offering someone a 'Dickson'. She traipsed off through one of the walnut panelled doors, which lined the North end of the great hall. Several minutes later she reappeared, clutching a small silver tray in both hands, on which was placed an empty glass, a bottle opener and a bottle of Guinness. She put the tray down on the table, clearing away several back copies of Country Life and fallen peony petals as she did so. Pouring Guinness from a bottle is a bit of an art. Great things come to those who wait, and all that. Pour it too fast, and it erupts and explodes out of the glass like an anaemic Donkey's tongue. Pour it too slowly and you don't get the required, smooth inch deep and satisfying head that every savvy stout drinker demands and expects. I was looking forward to demonstrating my Guinness pouring technique to Sabrina, I was so sure she would be impressed with my youthful and experienced wrist action. As I made my move towards the table to begin the ritual, I was more than a little disappointed to see her grab the bottle herself. She picked it up off the ornamental silver tray and immediately cracked off the top with the bottle opener in one swift flick of the wrist.

"God, I hope I'm doing this right!" She exclaimed.

Without any further warning, she up-ended the bottle 180° into the glass. The resultant explosion was immediate and embarrassingly brutal. Half a pint of precious brown foam shot up the sides of the glass and began at once, to cascade onto the antique Persian rug at our feet. The smell of hops and malt was overpowering. She shrieked, dropped the bottle and flung the glass out of her hand. I stood and stared in utter disbelief. This legendary beverage had provided the means to afford her an expensive English convent education and had allowed the trappings of wealth that few in Ireland could imagine, yet it seemed she hadn't ever poured one herself. It was unbelievable. I have to say, she covered her faux pas and resultant obvious embarrassment well. We had a good-natured laugh about it and I opted for a safer glass of mineral water instead. I was driving after all. Sean thought the story most amusing and entirely typical. He'd seen the Duchess of Westminster do something similar with a bottle of Krug once and Princess Margaret, it is rumoured, on the private Caribbean island of Mustique delighted in balancing empty Bollinger bottles on male guests, including one infamous and well-endowed East End gangster! The aristocracy eh! Don't you just love 'em?

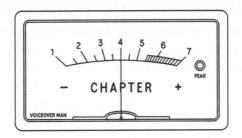

THE CHANCELLOR HAS JUST
ANNOUNCED HIS 'BUNNY MIDGET'

I got my first big break, age twenty-three, when I applied for a job, as an announcer at BBC Radio 2 in London. It had been advertised in Ariel, the BBC's in-house journal. Amazingly, I had two job offers – simultaneously. The other was to work as an assistant to a man called John Behague in Jordan, training Jordanian announcers and newsreaders. London though was *my* Mecca. I had dreamed of it as a boy in my small bedroom in Belfast for years. It had seemed so impossibly far away back then, almost like another planet. But now, I had my chance. I seized the opportunity and threw myself into it with all the enthusiasm I could muster.

I was called to an interview in London and sat in an imposing office near Broadcasting House in front of several important-looking men wearing sober suits, one of whom, Iain Purdon was to become my boss. The other was Bryant Marriott, the avuncular, pipe-smoking Controller of BBC Radio 2. As I was on the way to the interview and exiting Oxford Circus tube station, I recall slapping my thigh and giving myself a damn good talking to. Psyching myself up for what was undoubtedly the most important moment of my professional life to date. Nervous as a kitten, I waited in a small anteroom, waiting to be called. The interview went as well as I could have hoped for.

Two weeks later I got the news that I had dreamed I would hear. I was offered a six-month attachment as a radio announcer on national BBC Radio! To say I was overjoyed, would be an understatement. And so, when the time came, I packed a small suitcase and flew to London. My wife followed three weeks later. We never looked back and never returned.

I had rented a small basement flat in London's Pimlico, I had a brand-new BMW and a burning ambition to set the world on fire, or at least singe it ever so slightly at the edges. The BBC back in the early '80s was full of the most wonderfully colourful characters. It feels like it was only yesterday when I first stepped through its imposingly tall and heavy bronze doors in Portland Place at the top of London's Regent Street, beneath which was Eric Gill's imposing and controversial wraith-like statue of Prospero and Ariel. The doors led into the softly lit Carrara marble-lined reception, which was guarded by two uniformed commissionaires with the obligatory white gloves tucked under their shiny epaulettes. It was an entrance that had been designed to impress. The year was 1982. Several years before a corporate 'wrecking ball' demolished the institution. John Birt arrived like an uninvited guest at a rather classy party. The institution back then was run by

From:	Presentation Organiser, Northern Ireland.		
Room No. & Building:	402 BH Belfast	Tel. Ext: 202	date: 26.01.81
Subject:	RESIGNATION		
To:	Peter Dickson	Copy to:	HPNI; HRU; HANI; S.Pers.O.; Pers.O.1

I acknowledge receipt of your resignation copied to me and dated 26.1.81.

Your last day with this department will be Friday 27 February 1981, but as you will have 4½ days leave (3½ Annual + 1 PHL New Year's Day) your last effective duty will be Friday 20 February 0530-1500, Radio Ulster Continuity.

PMB/SAC   (Michael Baguley)

BBC resignation – 1981 – Belfast.

ex-military, ex-public-school types with a strict regard for protocol, but with a huge tolerance for individual eccentricity and it must be said, alcohol. Most of them were three sandwiches short of a picnic. You were, however, treated like a grown-up and given the unfettered freedom to be as creative and as bonkers as you like. As long as the job was done, to a high standard and on time, no one seemed to care how you went about it. Most of the truly great programme ideas and formats were dreamt up in three of the closest watering holes to Broadcasting House; the 'Crown and Sceptre' on Great Titchfield Street, the 'Yorkshire Grey' on Langham Street and the 'Horse and Groom' on Great Portland Street. Rather like Fleet Street the centre of the British newspaper industry in days gone by, the creative juices were all too often stimulated and indeed fuelled by alcohol. Today, the BBC is an altogether different beast. The time and motion apparatchiks, the unfocussed-focus groups and the marauding gangs of monstrously remunerated corporate analysts, consultants and accountants, have altered the insouciant ambience irrevocably. But back then, as a young man in swinging Thatcher's London, it was pretty much perfect. It remains one of the happiest periods of my career, and in many ways, it shaped the rest of my life in this crazy old business we call 'Show'.

There were roughly fifteen or sixteen staff announcers in the presentation department in the early '80s and they were indeed an odd bunch! There was Robin Boyle, God rest his soul, who was the voice of "Friday Night is Music Night." Robin, or Bob as he was known to his friends, was a tall imposing figure with a head of glossy pomade black hair and a pencil moustache. He had the air of a WW2 fighter pilot, and indeed I believe he may have served in the RAF during the war. He also wore silk cravats, smoked un-tipped Park Drive cigarettes and drove a fabulously expensive BMW motorcycle, which to my mind back then was about as exotic as you could get. Bob though, was clearly not the full shilling, there were a couple of Kangaroos loose in his upper paddock. He would explode without warning into beetroot red rants at the slightest provocation and then calm down as quickly as he started. He called everyone "Matey," possibly because he couldn't remember their name. He was though, a consummate broadcaster and lived life on the edge. He was a great mentor and I learned a lot from him. Sadly, he is no longer with us. Then, there was James Alexander–Gordon or JAG as he was known, the quintessential voice of the football results on BBC radio.

The calming cadences and gentle prosody of his lowland Scottish accented voice announced the final scores of every single football match played up and down the country on a Saturday in Britain. "Fife – 4, Forfar – 5" was his all-time favourite result, and he prayed for it to come up every week. Reading the football results was his main claim to fame, in common with Tim Gudgin and Len Martin, his counterparts on BBC TV's Grandstand. They had held their respective roles for so long, they retain a special and very unique place in broadcasting history. JAG's soft lilting voice transformed the football results at 5 o'clock on a Saturday into a kind of hypnotic poetry. Rather like the shipping forecast on Radio 4, it had its own distinctive cadence and rhythm. JAG had the uncanny ability to scan the result with his eyes first and then alter his inflection depending on the score. In other words, if the number of goals scored by the first team was higher than the number scored by the second team, he would inflect up on the first and down on the last and vice versa! It sounds easy, but you try doing it – often at first sight and at speed. Watching him in action, from the other side of the glass, was a masterclass. I still love watching other professionals at work and grab those increasingly rare opportunities when they arise.

For all his incredible competence though, JAG had his moments of fallibility, as all of us do from time to time. In live broadcasting, cock-ups are pretty much inevitable. There was a now-infamous occasion during a news flash on the Jimmy Young show on BBC Radio 2 when James had to announce the details of a mini-budget which had just been sent down the wires to the newsroom by the Press Association. James rushed into the studio, hit the talkback button and ordered the Jimmy Young Show producer to hand over to him for some important news. This, they dutifully did. He began:

"The Chancellor of the Exchequer has just announced that he is to present a 'Bunny Midget' to the Commons later today."

Howls of laughter could be heard from the newsroom, and presumably across the nation. Poor James. Spoonerisms were the announcer's worst nightmare; well second worst nightmare. Vomiting on an open microphone comes at the top of the list. The MP Jeremy Hunt, the often spoonerised Culture Secretary has fallen victim to many a misplaced phoneme on the BBC. JAG though, was one of life's characters. Only five feet, six inches tall yet with the disposition and sunny confidence of a much taller man, he was the departmental clown and played the role with aplomb. He was born and raised in Scotland, the son of a publican he had contracted polio as a young child. As a result of this devastating illness, which was rife in the 1940s, he was left with one leg shorter than the other and wore a prosthetic shoe to compensate for the difference. On one memorable occasion, he told me that as he arrived for work one morning and was ascending the marble staircase in Broadcasting House to begin his shift, he encountered Marmaduke Hussey who was the Chairman of the BBC, coming down. Old Hussey, an ex-guards' officer was a war veteran and had sustained a shrapnel injury to his leg at the Battle of Monte Cassino in 1944. This had left him with a permanent and pronounced limp. The two men met on the stairs outside the imposing oak door of the Director General's office on the first floor. Hussey caught sight of JAG limping and lumbering up the stairs in front of him. Not knowing quite what the protocol was, JAG proceeded on his merry way, huffing and puffing and bumping and clattering his way up the stairs smiling and laughing as he went, stick in one hand, briefcase in the other. When he drew level with the Chairman, JAG nodded and said "Mornin' Chief!" Hussey took one look at him, and bellowed:

"Are you taking the fucking piss?"

JAG dined out on that story for years. In truth, though he was full of the most wonderful, fanciful stories. Most of them, I suspect a product of his overactive and fertile imagination, nurtured during his long incarceration as a child in a Glasgow hospital bed. He allegedly; owned 'a water bottling plant on Lough Fyne', made 'TV commercials for Mercedes in the Sahara Desert' and 'owned a luxury penthouse flat overlooking the Mediterranean'. His main claim to fame though, and quite possibly his tallest tale was his legendary encounter with a ghost, in what is now the five-star Langham Hotel in London's Portland Place. The 'Langham' is a grand imposing building across the street from Broadcasting House and during the '70s and '80s, it was leased to the corporation as office space. It also housed the BBC Club and a variety of rooms on the fourth floor which were set aside as bedrooms for staff, who had to work shifts. The 'Langham' was originally one of London's grandest hotels and the scene, a hundred or so years ago of a gruesome death. JAG would relate the fanciful tale to whoever cared to listen with the open-faced wonderment of a small child. As legend would have it, a serving Prussian army officer was staying in the hotel, in the days when the streets were lit by gaslight and reeked of horse manure. The story goes that he was having an affair with a married woman, whose outraged husband had tracked them down to the hotel and had burst in on the shocking, adulterous scene. The Prussian, obviously a man of great honour, having been witnessed in the adulterous act took it upon himself to instantly hurl himself by his breeches out of the fourth floor bedroom window and onto the cobbled street below. It was, by all accounts an event that scandalised Victorian London. The point of this story is that our Prussian friend, or rather his ghost, took it upon himself to haunt the legendary room 401 and the surrounding corridors ever since.

On a cold late December night in 1982, JAG was scheduled onto the overnight announcer shift, which required him to stay in the Langham. He read the midnight news on Radio 2, said goodnight to the news editor on duty that night and made his way downstairs to the oak-panelled duty office on the ground floor, which was tucked discreetly away behind the main reception of Broadcasting House. He knocked on the door and entered. There, Roger Pearce the duty officer that night was waiting for him with a warming finger or two of Islay malt, in a Waterford cut-glass tumbler. It was a lovely tradition back then, the announcers from Radio's 2 and 4, whose midnight bulletins ended at similar times, would gather in the duty-office for a nightcap. The duty office was located in a fabulously cosy and very intimate oak-panelled room, with a thick red carpet, dark oak wainscoting on the walls and warm low lighting. The receiving room, as it was more formally known was designed to welcome important guests, stars of stage and screen and even royalty who would from time to time visit Broadcasting House. On a small desk to the side, next to a comfy velvet armchair, there was a black Mont Blanc fountain pen next to leather-bound visitor's book which contained the most amazing collection of autographs I have ever seen. Clark Gable, HM King George V, HM Queen Elizabeth II, Chaplin, Anthony Eden, Laurel and Hardy, Jackie Onassis, Margaret Thatcher, Churchill, Eisenhower, Marilyn Monroe, Fred Astaire. You could name almost anyone of significance in the 20th Century and you would find their name in there. It is, without doubt, the mother of all autograph collections and must be priceless. Anyway, back to the story. At 1.45am, after half an hour or so of companionable conversation and airy banter, JAG picked up his small overnight bag and headed for the 'Langham'. He walked across a deserted Langham Place via the zebra crossing, walked up the imposing staircase from the street, collected the key to room 401 from the commissionaire on duty, took the lift to the fourth floor, located the room and got to bed. At around 4am as the story goes, he inexplicably woke up, aware that something was not quite as it should be. It was a cold December night but the temperature in the centrally heated room had dropped to below freezing. By the cold light of a sodium streetlamp on Portland Place, which filtered its way into the small bedroom through a chink in the curtains, JAG could see his breath forming in distinct furls in the air. Uneasily, and not yet quite fully conscious, he sat up in bed and peered into the semi-darkness of the room. There was utter silence. Then suddenly at the foot of his bed, he made out the unmistakable figure of a man. A man, who was a good six feet tall – in full 19th Century military uniform, complete with sword and spurs. He was standing there, motionless and silent as the grave. JAG, called out.

"Who's there?" "What do you want?"

There was no response. He called out again. No reply. The man just turned away from the bed and slowly and noiselessly made for the window on the opposite side of the room. Terrified, JAG reached down to the floor and grabbed his hefty orthopaedic shoe and with an almighty grunt, he hurled it at the man. Either he missed, or the shoe passed straight through the man, but it slammed into the wall on the far side of the room next to the wardrobe, with a deafening clatter. That was it. JAG was up and heading for the door. Hyperventilating and heart pumping in sheer terror, he ran, in his pyjamas down the four flights of stairs, past a bemused security guard, out of the front door of the Langham, across the zebra crossing, into Broadcasting House, hobbled up three flights of stairs and only stopped when practically out of breath, he got to the newsroom. Whether he read the 6am bulletin in his pyjamas, isn't known. Like much of the fine detail of JAG's stories it was lost in the translation. But great stories they were nonetheless, and they kept us all entertained for years. Sir Terry Wogan was a fan of these outlandish stories and at social occasions, he could often be seen egging JAG on for more.

The remaining members of the department consisted of a rag-tag bunch of fine voice talent who at the time included: Jean Challis, Patrick Lunt, Colin Berry, David Geary, Richard Clegg, David Bellan, Steve Madden, Charles Nove, John Marsh, Hilary Osborne, Alex Lester and Alan Dedicoat. Alan became famous as the 'Voice of the Balls' on The National Lottery on TV and as well as being the last man to leave the Radio 2 presentation department as its senior announcer, he is at the time of writing the voice of 'Strictly Come Dancing' on BBC1 TV. I recall him saying to me once over a pint, how much he envied me for my freelance work when I was additionally working for BBC TV presentation as a live promo voiceover at Television Centre, in the evenings. Little did he know then, what great things lay in store for him. I guess it's a case of, 'beware of that on which you set your heart, for you shall surely have it', as Billy Shakespeare once wrote. Alan certainly set his heart on it and it was delivered – by the bucket load!

The Radio 2 presentation department was headed up by a Scotsman called Iain Purdon. A Celt – but Harrow educated, he had a Presbyterian work ethic like a Clydebank shipbuilder on permanent overtime. He ran the BBC Radio 2 Presentation department with ruthless efficiency. Automating everything that moved. He was one of the first to employ computers for administration tasks at the BBC. He had an overtly obvious passion and enthusiasm for his work; working longer hours than demanded by his contract and zealously guarding the standard of his department's output. He would fight your corner in any argument and then give you the mother of all bollockings privately afterwards. He was a great boss to work for and was hugely respected. In 1987 he wrote my annual report and commented as follows:

"I value Peter's performing abilities enormously. He puts a lot of effort into his work in terms of careful planning and actual delivery of the words. His contribution to the promotions unit is first class and he is making a name for himself as a presenter. He has a lot going for him we can field him widely in routine announcer duties while his 'Nightcap' Series is a good outlet for the zany side of this talent. His editorial judgement, however, is less advanced, although I have noted his recent efforts to soften his approach where appropriate. He is also not naturally tolerant of BBC administrative procedures, which can show in his dealings with those who operate them. Let this not unduly detract though from a good report, on a good broadcaster."

I have never and never will be tolerant of any administrative procedures! At least he had that spot on. I have a lot to thank him for though, he gave me my first taste of the big time as a Radio 2 presentation announcer and I will never forget the blind faith he put in me. When I look back on my extremely fortunate career, I must recognise and acknowledge the opportunity he gave me. Cheers Iain, I owe you big time!

The BBC in the 1980s was run rather like the Civil Service and its internal organisation and structure was conducted along very similar lines. Everyone on management grade had a title, which was abbreviated to an acronym. So, Controller Radio 2 became, C.R.2, The editor of news became Ed News R2, and Purdon as presentation editor Radio 2 became Pres Ed R2. In much the same way that emails are the curse of most organisations these days, inter-departmental memos were written in their thousands each day on typewriters and in triplicate, using carbon paper (remember that?). Rooms were set aside and filled to bursting with filing cabinets in which to store them. The BBC's carbon paper bill must have been enormous. The place, it seemed to me was run on fear with everyone from Alisdair Milne the Director-General down, covering their arses with memos. Purdon was no exception. He loved his memos and issued torrents of them daily.

One of the duties of the presentation department was to produce the various on air promos and trails, played throughout the day on shows on the network. Back then, this little outpost was located on the second floor of Broadcasting House in London, just across the corridor from the offices of BBC Radio 3, the classical music network. The room and studio combined were no bigger than a broom cupboard. In fact, I think it might once have been a broom cupboard or indeed a lavatory! We had great fun in there though. Unfettered and unregulated by the suits, some of us gave full reign to our imaginative, creative sides! The promo unit was presided over by a couple of clerks, who basically, kept us all in order and scheduled the promos for transmission. One of these clerks was a woman called Lesley Douglas, who rose up the ranks to become the Radio 2 channel controller. She fell on her sword however several years later following the Sachs-Gate Jonathan Ross / Russell Brand scandal. Back in the '80s though she was fresh from Newcastle Upon Tyne, her hometown and found herself, like me, trying to adjust to the rigours of life in London. We had much in common, including our shared slightly anarchic sense of humour and I can recall spending many a happy hour in her company. On one memorable occasion, I climbed up onto a filing cabinet during the lunch hour and hid in a large tambour cupboard behind her desk. I must have waited there for over twenty minutes, intending to jump out and surprise her on her return. She came back eventually, with Iain Purdon the Radio 2 departmental boss and I was forced to wait a further twenty minutes while they had a meeting! By this time, my knees were bleeding and I was short of oxygen. Purdon eventually left however and without any further delay, I made my surprise attack. The poor girl nearly died on the spot, but after regaining her composure, saw the funny side. Her rise through the ranks was meteoric, fast and quite unprecedented.

The corridor outside post-production suite number three in BBC Broadcasting House, London, was en route from the main reception hall, to the Radio 2 on air broadcast studios two flights down the stairs. Consequently, all the big name, celebrity guests of the day would pass right outside our door. From Presidents to Hollywood A-listers to royalty they all had to pass PPS3. Frequently, we would grab unsuspecting celebrities as they passed our studio to ask them for sound bites and other material for use later or simply for our amusement! On one such occasion, around the mid-eighties, I grabbed a bewildered Tommy Trinder, one of the best-loved war-time comedians in Britain and an equally confused Hollywood legend Dennis "Easy Rider" Hopper and persuaded them to enter the broom cupboard at the same time. I must have appeared insane, but they went along with it and obliged me with a quick interview and a few sound bites. It was a magical moment. There, squeezed into the smallest studio in the known universe was Tommy Trinder, one of the finest British music hall acts of the 1940s and Dennis Hopper, one of Hollywood's biggest stars. Neither of them knew who the other was, but that was the beauty of the occasion. I had Tommy shouting his ludicrous catchphrase "Ha ha! You lucky people!" and Dennis reciting passages as Billy from "Easy Rider." At the time, I couldn't see any way of getting these remarkable sound bites to air, but I was determined to find one. I was later to encounter Hopper again, in a different role, this time in a TV studio. He luckily didn't recognise me, and I am pleased to say that it led to an altogether more hilarious encounter. More of which later.

Radio 2 was a 24-hour-a-day radio station and our duties as network announcers were threefold. We rotated between news-reading duties, through continuity announcing, to live programme presentation. News reading shifts were characterised by fifty-five minutes of sheer boredom – reading the paper and drinking copious amounts of coffee; followed by a breathless last-minute dash to the studio and five or ten minutes of sheer drama. The announcer's rota was issued weekly and had all the complexity of an airline timetable. Working out when and where you had to be, on any given day was a feat in itself. Finding the right studio was another matter. BBC Broadcasting House in London is a hugely complex, labyrinthine building which was constructed in the 1920s. There are basements and sub-basements, sub-sub basements, mezzanine floors, underground tunnels, dozens of elevators and extensions and miles of drab, uniform corridors, all painted in the same regulation standard magnolia. When you walked along them, the floors rattled as underneath the carpet, were trap doors through which hundreds of audio and communications cables had been laid. It took me almost a whole year to be confident enough to find my way around and reach any given destination. Guests of shows on Radio 2 would sometimes inadvertently lose their minders, who escorted them from reception, and they would get lost for days at a time! In the late 1990s, Frank Bough disappeared for years but that had nothing to do with his sense of direction, more his lack of good sense and discretion.

Continuity announcing was by far the most taxing of the roles undertaken by the announcers in the Presentation department. It was rather like being in charge of a small railway network, making sure programmes arrived and departed on time with a seamless transition at every junction. It was one of those jobs where you had to be prepared for any eventuality. From the Queen dying, or her Mother choking on a fishbone (as she often did) to something as mundane as a tape machine misfiring. I loved it, but not as much as live programme presentation. As I said, Radio 2 was a 24-hour station. The overnight sustaining service was run by the staff announcers, who presented the music programmes between 1am and 6am. The show was imaginatively called: 'You And The Night And The Music' or YATNAM to use the BBC acronym, or as we called it 'You And The Shite And The Mucus'. Back then, the BBC had an agreement with the all-powerful Musicians Union to guarantee a quota of live in-house recorded music sessions per year. This was to show the licence payer and the government of the day, that all those expensive in-house orchestras and bands really were value for money. It was, of course, utter bollocks. Most of this crap ended up on 'YATNAM', along with a high proportion of what were called, 'Radioplay' recordings. These ended up on vinyl LP's produced by the BBC for its own use, to satisfy the strictly imposed restrictions on commercially available recordings, or 'needle time' as it was known. The Radioplay recordings were in some respects, worse than the session music. These records were rammed with dire instrumental cover versions of well-known tunes. Anyhow, the result of all this red tape bullshit was that the presenters were given the job of making a silk purse out of a sow's ear. 'YATNAM' was a baptism of fire for new announcers. We had to fill five hours of national radio airtime, with no more than a box full of crap records and session tapes, an A4 writing pad, pen, stopwatch, a pair of bicycle clips and a fistful of shakily written letters from bewildered and frequently clinically insane listeners. Needless to say, the recipe called for mischief, and I was happy to provide it by the shed load.

One of the big attractions of through the night broadcasting is that the Radio 2 management were all tucked up in bed dreaming about retirement or pencils or whatever it is that bosses dream about, so you pretty much had free rein on what you did and said. As I sat at the microphone, in the warm glow of either continuity studio H or J on the first floor of Broadcasting House, I would visualise my voice drifting out across the inky darkness, radiating from a hundred rusty transmitter masts, perched atop hillsides and remote crags dotted around these islands. From the misty glens, in the far north of Scotland to the Atlantic ravaged coves of Cornwall to the mast at the pinnacle of the Black Mountain in County Antrim, Northern Ireland. Broadcasting at night has an almost indefinable, magical quality about it. For a start, the night time listener is radically different from the daytime one. The intangible bond between presenter and listener seems somehow intensified at night. There is a siege mentality at work here, the sharing of a common predicament. It's as if we are as one thinking, we must get through this together. The darkness, the sense of isolation, the feeling of being different from everyone else. The audience for radio at night comprises, basically four types. Those who are working and trying to stay awake, those who are awake and trying to get to sleep, those who are ill or tending to young children and those who are clinically insane. There's a pull, a friction, an edginess that's just not there during the daylight hours, a breeding ground for anarchy and mischief – especially when there's a full moon! The truth is, and I am ashamed to admit this, but I never prepared for any of my shows. I just turned up, looked at the clock, and thought:

"Sweet Jesus, how am I going to get through this? What on earth am I going to say for the next five hours?"

There was no script, no producer, no nothing. Luckily, we had company. By that, I mean company in the studio. 'YATNAM' was assigned a studio technical operator or T.O to use the BBC acronym. These were the boys and girls with the technical know-how to operate the gear and get your show on the road and keep it there, sounding as sweet as possible. They were trained to an extremely high standard by the BBC's engineering training school at Wood Norton in Oxfordshire – or, Camp X-Ray, as it was known. They also provided in the most part, amiable company and acted as a sounding board for some of the more outlandish schemes I often devised for the shows I presented. On one occasion, and for no other reason than I was bored, I decided to start the programme from the toilets down the corridor from the Continuity Suite. Andy Walmsley, my T.O that night, looked at me as if I had two heads, but dutifully obliged by obtaining twelve metres of outside broadcast microphone cable from the London BH control room supply store and ran it from the studio to the number one toilet cubicle in the Unisex Loos. It was in these loos incidentally, that you were just as likely to encounter David Bowie or Sophia Loren as Gloria Hunniford, Terry Wogan or Jimmy Young. Being a tight fit, the layout of the London Control room and continuity suites on the first floor of the extension of BH overlooking Hallam Street, meant that the unfortunate architect had no room on his blueprint for two bathrooms. So, the door had both a Male and a Female access symbol! This caused much consternation and confusion for the high-profile guests who visited each day. I can only wonder at the encounters that must have taken place in there. Imagine settling yourself in front of one of the three urinals on the wall and just getting into your stride when in steps Margaret Thatcher, before appearing on the Jimmy Young show? The cleaners must have had at their work cut out at closing time.

One of the benefits of through the night working at the BBC was the hospitality or 'hostility' tray, as it was known. This was a large orange plastic tray on which could be found: cheap Bourbon biscuits, barely filled almost stale sandwiches and a flask or two of undrinkable coffee and tea, which would be delivered to the studio before transmission. It was like a magnet for any passing and hungry soul who had security access to the heavily guarded continuity suites. The 'YATNAM' show production control room became rather like a late-night social venue. People would drop by on their way back from gigs and parties in London. It was not uncommon, to look through the glass and see Simon Bates standing there, wolfing down a ham sandwich and quaffing black coffee out of a polystyrene cup at 2am!

"What the bloody hell are you doing here Bates?" I would ask on the talkback.

"Couldn't sleep love," was often the reply. He lived in a flat, conveniently located just across the road. Goodness knows how he kept going. He was on air on Radio 1 the next morning – always bright as a button. The man was a machine, strong as a bull.

Simon Bates is one of those people you either love or hate – a real Marmite personality. There are a great many people whose reaction to and opinion of him falls into the latter category. The response, when you mention his name, is rarely ambivalent. I remember the first time I encountered him. It was during a hot seat changeover in one of the old Broadcasting House continuity studios. He had just finished recording a show for Radio 1 and I was due to occupy the studio after him for Radio 2. Fifteen minutes were allocated for the changeover, to allow me time to settle in, give voice levels and so on. I waited patiently with the engineer in the outer control room for him to leave. After five minutes of this, I decided to go in anyway and start setting up. He was on the phone, to his stockbroker or wine merchant – it was often hard to tell. I nodded to him and began to spread my stuff around. He glared at me, slammed the phone down and before I could explain, launched into a tirade of vitriolic abuse, directed at me like a hairdryer on full power with the twin-turbo engaged. His parting words to me were:

"I don't know who you are, but I can only assume you are having a bad day, otherwise you wouldn't be so fucking rude!"

It was a line delivered so perfectly and with such forceful aplomb that now I can almost forgive him for it, but as a junior announcer, it left me pretty shaken with just five minutes to go before a live broadcast. But that, as they say, is show business! We have since incidentally made up and Simon and I are now friends. After Radio 1, Simon spent nine years as the breakfast presenter on Classic FM and did a fine job – at least after he bought 'The Bluffers Guide To Classical Music'! He later returned to doing what he does best – pop-jocking on Smooth FM in London. He now spends his time on his estate in Devon howling at the moon and shouting "Stop That Train" to guards at Plymouth railway station. When Simon was on Radio 1, I would often swing by his studio just to watch him at work. In the same way, he would watch Sir Terry Wogan in his studio. I have always believed and still do, that the best way to learn any trade or skill, is to watch a master at work. Watching Bates at the height of his powers was an education you just couldn't buy. It was worth a thousand media courses. My good friend Adrian Juste and I to this day, share memories and recollections of Bates, in his element.

In 1985, Simon was on the front cover of the 'Radio Times' magazine, promoting an anti-smoking campaign as part of a general BBC-wide health education initiative. The health risks associated with smoking were obviously playing on his mind – or so I thought. Adrian and I wandered into his studio one morning and were more than a little surprised to see him sitting at the desk shrouded in light grey smoke, fondling a huge Cohiba between his fat fingers.

"I thought you'd given up," I said, gesturing to a copy of the Radio Times that had been casually and probably deliberately left next to one of the turntables.

He looked up and with a twinkle in his eye spoke in that wonderful resonant, basso profundo voice of his;

"Oh come, come! Do get into the real world, love!"

I was perhaps being naïve but the hypocrisy of the scene, not to mention the fug from the Cohiba, was quite literally – breath-taking. But that was Bates. He was and still is an anachronism. Delightful company one minute and a complete monster the next, full of bluff and bluster. It's what makes him all the more interesting but to those who don't get him and there are plenty of them, he's absolutely unbearable. I only saw him rattled once. Simon's modus operandi was straight out of Machiavelli's best-selling management handbook. His finely tuned social and corporate antennae reached deep within the corporation and if you ever needed to know anything about anyone, he was your man. He ran an unofficial network of spies and informants within Broadcasting House, who came chiefly from the upper secretarial and personal assistant level. It seemed to those who knew him and those who didn't, that he had eyes and ears everywhere and that he was somehow always one step ahead. On many occasions, he had advance intelligence of senior management personnel changes, even before the channel controllers had been informed.

One evening, after reading the midnight news on Radio 2, I paid my customary whisky visit to the duty office on the ground floor which was tucked away behind the main reception. I breezed in to discover Bates hunched over a large blue file on the desk. It turned out that this file contained the log of complaints and comments from the public, who telephoned the BBC daily. The contents of this file were not intended for general consumption or indeed for his but as a source of intelligence, it was invaluable to someone like Bates. This information would routinely be made available to the channel bosses the next day, as the duty log was published every morning and distributed to the management. He though, always liked to be one step ahead. Looking somewhat flustered at being discovered reading it, he briskly closed the file and initiated an unrelated line of conversation. Bizarrely, he told me that he had just bought a tomato canning factory in Belize! I shudder to think what would have happened if he had ever got together with James Alexander Gordon!

Legendary BBC Radio 1 producer, Malcolm Brown was Simon Bates' producer for a significant period in the early '80s. Malcolm recounts many stories about their time together, but my favourite is the one relating to the Radio 1 visit to the city of Bath in Somerset. The planners at Radio 1 had decreed that the whole of Simon's show was to come from this famous spa town with topics and features to include the ancient Roman baths, the Royal Crescent and the wonderful Georgian architecture. Malcolm, who is a practising Christian, was also aiming to have Simon report live from within the majestic Bath Abbey in the heart of the city centre. The planning was going well, until one day about a week before the scheduled trip, Malcolm received a letter from the Bishop of Bath and Wells. It was not good news. The Bishop it seems had severe misgivings about granting Radio 1 access to the Abbey. It was something to do with pop being the *'devil's music'*. Undeterred, Simon persuaded Malcolm to carry on. The plan was to sit in the Outside Broadcast vehicle, parked outside the Abbey, and *pretend* he was inside. I have to say, that this kind of duplicitous practice would never be countenanced within the current BBC, but this was the 1980s when the truth was just an inconvenience to be simply circumvented. Malcolm was to pay a visit to the Cathedral the day before the broadcast and write a couple of scripts for Simon, painting a nice descriptive picture of the scene within. Malcolm has a classics degree and a love of good writing. His scripts though were often too flowery and elaborately elegant for the average Radio 1 listener, so Bates frequently had to tone them down, often sight-reading them.

Back in London for the broadcast, Radio 1 DJ, Adrian Juste was ensconced in the studio, tasked with adding a faint touch of reverberation to Simon's voice and mix it with sound effects of a large church interior. Knowing Adrian as I do, he probably had the actual sound effect of the interior of Bath Abbey, he's that much of a professional perfectionist. It's true to say that Simon had what you might call 'form' in this sort of fakery and had done this kind of thing many times before. Never letting the truth get in the way of a good story, he had broadcast from a New York lower east side deli, from the comfort of his Surrey drawing room and been on top of the Telecom Tower, when he was actually safely back in the studio quaffing coffee and doughnuts. This is the beauty and simplicity of radio; without the pictures you could be anywhere. In the current enlightened politically correct times, of course, this sort of practice would be considered totally and wholly unacceptable.

The big day arrived. The broadcast was going swimmingly. Then, half an hour into the show, the moment that Malcolm had been persuaded by Bates to fake, reared its ugly head. It began convincingly enough. The sound effects were there right on cue from Adrian back in Radio 1 HQ at Egton House, the reverb on Simon's microphone indistinguishable from the real thing inside the Abbey, a few hundred yards from the radio car, parked outside. Adrian was weaving his magic like an audio alchemist and when the music ended, Bates launched into the first piece of flowery prose that Malcolm had written in the bar, the night before. One can only imagine the good Bishop's reaction on hearing it, though Radio 1 probably wasn't one of the pre-sets on the dial of his vintage walnut-cased Roberts radio on his desk, back at the Manse. He continued:

"OK. That was Kim Carnes and Bette Davis Eyes, number one again for the third week in a row. It's 11:24 on Radio 1 and here we are again, inside this most majestic of Medieval English churches, Bath Abbey. Founded in the 7th Century, with additions in the 10th, 12th and 16th centuries and major restoration carried out by Sir George Gilbert Scott in the 1860s. The scale is immense. Simply immense. Breath-taking. In front of me, the great towering knave, with its majestic stain glass window depicting..."

He turned the top page of the sheaf of papers that was balanced on his knee in the back seat of the radio car. It was blank. A sheet of virgin white paper loomed up at him. There was the briefest moment of hesitation, from one of Britain's most consummate broadcasters as his brain registered the fact that the script had run dry. He continued,

"Let's take a moment here for some music." And closed his microphone.

As Depeche Mode's latest single blared out of the monitors, Simon turned to Malcolm, sitting beside him in the cramped confines of the vehicle.

"What the bloody hell's going on. Where's the rest of the fucking script?"

A chastened Malcolm who, like the Annie Lennox record that was lined up to play next, had turned a lighter shade of pale and meekly confessed that he had spent the majority of the evening in the hotel bar and that having consumed one too many pints of Wiltshire's finest Exmoor Gold, he had forgotten to complete the remainder of the script! The rest of the 'visit' to the Abbey was rapidly abandoned without excuse, apology or explanation.

One of the main features of Simon's show on Radio 1 was the legendary 'Our Tune'. This involved Simon reading out a letter from a listener describing a significant and often emotionally charged event in their life, to the accompaniment of Nino Rota's lachrymose love theme from the movie 'Romeo and Juliet'. At the culmination of the feature, old Master-Bates as he was affectionately known, would play the tune that held the key to the listener's memory. Was it schmaltzy? Yes. Was it cynical? Absolutely. Whole factories across the UK would halt production for the ten or so minutes that it was on and hairy arsed lorry drivers would pull themselves off at Scratchwood services and weep into rags impregnated with Swarfega. I'm not entirely sure I've phrased that correctly, but you get my drift. Bates' performance was so polished, so commanding, that most people listening were entirely unaware of how disorganised it was behind the scenes. On my occasional visits to his studio, I recall being completely mesmerised as I sat opposite him. He would invariably be on the phone during the preceding record, either instructing his stockbroker and barking "buy" or "sell" or dictating some piece of salacious showbiz gossip to the entertainment editor of a red top tabloid five miles east of Portland Place, in Fortress Wapping – News International's HQ – where 'The Sun' and 'News of the World' newspapers were published. Throughout all this, he would be chomping and puffing on a king size Cohiba and scanning the various TV monitors he had dotted around the studio, tuned to every single channel you could imagine. At the appointed time for 'Our Tune', he'd give the letter a cursory glance over in the seconds before opening his microphone fader, then launch into the piece with all the enthusiasm of a dog with two dicks in a kennel full of bitches on heat. Altering the story for dramatic effect, embellishing on the fly, making most of it up as he went along – with the music swelling, in all the right heart-tugging places. *"And the baby died,"* became the alternative unofficial privately shared name for the most talked-about feature on British radio. More often than not, Bates would become so carried away with the story, and go off-piste to such an extent, elaborating here and there that he would forget the names of the main protagonists. He would close the mike and shout on the talkback to Fergus Dudley his producer:

"What the bloody hell was this woman's husband's brother's name?"

Fergus, looking at Bates through the control room window would more often than not shrug his shoulders. Bates would have to quickly, make up more stuff on the spot to cover his lapse and carry on referring only to the relationship until he could scan back over the letter to find the names again. It was a seamless daily performance. The 'Our Tunes' became more and more outlandish as the years progressed. He swears they were all bona fide, but rather like the readers' letters to some magazines and newspapers, I have my private doubts. Bates though, rode his show proudly and without apology across the sanctity of Her Majesty's hallowed BBC airwaves, like one of the fearless horsemen of the apocalypse. He was a master of the art, at the top of his game. Supremely confident and never lost for words. I envy and still greatly admire his talent.

Former Radio 1 DJ and good friend Adrian Juste takes great delight in the story of how on one occasion, Bates calculated Adrian's mortgage repayments to within three pence while Bates was presenting the Top 40 show, live on Radio 1. Bates never wore headphones. He used to crank up the volume on the cans and leave them on a hook beside the desk. He also turned off the studio loudspeakers. This left the studio almost eerily silent and gave him the peace he craved to get on with reading books, writing newspaper articles, making phone calls, watching TV and firing up the large Havana cigars which he kept in a locked mahogany humidor in the studio. It was often said by the technical boys who engineered his shows from the control room next door, that the only way Bates knew it was his turn to speak, was when the PPM volume needles showing the main output signal on the desk in front of him, stopped moving! It wasn't far from the truth. Bates' legendary multi-tasking abilities only surpassed that of the great Eugene Fraser the infamous Fijian Radio 4 continuity announcer, who unbelievably used to audibly fart his way through the sanctity of the shipping forecast and recite rude jokes and limericks, during pauses while his microphone was closed. I saw him perform this jaw-dropping routine once and have never forgotten it. A small, but appreciative crowd of his fans and admirers had gathered to watch the great man at work. As the strains of 'Sailing By', the BBC Radio 4 shipping forecast theme tune faded, Eugene launched straight in.

"Here is the shipping forecast issued by the meteorological office at 22.00 today. Rockall 1003, rising slowly."

He would then quickly close his microphone and the private sideshow would begin. Keying down the talkback to the control room in the continuity suite, he started:

"There were these three nuns."

He would then open the main studio microphone.

"Malin Head, 1006 falling, visibility good." Close his microphone again...

"Riding down a cobbled street on a bicycle."

He would open the microphone again.

"Cromerty, 1002 rising slowly, visibility good." Then, close his microphone.

"One said to the other, have you ever come this way before?"

He then let out the most enormous fart, which he set promptly on fire with a cigar lighter held in his hand. The emanating methane gas, burst violently into a beautiful ethereal blue and indigo coloured arc, nearly ripping off the seat of his pants and destroying the fabric of the very chair on which he was sitting. He would then carry on reading the rest of the shipping forecast as though nothing had happened. He was Mr Cool alright, even if his arse wasn't and his antics are a perfect example of how the devil finds work, for idle hands to do. Eugene was a one-off. A Fijian by birth with the physique of an All Black prop forward, the sun literally shone out of every one of his orifices. Or should that be orifi? Anyhow, radio needs and deserves more characters like him. Sadly, these days, they have all either retired, died, been sectioned or arrested and imprisoned.

Nowadays, BBC Radio 1 is located in a brand spanking new complex within New Broadcasting House. Before the move, the station occupied a very unassuming building called Yalding House, several blocks away from Broadcasting House. From the outside, it resembled an office of Her Majesty's Revenue and Customs. Bland, nondescript and terribly boring. Its dull exterior gave no clues as to what went on inside. Back in the 1980s Radio 1 was relocated from the old Broadcasting House Control room to Egton House, just across the street from Broadcasting House in Riding House Street and was linked to the mother ship by a secret underground passage, which had card-key activated security entry doors at either end. All very James Bond. This was the preferred route for elusive pop stars, A-Listers and guilt-ridden government ministers who wanted to slip out of the building unnoticed and for DJ's and other operatives like me who couldn't be arsed crossing the street in the rain. Using this route, you could effectively exit Egton House underground, enter Broadcasting House basement still underground and weave your way through the labyrinthine corridors in the bowels of the main building and exit at street level in either Portland Place or Hallam Street, away from the great unwashed hoards and paparazzi and into a waiting fast car home. The more publicity hungry turns and the B and C listers, who were guests on a show preferred to exit via the Egton House main entrance, which opened onto Riding House Street next to Wren's famous All Souls church. Here were often to be found, the paparazzi of the day and the usual sad bunch of disposable camera touting groupies and club-footed, biro wielding, custard cream eating, piss soaked autograph hunters. You could smell them from the other side of Regent Street if the wind was in the right direction! An unforgettable aroma, of damp knickers, bubble gum, unwashed hair, cheese and onion, cuppa soup, cheap biscuits and orange peel. Heady stuff indeed.

Radio 1 in those days, was at the very epicentre of the music business in the UK. These were the days before Spotify, Apple iTunes and even Napster. The station's profile was sky high and the profiles of the individual DJ's were equally stellar. They were true radio stars. The line-up consisted of the two Simons, Mayo and Bates, Dave Lee Travis, Gary Davies, Bruno Brookes, Steve Wright, Adrian Juste, Paul Gambaccini, Tommy Vance, Andy Peebles, Noel Edmonds, Annie Nightingale and veteran broadcaster John Peel who is sadly no longer with us. Peely and Nightingale were the only ones who survived the Stalinist style Bannister putsch in 1993. The station was headed up by Johnny Beerling, a diminutive man with a full head of tousled blonde hair and a fondness for old school Henley-style rowing blazers. John-ny was a dyed in the wool BBC man and had risen up the ranks from studio manager in the Aeolian Hall, to producer and on to the executive floor, culminating as the Controller of BBC Radio One. Because of his pedigree, he commanded enormous respect from mostly everyone who worked for him. He knew the business inside out. Johnny is credited with inventing the legendary Radio One Road Show – a huge circus that plied its way with its tacky wares aboard the infamous 'Goodie-Mobile," around Britain's seaside towns in the summer months, leaving a trail of mayhem in its wake. I'll get to the Road Show later. Believe me, it'll be worth the wait!

Directly under Johnny on the executive board at Radio 1 was a woman called Doreen Davies. This pair of grand fromages was an odd double act to be at the helm of a supposedly "yoof" orientated station. Doreen, by 1983 must have been in her late fifties. I have a particular fondness for and intimate knowledge of BBC Radio 1 at this point in its history because al-though I was at this time a staff announcer on BBC Radio 2, I was to play a small role in its output.

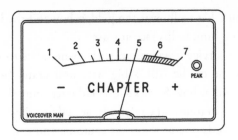

HE'S GOT A BACKSIDE LIKE
'A PAPERHANGER'S BUCKET'

T he long and often dull shifts, spent in Radio 2 continuity or in-studio 3F located on the third floor of Broadcasting House adjacent to the Newsroom, reading news bulletins, would be broken by welcome meal and rest breaks. It was a chance to stretch one's legs and sample a plateful of fayre at the legendary and infamous BBC staff canteen. One fine sunny Sunday in 1983, I took my place in the lunch queue in the staff canteen on the seventh floor of Broadcasting House. The view of the London skyline from the big picture windows up there was one of the best views in London. I was gazing out to the south over the spire of All Souls Church and admiring the vista down Regent Street. The big red Routemaster buses and iconic London black taxis slowly lumbering their way south towards the statue of Eros at Piccadilly Circus. My reverie was interrupted by a commotion further down the queue. Steve Wright and his posse of afternoon boys were in the process of noisily ordering lunch. Steve, at the time, was one of the biggest names in radio and I was one of his biggest fans. His afternoon show, traditionally in the graveyard slot for radio, was commanding huge audiences and he was riding high on a wave of popularity. It's hard to overestimate how important he was to Radio 1's success and profile. He really was the golden boy and the bosses kept him sweet by indulging him, to his face at least.

Being a public service broadcaster, with its mandate to inform, educate and entertain; some of the BBC's big wigs and grand fromages became somewhat unnerved at how Steve's show had over time, slowly turned ever so slightly anarchic in tone and content. In actual fact, it was just an illusion of anarchy, as Steve is one of the most cautious and conservative people I know. Nonetheless, Malcolm Brown, his producer took the daily brunt of assaults from management and kept most of the unpleasantness from Steve and his posse. It really was a thankless task for Malcolm, but he eased his burden by pointing himself at the Yorkshire Grey, a well-known nearby watering hole, at the slightest sign of trouble! The Yorkshire Grey, just around the corner from Egton House was in effect, Malcolm's real office. Over the years, considering the amount of money he must have thrown across the bar, he could probably have bought the premises, lock stock and all the barrels in its capacious cellar. Anyway, back to the canteen. I wandered over towards the commotion at the back of the queue to see what all the fuss was about. Steve was demanding that his three scoops of vanilla ice cream be served in a chilled stainless-steel bowl, not a glass one. It was, as I was later to discover one of his many eccentricities. As one of the hapless serving staff went off to find one, I engaged him in conversation and when we reached the cash register, we were getting on like a small supermarket on fire. I joined his table and for the next hour, along with Dave Wernham (aka Mr Angry) we traded insults and jibes, took the piss out of other diners, and generally mucked about. It was all hugely entertaining.

Quite how it happened, I don't know but it was at this lunch that the idea for a character I was to play on his show was born. Steve's afternoon show on Radio 1 featured a series of telephone characters who were incredibly popular. In fact, one could argue that they defined his show, at a time when the Zoo format was largely unknown in Britain. There was Mr Angry, Sid the Manager, Gervaise the Hairdresser, Damian the Social Worker and Fred Cresswell the Cinema Manager, to name a few. Most people who listened to the show thought that Steve performed these characters himself. In the very early days, he had voiced some of them, but as the show evolved and more people came on board the newer characters were played by a variety of people. Gavin McCoy, a DJ and presenter had met and worked with

Steve when they were both on the payroll at a radio station called 210 FM in Reading, Berkshire. Gavin is one of the funniest and most talented people I know and over the years has been responsible for some of the funniest most entertaining 'radio character' moments on Steve's show. Gavin was the inspiration and the voice behind Sid the Manager, Gervaise the Hairdresser and Fred Cresswell the Cinema Manager, three of the all-time great modern British radio characters. As I briefly mentioned earlier, Steve's afternoon show gave the impression of total anarchy. However, it was all carefully engineered. Apart from the music and the news, around forty percent of the speech output was pre-recorded on tape, not that anyone listening would have known. Steve is one of the most skilled presenters but he's also a stellar radio producer and could deftly weave, live and pre-recorded material into a single seamless link, like a spider on acid.

All of these comedy elements and sketches were recorded in the pre-show preparation hour between 2pm and 3pm. Gavin, at the time, was a breakfast presenter on BBC Radio Bedfordshire, and returned home after his show to his house in Luton to receive the phone call from Steve at around 2.45pm. They had fifteen minutes to record two or three character inserts for the show that day. It was inevitably a pretty fraught fifteen minutes too. Gavin is a hugely mischievous character and enjoyed winding Steve up by mucking around and deliberately wasting time so that as the clock ticked inexorably towards transmission time, tensions invariably rose. During one of these pre-record sessions when Gavin was playing the part of Gervaise the Hairdresser, Steve and he were discussing a fellow Radio 1 DJ, who shall remain nameless. In the first of the recordings that day, Gervaise, came out with the line,

"Yeeees! Do you know Steve, he's got a backside like a paperhanger's bucket!"

The quarter-inch tape that was spooling over the heads on the huge A80 Studer tape machine at the back of the studio captured every word, and the studio engineer who was manning it immediately took out his Chinagraph pencil and marked the offending section of the tape for editing, as it passed over the recording head. I'm quite sure that twelve foot length of tape ended up in someone's private collection. Every single day was like this and it was a wonder to me how some of these out-takes didn't somehow, at some time accidentally get to air. It's a testament to the professionalism and skill of those brilliant technical operators from the London Control room, who were always on the ball, always got the joke and were ever vigilant. All of these pre-recorded inserts were then carefully reviewed and edited. Once the expletives and libellous comments had been expurgated, they were spliced up and transferred to small five-inch reels, labelled and stacked into a neat pile on the control room desk. Once the show started, Steve would bark commands via the talkback, like some latter-day General, ordering up each one of these pieces of comedy ammunition as and when he needed them. The operator would load up the tape on one of the big Studer machines at the back of the control room and switch direct control of it to Steve's on air desk, in the studio next door. "Light me up on three," Steve would shout and the engineer at the back of the control room would oblige by switching direct control through to the studio. "You have control." A green light would illuminate on his desk. "More level in the cans!" "Give me more top end love!" "Crank it up friend!" were three of his favourite commands that he barked incessantly over the talkback. All the while, planning his next segment, that would include jingles and inserts from five cart machines and CD players. The second engineer, who was driving the on air desk in the control room had the task of smoothing out all the incoming output levels of these audio sources into a uniform PPM 6. PPM 6, stands for Peak Programme Meter 6. This was the standard peak level, which the big black needle on the output meter should never exceed, for all outgoing material, on its way to the transmitter. It was a difficult enough job. Sometimes the levels were all over the place like a mad woman's shite but rather like throwing mud pies at a brick wall, some of it stuck. Most days, the operator on the sound desk was laughing so much that it's a wonder any of it got heard at all! The big Orban-Optimod signal processors up at the transmitter must have been on permanent overtime trying to sort it out and becoming so hot, you could fry a truck driver's breakfast on them.

After our chance meeting in the canteen, I went away and developed the character we had conceived at that memorable lunch. Several days later, I called Steve from the newsroom and told him what I had come up with.

"Let's give it a go friend," he said.

"Are you sure?" I replied. It still seemed kind of half-baked to me.

"No, you'll be fine," he said. "We'll pre-record it tomorrow at 2pm."

And that was it. The character I had christened 'Mr Mad', was born. The next day I was enjoying a day off at home. The phone rang, it was Steve. We briefly discussed what I was going to do and say. He ran through his responses and I outlined what I would say.

"Perfect." He said." "You ready?"

"Ready as I'll ever be," I said. In the background, I could hear the engineer.

"OK. We're rolling."

One of the five big Studer machines at the back of the studio clunked and whirred into life with a new pristine reel of quarter-inch tape, rolling over its gleaming aluminium enshrouded recording heads, at a steady fifteen inches per second.

Silence. Then, "Hello, who's this on the line?"

"Brr... Brr... Hello, it's Mr Mad 'ere, I'll tell you who's mad."

I launched into my pre-arranged rant. Sixty seconds later it was all over. The posse in the studio had been laughing all through the piece and Steve seemed pleased with the way it had gone.

"That's great!" he said. I'll stick it on later, at about 3.45pm. Talk to you tomorrow at the same time?"

I had forgotten that this was a daily show and that it would require me to come up with material five days a week. We hadn't even discussed remuneration, but that was the way it was in those days. Spontaneous, joyous and unpredictable.

Most of Steve's contributors in those early days worked on the show just for the hell of it and for the craic. We were the biggest collection of rank amateur radio anoraks ever assembled on earth. That was what gave the show such energy and immediacy. We didn't have to wait for contracts to be signed or have meetings, hold focus groups or consult the consultants. We just did it – and to hell with the consequences. The motto was 'never ask permission, only forgiveness'. We trusted in Steve's judgement and in any case, Malcolm would be back in the office, or should I say, the 'Yorkshire Grey', to take the flak, of which there was plenty! Things pretty much continued this way for several months. On the days that I was working in the newsroom and reading news bulletins on BBC Radio 2, I would take a call from Steve just after lunchtime and I would disappear into the news booth, to get some peace and quiet to record my bits as Mr Mad, down the internal phone line. I didn't want my news colleagues to hear me. Then moments later, at

2 o'clock, I would be reading the news on Radio 2! To the casual outside observer, it was mind-blowingly schizophrenic. Sober sounding voice of authority one minute and dribbling lunatic the next. But it was all voice acting to me and I loved every delicious moment of it. In between the bulletins, I would take the lift to the sub-basement and wander over to Egton House via the tunnel that ran under the road, to join the Posse on Steve's show and swell the numbers. We would whoop and clap like sycophantic monkeys at Steve's jokes, all adding to the atmosphere of what was undeniably the biggest show in radio at that time, in the UK. The audience figures were huge. Someone once calculated that in any given week, half the population of the UK was tuned in at some time to Steve's show. That's over 27 million people!

A relaxed, creative atmosphere in the studio was something Steve was very keen to create and preserve. If the atmosphere was good and the team were relaxed, flashes of brilliance would often ensue. The corollary of this, of course, was when people, Steve labelled "the atmosphere Hoovers" turned up. These were the kind of people who, by their very presence in a room, would suck the atmosphere right out! The atmosphere Hoovers were banned from the studio and the corridor outside. Steve even went to the extent of temporarily obscuring, with copies of Melody Maker and bits of cardboard, the large triple glazed window that looked out over the Radio 1 transmission reception area, so they couldn't see in. More particularly, he didn't want to see parties of senior management and visitors trooping through, gazing at him through the glass-like he was some kind of performing monkey. That really put him off. The suits upstairs were also banned from visiting while we were on air. The thick, double airlock control room doors were more often than not on lock-down, to prevent any unauthorised access by 'atmosphere Hoovers' during transmission. Steve is credited with introducing the zoo format to UK radio, a style of broadcasting that was first pioneered in the USA by radio greats like Howard Stern in New York, Rick Dees in LA and 'The Greaseman' – Doug Tracht out of Washington DC. It was a 'zoo' alright and we were the monkeys, but we weren't on public display.

'Mr Mad' seemed to be going down well with the great British Public. I knew this because on many occasions on the street and on trains and buses, I would hear groups of lads reciting my lines from the show. "I'll tell you who's mad" they would say and then shout out a list of their mate's names. It was odd for me to hear that. On one occasion, I was on a train on my way to Leeds in the North of England and was sharing a carriage with a group of young people who were clearly fans of the show. They were discussing at great length what they thought of his many show characters. The subject of Mr Mad came up.

"I wonder what the bloke who does him really looks like?" said one. I had to turn away and look out of the window.

They clearly didn't know that the bloke who did him was sitting only three feet from their table! But that's the beauty of radio. All of the fun, with none of the hassle (and none of the money I may add!). Incidentally, travelling North with me on that day was the actor Ian Kelsey who used to be in Emmerdale and who was then in the BBC TV series 'Casualty'. He was recognised by fellow passengers passing through the carriage, about twelve times in the space of an hour. I have been out in public in the company of many famous faces over the years and I can't imagine what it must be like living your life in a goldfish bowl, day in and day out. It must be ghastly. Fame? Not for me thanks. As popular as he was with the great unwashed British public, Mr Mad, however, did not go down well with everyone. The distinguished actor Sir Brian Rix was president of MENCAP

In character as 'Mr Mad' with Simon Mayo and Steve Wright – 1984 – BBC Radio 1, London.

'Mr Mad' showing off his new mobile phone – 1985 – BBC Radio 1, London.

PETER DICKSON

the well-known mental health charity. I had a lot of time for Brian and the good work he did but unfortunately, he took great exception, it seems, to my Mr Mad character. On an almost daily basis, he would call the BBC, demanding that he be taken off air. Brian argued that it was harming the charity, which was engaged in a hearts and minds PR battle to address the stigma of mental illness. Now, I have a lot of sympathy with his argument, but I couldn't quite see where Brian was coming from. At the time I wasn't aware of all these rumblings, none of us were. Malcolm saw to that.

Malcolm was a bit of a genius. Born and raised in Liverpool, he went to school with Paul McCartney (didn't everyone from Liverpool?) and was a bit of a closet intellectual. Having several degrees, one of which was in the Classics, and a background in classical music he was no mental midget. He fended off this daily barrage with all the skill of a grassroots politician, in the run-up to a general election. Meetings were held at the very highest level. The Controller of Radio 1 was involved as was the Director of radio and who knows, even the DG himself. Malcolm, it seems, persuaded them that 'Mr Mad' wasn't *mad*, in the sense of being mentally ill. He was only "*mad*," in the sense that he was upset or angry "*mad*" with certain people and issues, by pointing out the little absurdities and annoyances of daily life. How Malcolm presented this to a board of sombre-faced, dark-suited media executives summoned to discuss a fictitious character on a radio show, is almost the subject of a comedy show in itself. You only have to have watched an episode of the brilliant satirical comedy 'W1A' on BBC TV to understand where I am coming from. As always though, truth is infinitely stranger than fiction. I would have loved to have been a fly on the wall at one of those gatherings though. Quite how he kept a straight face, is anyone's guess. Being a bit of a closet anarchist himself, Malcolm viewed the whole episode as a game of mental chess. Moving his knights and castles, around the board, with consummate skill and ease. The fact that Mr Mad remained on air for as long as he did, is all down to him. I know he loved every minute of it and would sit in the pub at lunchtime dreaming up more ways in which, like Don Quixote, he could prick at the underbelly of the BBC establishment. He was the perfect foil for Steve's and my antics. I was sad to learn that Malcolm was let go, by the BBC a few years ago. Pensioned off, early it seems. It's their loss, not his. He was and is one of the best producers I have ever had the good fortune to work for. God bless him!

Radio Times profile picture – 1985 – BBC Radio 2, Broadcasting House, London.

Standing in for Gloria Hunniford
1986 – BBC Radio 2, London.

With Gloria Hunniford
1987 – BBC Radio 2, London.

'Mr Angry' was one of Steve's favourite characters. Indeed, the fact that he is even today remembered by most people over a certain age, is a good indication of the extent to which he became embedded in the national consciousness. Ironically, for such a forthright character, he was played by a rather shy and modest BBC employee, called Dave Wernham. Dave was one of the technical operators in the Broadcasting House control room and was often scheduled onto Steve's show. In a similar experience to mine, Dave quite unexpectedly stumbled onto the air with his character, Mr Angry from Purley. In common with my character Mr Mad, it was a rant – a bile-filled rant – from a very angry man indeed. As Mr Angry, Dave would let rip with whichever of life's irritations was bugging him that day. It could be anything from late-running trains to the wrong type of filling in his sandwich! Then, at the end of this explosive telephone outpour, he would end with the infamous words, *"I'm so angry, I could throw the phone down."* And, five times a week he did. So forcefully, that he annihilated three or four perfectly good telephones in the first week alone, smashing them all into tiny fragments of grey metal and plastic! One of the brown-coated boffins in the BBC engineering department was summoned to come up with a solution. It arrived the next day in a wooden box. It was a standard plastic-cased British Telecom phone with a bell inside, which would loudly chime when the receiver was slammed down. The upper surface of the cradle, however, was specially modified with reinforced steel plates. That phone belonged to Mr Angry for many years and the sound of its bell still reverberates in my mind to this day. Mr Angry became possibly the most famous and most loved of all the characters on Steve's show, but after a few years, Dave ran out of steam. His voice was taking a daily battering. Consequently, he and Steve decided to kill off Mr Angry in spectacular style. He was to be shot, live on air! The plot was shrouded in the utmost secrecy.

On that final Friday, I remember as doubtless millions will, the dark and terrible moment of his demise. The segment began in the usual way with Mr Angry, embarking on his full-on, no holds barred rant. Then in the background mid phone call, a distant doorbell was heard. Dave, or should I say, Mr Angry, paused and said he had to go and see who was at the door. As an audience of millions listened in turning up the volume on their radios to hear, we heard him put the phone down on the hall table and amble off towards his front door to see who was there. The Nation held its breath. A door could be heard opening in the distance, and then… a volley of shots rang out. The line went dead. Steve, feigning consternation, told his listeners not to panic and linked in true DJ fashion, into the next record. Several minutes later, Steve broke the 'sad' news that Mr Angry from Purley had been shot dead. The nation went into mourning. The next day, The Sun newspaper one of Britain's biggest red tops, carried the headline: "MR ANGRY FROM PURLEY – SHOT DEAD!" It was, of course, ridiculous and it must have been a very light news day, but it served to demonstrate the power of radio in general and the influence of Steve Wright, in particular. To this very day and it must be all of twenty-five years since this all happened, people still remember Mr Angry and ask me endless questions about him. Mr Mad and every other character on that show continually lives in his deep shadow.

In the Summer of the year that Mr Mad was created, Steve was scheduled to appear at a Radio 1 roadshow in Brighton. Steve has always loved the idea of show business, and always used to marvel at the entourages who accompanied the biggest stars of the day when they made their public appearances. With this in mind, we came up with the idea that *he* should be accompanied by his own security team at the Brighton venue. I foolishly volunteered. I came up with the idea for a character called 'Les Miserables', a burly, stubble chinned, sunglasses and medallion wearing, black-suited minder. We introduced him on the afternoon radio show, a few weeks before the event. He spoke with an obligatory south London estuary drawl and was as unpleasant a character as you could ever imagine. The radio audience loved him. I would noisily barge into the studio, unannounced to introduce guests and generally be as obnoxious as possible. I even grew a beard for the part, such was my quest for authenticity. The big day arrived, and I was backstage in the roadshow vehicle, waiting for my turn to be introduced to the crowd. There must have been 20,000 people out in front and the noise was quite literally deafening. The Brightonian Seagulls had given up and had headed east to Hove for the afternoon, to terrorise a less intimidating target. What I didn't realise, was that the well-known journalist and broadcaster John Craven was also there on stage, with a camera crew from his show – the BBC TV children's news programme, 'Newsround'. As I swaggered onto the stage with Steve in my best pantomime bad guy style to the sound of booing from the crowd, Craven with his microphone in hand leapt forward to grab a word with Steve. I was committed. Not wishing to stand there like a spare prick at a wedding, I launched myself forward in as menacing a fashion as possible. I grabbed Craven by his tie, drew myself up to my full height, pushed my face to about one inch from his, nose to nose and as the cameras were rolling, I uttered the words, *"Steve don't do interviews."* Steve was as taken aback by this as Craven was and began to laugh, in that high-pitched nervous way of his, but I was now deeply and irreversibly fully committed. The Character of 'Les Miserables' had completely taken over, I was immersed in the character – there was no going back. I could see the look of bewilderment and horror on the faces of the first few rows of the crowd as I twisted Craven's arm through 90° and marched him off the stage with the cameras following our every move. He never got his interview, but the entire episode was shown on BBC1's Newsround later in the day. Luckily, Steve saw the funny side but as for Craven, I haven't seen him since, except for a brief encounter at Champneys Health Spa in Hertfordshire in 1998, when he had long forgotten the episode – and I didn't remind him of it. I have been a member of Champneys for many years and the steam room in the spa is always the place for a chance encounter with a star. I've witnessed Sir Yehudi Menuhin on all fours in the changing room reaching for a lost shampoo bottle (as horrific a sight one could never wish to see and one I shall never be able to un-see), Ian McShane's mesmerising vocal performance in the Turkish bath, Ronnie Wood and Charlie Watts sipping mineral water (who knew) in the drawing-room, Frank Bruno upon whose lap I almost accidentally sat in the steamy gloom of the Laconium, John Cleese's silly walk outside the thalassotherapy pool and afternoon tea with a then virtually unknown Simon Cowell and his friend Jackie St Clair on the Wisteria covered loggia.

Amazingly, almost a year later, Mr Mad was still going strong. What's more, he had been asked to appear on a charity record, called *"The Spoken Word of Rock and Roll."* The record producers had managed to press-gang every single name in British light entertainment to appear in it, from Sir Michael Caine and Robert Powell to Sir David Jason and Warren Mitchell. I was the only one I hadn't heard of! Again, this was a testament to the popularity of Steve's show and the characters on it.

In the mid-'80s, John Cole was the BBC's Political editor. A genial Northern Irishman, whose impossibly contorted vowels, English ears found so difficult to interpret. As a native of the province myself, I, of course, had

BBC 1 TV live promo booth – 1987 – 'Pres A', BBC TV Centre, London.

no problem understanding his dialect. He was though, the perfect target for mimicry. I decided to introduce the idea of a daily telephone call from 'John' on Steve's show. We called him 'John Bole', and he became a regular fixture – commenting on almost anything, as long as it wasn't political. He would discuss a wide range of topics from; the plot of 'EastEnders' to the state of the railways and the scarcity of a decent sausage roll in Northampton. I thought it was hilarious but subsequently discovered that John Cole himself hated being lampooned in this way. During this time, I was also prostituting my vocal services in West London's White City, as a promo announcer on BBC Television. This little gig on the side required several trips a week to BBC TV Centre in Wood Lane – or 'The Concrete Doughnut', as it was known. A moniker inspired by the now iconic and at the time, radical '60s design of the building, uncompromisingly circular in shape. On one of these visits, I was taking the South Hall lift to the fourth floor, when it stopped at the second floor to admit some more passengers. Who should walk in? Yes, you've guessed it – the very man himself – Mr Cole. Little did he realise that he was sharing the lift that afternoon with his nemesis, his aural doppelganger! As he exited the lift at floor three and just as the doors were closing behind him, I couldn't help but capitalise on this serendipitous encounter. At the top of my voice, I shouted out his character's catchphrase "Cheerio Now," in my best John Cole voice. As the doors closed, I just caught a glimpse of him turning on his heels and glaring back. It was too late – I was gone.

The promos on BBC1 and BBC2 television were made and scheduled by a division of the TV presentation department, headed up by a bloke called Pat Hubbard. In consultation with the channel controllers and schedulers, the department's function was to devise short thirty or forty-second trailers for whichever programmes had been identified as requiring a bit of a publicity push. Pat was an incredibly talented yet highly eccentric individual, as were most who worked for him but overall, they were a hugely likeable and dedicated bunch who spent all their waking hours thinking about and making promos. Promos are to TV what trailers are to the movie business.

Back then, in the 1980s the promos on the BBC were voiced by just three people. There was the wonderful Ray Moore a colleague from Radio 2, the brilliant John Braben and little old me! I learnt everything I know about promo voicing from these two guys and I owe them a huge debt of gratitude. Ray and John were masters of the art. Those who work in TV promo production today, find it almost incredible that as recently as the late '80s a good proportion of the on air promos and evening menus on TV in the UK, were voiced live. This required the voiceover artist to be there, in situ for most of the evening. It also gave the channel controllers the flexibility to change the schedule at short notice, which they sometimes did. The evening run-down or menu was a thirty or forty-second resume of that evening's programmes on BBC1 TV. Visually, it was a simple montage of short clips extracted from the programme content, ending with a still sequential graphic showing the start times of the individual shows. The script was invariably packed with detail and so it had to be read at breakneck speed and with split-second accuracy. While reading, I had to keep one eye on the transmission monitor in front of me, in order to see the shot changes and so keep to the correct pace and the other firmly on my script. If you fluffed a line there was no going back, you just had to keep marching on! The evening rundown usually occurred right after the 6 o'clock news on BBC1, just before 'EastEnders'. It was felt that this was the time of peak viewing and so delivered the maximum possible audience. Bear in mind that this was before the true multi-channel environment we know today, so audiences of 15 to 16 million viewers were not uncommon. I have tried many times to imagine what 16 million people would look like when gathered together in one place. The only problem is that Wembley stadium is the biggest venue I have ever been to and that only holds 100,000. To conceive of an audience of a magnitude many times that size is not only impossible but quite terrifying! The best advice given to me by Ray Moore was to put all thoughts of a mass audience out of your mind otherwise your mind, and legs will turn to jelly! One evening while watching BBC1 at home, I heard Ray launch into an evening menu rundown. It started brilliantly. Ray was his usual forthright, commanding self with a typical huge commitment to the script in hand. His phrasing impeccable and his deep rich baritone voice, playing with the roundness of every carefully honed syllable, it was a joy to behold. Then, without warning it all went pear-shaped and I knew only too well what must have been running through his mind.

The script called for Ray to say, "After EastEnders, it's Top of the Pops."

What came out of Ray's mouth was "After EastEnders, it's Top of the Wops!"

Boom!! At the speed of light, it had left the transmitter and was now halfway to Mars. There was nothing he could do but carry on as though nothing had happened. Some chance! 16 million people heard it. The trail was so fast-paced, there was not the luxury of even thinking about correcting his error, so poor Ray had to soldier on, with the sound of laughter from the control room and living rooms up and down the land ringing in his ears. These days, all TV promos are recorded days if not weeks in advance and are neatly packaged for transmission. The spectrum of voice talent has broadened. Promo producers now have the luxury of hiring the voice they want, to compliment the promo they are making.

There has been much talk over recent years of the BBC dumbing down its content. In common with the written word, the spoken word is in a constant state of flux – the zeitgeist moves inexorably forwards. The vocal style known as 'Estuary English' continues to rear its head on much broadcast TV and radio. Regional accents; egregious glottal stops, snarky Mancunian, reassuring Yorkshire, evocative Irish, comforting Brummie and cheery Geordie, are everywhere. Nowadays, it seems that anyone speaking with what was once quaintly known as *'received pronunciation'*, is to be at best distrusted and at worst derided. This is change and as we all now know;

change is the only constant. I'm not saying it's a bad thing. It's just that the pendulum has swung in the opposite direction and appears to have stuck there. The result is that much of the time, I hear voice actors with RP accents deliberately dropping their "H's" and glottal stopping or producing consciously created morphological or articulation disorders, just so they can get work and appear to have that all-important cool 'street' sound, so craved by those Gen Z producers and creatives. My style is more 'boulevard' than 'street' but thankfully, to date, I haven't had a day without work for over forty years! Call me old fashioned, but I 'aint droppin me aitches for no bitches', unless of course, the part demands it darling! As Noel Coward once remarked: "There are many actors sleeping under bridges along the embankment tonight, for want of an upward inflection." How true, no matter how you dress it up, we are all vocal prostitutes.

The roll call of whacky characters on Steve's show was beginning to grow. Gavin had extended his repertoire and added a few more into the mix at the afternoon radio zoo. I had introduced the character of 'Dickie the Exec', a pompous radio producer from the old school. Meanwhile, a young lad called Richard Easter had joined the team. Richard had been working in the BBC post room, in a gap year between school and university, delivering internal mail to offices and studios throughout BBC Broadcasting House. One of his daily calls was to the Radio 1 transmission reception, located just outside the on air studio. I'm not entirely sure how it happened, but in much the same way that I ended up on the show, he and Steve met in reception one day and Richard progressed to performing a high pitch voice character called 'The Maggot'. In due course and after much deliberation Richard declined his place at university, left the post room for good and joined Steve and Radio 1 full time, writing and compiling elements for the show and performing various characters. He became an invaluable asset to Steve and eventually became one of his co-presenters for a good few years. Richard is one of the nicest people you could ever hope to meet. He is a gentle soul, but with a rapier fast wit and excellent comedic reflexes. He ended up in Manchester and became the lead writer on Chris Tarrant's 'Who Wants to Be a Millionaire' among other shows. He also spent some time working with Syco in the TV development department. Good for him. He deserves all the success that comes his way.

Meanwhile, back at Radio 2 in a hypnotic and seemingly never-ending game of musical chairs, the music was about to stop, and the wheels fall off.

Backstage with Steve Wright – 1987 – BBC Radio 1 Roadshow.

PETER DICKSON

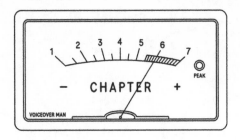

THE EPISODE CONCLUDED WITH HIM WAVING HIS PENIS AT ME

W ogan was on the move. The rumours of his demise in 1984 though, had been greatly exaggerated. Lord, how I miss that man. He had been the doyen, the eminence grise of UK breakfast radio for more years than anyone could remember, some less sympathetic might say; too many years. He had now decided to leave Radio and concentrate on his TV career. Terry always had his eye on the bottom line and TV has always been radio's richer cousin. Habits learned as a junior bank clerk in Limerick all those years had not entirely deserted him. This was show *BUSINESS* after all. He had been contracted, to host an early evening live chat show on BBC1 TV, three nights a week. This was great news for him but disappointing news for me, as I had learned much from the great man and enjoyed his company. During his breakfast show, we would often be on the phone to each other while the records played. He, in his studio on the first floor and I, two floors up in the newsroom. One morning, just after the 7am news I called his internal extension in Continuity Suite H. He answered the phone. Putting on my broadest East Belfast accent I said,

"Hello, Wogan is that you?"

Terry, who could do a mean Ulster accent himself because his Da was from the province, replied similarly.

In character as Reg Ramsey-Street with Adrian Juste, Steve Wright
and Mark Goodier – 1988 – BBC Radio 1 Roadshow.

Steve Wright at work – 1989 – BBC Radio 1, London.

"Yes, mucker. Who's this?"

"Never mind all that," I said, "this is Captain Black, from the East Belfast UDA. When was the last time you saw your wife and kids?"

There was the slightest hesitation in his voice, then realising it was me, he roared with laughter. On many other occasions, we played telephone roulette. This was the most juvenile of games. Many of these phone conversations occurred with the big studio clock ticking inexorably towards the 8am news, which I was due to read. Radio 2 transmitted the Greenwich time signal, or pips at this time and Terry had to synchronise his last record of the hour so that it ended just before the pips at 07.59.55 – five seconds to 8 o'clock! The four or five minutes before this were critical if he was to get the record started on time. I would call him at about ten to eight and try to distract him as best I could. I was very rarely successful; such was his professionalism. Then at around thirty seconds to 8 O'clock, we would begin to play roulette. It was essentially a game of dare, to see who would slam the phone down first. Who would lose their nerve and bottle out? He had to speak first and introduce the news, but I had to make the short five-yard dash from the telephone to the microphone in my studio, while the last record ended, and the pips and news jingle played.

It was childish and irresponsible I know, but it livened up many otherwise dull mornings. Terry was also one of the most generous souls when it came to mentoring nascent junior broadcasters like me. I don't know whether it was the fact that we both came from Ireland and our fathers both came from Belfast but Terry it appeared, took a genuine interest in me and my broadcasting ambitions. We had both followed similar early career trajectories which I guess made him fairly sympathetic to this young whippersnapper. Anyway, in the spring of 1985 he very kindly arranged for me to meet his agent and manager, Jo Gurnett at her offices, in a mews house tucked away behind the Royal Albert Hall in the deepest nether regions of affluent Kensington. I turned up on the appointed day and unexpectedly, the great man himself was also there. I subsequently discovered that he co-owned the agency that negotiated his contracts and subsequently he got to keep the fifteen percent commissions he charged himself – talk about a savvy businessman!

"Come in my boy" he bellowed from across the office in those soothingly wonderful, avuncular Anglo-Irish tones he had.

"Jo, this is Peter, who I was telling you about. I was thinking we might get him started with a little ballroom dancing!"

Ballroom dancing? I was getting more than a little concerned. I had two left feet and couldn't dance for toffee. What was he on about?

"Jo – put him in touch with the BBC producer on the World Dance Championships. They are looking for an announcer and commentator and I can't do it, I'm just too busy."

I began to relax – slightly. However, my concern quickly resurfaced when I realised, I knew absolutely zilch about dancing. I have naturally got two left feet, most Irishmen have, except Michael Flatley. Alarm bells were ringing on every single floor inside my head. As we shall discover later, it was not the only time I would commit to a project while knowing absolutely nothing about the subject. I have always said yes and then tried to work things out afterwards! I will never learn. Before I had time to raise an objection or to even begin analysing Terry's proposal, calls were placed and appointments made and a few days later I found myself in yet another office in West London, this time about a mile from BBC Television Centre. Behind the desk in front of me, was the executive producer of 'Come Dancing'. In common with 'Strictly Come Dancing' it's more recent reincarnation, the original show was one of the most popular on British TV at the time. It first aired in 1950 and was transmitted almost continuously until its demise in 1998. It was delightfully old fashioned, solidly Middle England and was seen as a programme that upheld the BBC's core Reithian values. Terry Wogan was the show's star presenter who had himself taken over presenting duties from the urbane Peter West. The redoubtable Ray Moore, Terry's and my colleague on Radio 2 was the announcer.

The 'World Dance Championships', capitalised on the success of the seemingly insatiable appetite of Brits who like to watch people dancing on TV, though why anyone would want to watch other folks gyrating in garish costumes, is a complete mystery to me! The W.D.C is an annual tournament where professional and amateur dancers compete in both Ballroom and Latin dancing. It's a big, impossibly camp and slightly ludicrous affair. The championship is at the time of writing, now in its sixty-seventh year at the Royal Albert Hall in London. The best dancers from across the world compete, with the obligatory rictus smiles and impossibly erect postures at this glittering annual camp-a-thon. After the most perfunctory interview, and much to my subsequent alarm, I was handed the job of being the announcer on the show, which was to transmit live on BBC1 nationally, from the Royal Albert Hall. This was my first big break on national TV! I would be catapulted to stardom and become rich and famous... I would buy a large house in Chelsea and drive a Ferrari and...

"HOW MUCH?"

One hundred and twenty Pounds! Buyout. No expenses. Boom! Back-to-reality.

People often assume my professional life must be quite glamorous and fun. They imagine it to be a constant round of parties and hanging out with celebrities. It must be fabulous they say! I let them believe it of course but the reality couldn't be further from the truth. As I approached the Royal Albert Hall on the day of the broadcast I imagined, as I climbed those hallowed stone steps, that I'd be directed by a uniformed, white-gloved commissionaire to my well-appointed dressing room. There, waiting for me would be a bowl of exotic fruit, fresh flowers, the day's newspapers carefully pressed and attractively laid out, a fridge full of Krug, a table groaning with a smorgasbord of delectable comestibles delivered that day from Harrods and a leather La-Z-Boy recliner.

"Stage door, son!" Barked the tight-lipped guard on the door.

"You have no right coming in this way."

Duly admonished, I trudged dejectedly round the back of the world-famous venue and made my way in via the less glamorous stage door. To my abject disappointment, there was no dressing room. It was worse than that...there was no room at all. The place was rammed to the rafters with exotic looking orange-faced dancers draped in dazzling, bejewelled and feathered costumes. Every single dressing room in that great building was occupied. What was worse – my commentary position was literally in the middle of the quick-change area immediately off stage and I was surrounded by sequins, rhinestones, feather boas, clouds of talcum powder and Latino women with impossibly slender waists and unbelievably long legs. Concentrating on the script and the task at hand was a real challenge I can tell you. But it was quite an introduction for a boy announcer, on a big, live national TV production. I have to thank Terry for that.

Terry Wogan was one of radio's natural broadcasters. As at home in front of a microphone, as you or I might be in front of a log fire wearing a pair of

'Nightcap' with Colin Marshall (Engineer) and Andy Aliffe (Producer)
1987 – BBC Radio 2, London.

comfy fur-lined slippers while nursing a finger of fine Highland malt.

I have always believed that some people are natural radio performers, while others are more at home on TV. Few have ever mastered both. Wogan fell into the former category, while Gloria Hunniford, who is a natural TV performer, fell into the latter. Derek Jameson on the other hand, who eventually replaced Terry at breakfast, fell flat on his face. While he had the perfect face for radio, he also had the most imperfect voice. Rasping, wheezing and practically bronchitic, his phlegm filled, Cockney flavoured vocal delivery was the most unattractive sound imaginable especially at breakfast. Unlike Wogan, he will be remembered not for his easy charm and friendly, airy, educated banter but for his coarse bullishness, malapropisms, ignorance and constant mispronunciations. I once heard him pronounce the central American country Belize as 'Bell Eyez' and confuse combustibles with comestibles, though, if his culinary skills were anything like his microphone technique, his confusion was understandable though hardly forgivable. He took over the reins of the breakfast show from Ken Bruce, a safe pair of hands who had graduated from the BBC in Glasgow and who had acted as an interim and immediate replacement for Terry when he moved to television. Jameson was a dyed-in-the-wool, inky fingered print journalist, a former Fleet Street tabloid editor who came to Radio 2 with practically no broadcast experience, at the behest of the then Controller of Radio 2 – Frances Line. He certainly wasn't one of us and never would be. He would undoubtedly have had a similar uncharitable opinion of me, had I invaded his turf and begun to write a grammatically correct opinion column for the Daily Star.

The late and great Ray Moore, a true broadcasting legend, preceded Jameson on the BBC Radio 2 early show. Ray was a much-loved broadcaster, of immense talent and charm who genuinely deserved the bigger breakfast audience and they deserved him; yet he was passed over by Frances Line in favour of Jameson. All of us on the announcing team simply couldn't understand her reasoning. Ray, being the true gent he was, shrugged it off saying that he preferred his graveyard slot and his band of incredibly loyal if slightly unhinged listeners. It was an incredibly modest response that was typical of the man. As you have probably already worked out, Ray was another one of my heroes. I used to listen to him, in the years before I joined the network and marvelled at his extraordinary ability to paint the most vivid pictures

With Steve Wright and Mark Wells – 1994 – BBC TV Centre, London.

with words. Someone once said that radio will always have the edge on TV because the pictures are better on the radio. It's true. All you need is a little imagination and someone like Ray with the verbal dexterity to ignite it and turn those pictures into colour. Ray was that 'fire-starter'. The son of a Liverpool tugboat captain, he rose from a relatively impoverished background, to become one of the greatest live radio talents Britain has ever produced. A man who when he was on air, was always in the flow, never lost for words and what words! Ray was a real inspiration to me and so many others. I was honoured to have known him, to have worked alongside him and to be mentored by him. He was one of my all-time heroes and a true star and like Terry, I miss him greatly. I remember, in my early days as a radio announcer, popping downstairs in between news bulletins to the continuity suite, to watch Ray at work presenting the BBC Radio 2 early show. It was 5 o'clock in the morning. A soft orange glow from the sodium streetlamps on Duchess Street outside could be seen through the windows. The studio itself was bathed in the warm, dim light of a couple of 40-Watt angle-poise lamps. I went into Ray's inner sanctum while a record was playing and introduced myself. Ray seemed a little distracted. An un-tipped Park Drive cigarette lay softly smouldering on the lip of a 50s BBC Bakelite ashtray, beside one of the big EMT 750 turntables. A cup of half-consumed black coffee sat, steaming on the desk. Ray was a man who clearly lived on the edge and as I subsequently discovered, suffered terribly from nerves. To listen to him though, you would never have known it. His delivery was supremely confident, but underneath it all, he was terrified. Like a swan, graceful on the surface but underneath crazily paddling to keep afloat. During his show, he chain-smoked and drank industrial-strength BBC coffee with lashings of sugar out of a polystyrene cup. Another of his interesting and thankfully unseen habits was that when he was broadcasting, he undid the belt on his trousers, loosened the zip on his flies, and un-tucked his shirt. I recall with some alarm seeing this for the first time when he rose from his chair to pour himself another cup of coffee. He had to pour the coffee with one hand while clutching his belt buckle with the other to prevent his trousers from falling down around his ankles! The reason for this ritual, I since discovered was that Ray preferred his trousers to be on the tight side. In order for him to control his breathing properly and reduce the pressure on his lower abdomen and give his diaphragm room to move, he always loosened his trousers at the microphone! To those who worked with him regularly, including several female technical operators, it was unremarkable but to a newbie, like me, it was a startling yet totally wonderful revelation and something I now do myself. So, if you ever see me with my trousers unfastened, don't be too alarmed – unless I'm not at a microphone of course. Then you should be worried, very worried!

Ray possessed the most wonderful, God-given vocal instrument. The microphone loved him – any microphone, from the least to the most expensive, he sounded like the dog's back wheels! He had perfect diction, a rich chesty resonance that any voice talent would die for and with practised vocal dexterity, could lurch from received Queen's English pronunciation into the broadest impenetrable Scouse accent, at the turn of a hat. Aided by his fifty a day habit which sadly eventually caught up with him, he would be all over the airwaves each morning like supercharged chocolate-laced treacle pudding with extra treacle… and chocolate. His voice, especially at that time of the morning, was beautifully round, intensely resonant and lubricated with coffee and nicotine. His was the perfect voice for that time of the day, warm and reassuring, intensely British. When Ray was on the radio, the world

Cast and crew with Lulu and Steve Wright
1994 – Studio TC1 BBC TV Centre, London.

just seemed a much better place. It was Ray's creative ability, his extensive and sometimes arcane vocabulary and total command of the English language, his vocal gymnastics and sense of the absurd that really set him apart from his contemporaries. He invented 'The Bog Eyed Jog', a sponsored early morning jog for charity, which he would champion each year if it *"wasn't too black over Bill's Mother's"* – another of his favourite expressions when the clouds thickened, and the weather turned nasty. He enjoyed introducing the drum solos on Phil Collins' records as though we were hearing some hapless man falling downstairs while simultaneously clutching a large wooden wardrobe. Then there was: *"the walnut what-not in the corner,"* where Ray kept his records and he would use the instrumental intros of many tunes as the backdrop for his various nonsense poems. The one I remember best went like this,

"My father had a rabbit and he thought it was a duck, so he put it on the table with its legs cocked up!"

I loved that one. We all loved Ray and were dazzled each day by his sheer brilliance. He was also supremely talented at painting pictures in your mind with words, conjuring up the most brilliantly dark Hogarthian mental images. His use of language was breathtakingly, achingly brilliant. Couple this, with a near-perfect sense of comic timing and the judicious use of jingles, sound effects and records as the punctuation to this audio tableaux, and you had something that was very, very special indeed. The contrast, each morning between the fleet-footed elegance and assuredness of Ray and the elephantine clumsiness of Jameson, was at its starkest during the handover at half past six in the morning. For me, it was just too depressing for words. I confess that I turned the volume down. From Portland Place, with the wind in the right direction, you could hear the sound of radios being switched off across the entire country.

Jameson's show was billed as a breezy morning mix of light pop and topical interview. The brief from Controller Line was for it be like Radio 4 and a half but, unlike Radio 4, it not so much fell, but tumbled catastrophically like an arthritic pensioner between two carelessly placed stools. It was neither, a pop, personality nor news show. It was in short, a shambles and a total disaster for the station. Frances Line, I fear, will be remembered as the most ill-fated Controller in Radio 2's history. Her policy on the style of music Radio 2 should be playing was also risible. She issued every producer with an in-house music policy manual. This tome contained examples of the type of music she believed the station should showcase. She even produced a cassette, called *'something for the weekend'*, onto which she had dubbed samples of the music styles she wanted to hear. Diversity was the key, she explained to an assemblage of stony-faced producers at the policy launch. She insisted that her new initiative should celebrate the breadth and diversity of all available recorded music – and how the biggest radio station in Europe should utilise the breadth of the BBC's immense and globally coveted music library. Consequently, and slowly at first Radio 2's audio signature began to change. A gentle babbling brook, however, soon turned into a gushing sewer. Instead of the familiar contemporary Middle of the Road (MOR) – Adult-oriented Rock (AOR) profile, we got 'Sid Shuttleworth and his Jewish Harp', 'The Amazing Pan Pipes of the Andes', 'General Lafyette and His Incredible Pumping Trumpet' and the occasional Scottish bagpipe solo. The new music policy of comrade Line certainly had breadth, but there was no integrity, no cohesion, no brand identity. At the time, I thought of an advertising strapline for Radio 2. It went like this: "Radio 2 – It's all over the place." It quite literally was, but not in a good way! The poor presenters, like, Ray Moore, Ken Bruce and Jimmy Young who had to present this daily, eclectic musical miscarriage, were beginning to sound disenchanted on air. Those who wanted news, tuned to Radio 4 in the morning. Those who wanted music tuned to either Radio 1, Radio 3 or the burgeoning independent radio network. As Radio 2 had now radically altered its winning formula, listeners began to vote with their feet, or rather with their fingers and tuned out. Many of them ran across the bright sunlit uplands to the glowing, welcoming bosom of commercial radio and were never seen again.

Following a management putsch several years later, Terry's successors Chris Evans and Zoe Ball have built an audience at breakfast and I am pleased to say that Radio 2 is now once again the most listened-to radio station in Europe. Quality will always win, and Terry Wogan was a quality act. He was and will remain a broadcasting icon and I am honoured to have known him as both a friend and colleague.

In the final days of 2015, as the Christmas lights on London's Regent street still twinkled and ruddy-cheeked children pressed their noses against Hamleys' toy shop window, I invited Terry and our mutual pal Alan 'Dedders' Dedicoat to lunch in a Spanish Tapas restaurant near Broadcasting

House. It was a Sunday and the lunch segued nicely for Terry as it followed his Radio 2 Sunday morning show. It was one of the most enjoyable, gut bustingly funny and heart-warming lunches I can remember. As we sat down and the waiter delivered the menus, Terry proclaimed:

"Well, isn't this just grand lads? Me – sitting down to lunch with two of the finest voices in Britain!"

During the three hours we were together, it seemed more like three minutes – copious drinks of various hues and vintages were enthusiastically imbibed, and as we got to the coffee, I did something I hadn't planned to do but which seemed appropriate. I seized my chance to tell the great man something which I should have said to him years ago but hadn't.

Plucking up the courage and emboldened with the drink, I said "Terry, to be serious for a moment. I just…"

I could hardly get the words out…

"I just wanted you to know… how much your friendship and mentorship during my early career meant to me personally."

There I had said it. He looked at me with a quizzical Celtic eye, one eyebrow raised.

"You know." I continued, "you're the reason I got into this business in the first place. We're both from Ireland and our fathers came from the same city, Belfast. While growing up in Ireland I listened to you on the radio and I felt a strong affinity and connection to you. Because of that and because of your early mentorship, encouragement and practical advice which you freely gave to me, I owe you a real debt of gratitude." Slowly, he put his coffee cup back onto the saucer on the table, looked out of the window onto a windswept Great Portland Street where the slightest flakes of snow were beginning to fall on shoppers laden down with bags, faltered slightly and with what was unmistakeably a tear in his eye, told me that he hadn't realised the role he had played in my career but that it was one of the nicest things anyone could have said to him. I extended my hand and placed it on his lower arm and squeezing it gently, I said,

"Well, now you know. Come on, let's have another Brandy."

And we did. In fact, we had several more. As lunch came to its natural conclusion at 4.30pm, his kindness of spirit and generosity surfaced again. He offered me a lift in his chauffer driven car home. We lived not that far from each other, he in Berkshire and me in Buckinghamshire, neighbouring counties. The journey home in the back seat of the car was one I will never forget. I said goodbye to him, thanked him for lunch, which he had insisted on paying for and agreed to meet again for a reprise in the new year when the lunch would be on me. I closed the door and we waved to each other as I stood and watched his car depart down the road towards the village of Taplow. It would be the last time I would see him. Eight weeks later he was dead. It was a profound shock to me and to a Nation who had embraced this most special of Irishmen as one of their own, for the best part of half a century. I miss him terribly and as I write this I still can't come to terms with his loss. I can still hear his voice though – as George and Ira Gershwin, two of Terry's favourite songwriters once said – 'they can't take that away from me'. I feel really lucky to have known him. His family kindly invited me to his memorial service in Westminster Abbey. I sat with Dedders and a thousand other friends and family and former colleagues in that great space, reserved for the remembrance of royalty and statesmen and listened with gratitude to those who had the fondest memories of the great man. It was quite an occasion, which was also broadcast live to the nation. Shortly afterwards, the BBC renamed the building which now houses BBC Radio 2 – 'Wogan House', in his honour. A more fitting tribute I could not imagine. His name and memory now live on above the portal that every broadcaster in the nation worth his or her salt would ever wish to cross.

One unremarkable Monday afternoon in December 1986, I was on duty in the newsroom when I received a call from Iain Purdon, the departmental boss. The weather outside had turned nasty. Heavy snow was falling on Regent Street, borne by a stiff wind sweeping up from the South West and Gloria Hunniford I was told, was snowed in at her home in Surrey. At short notice, I was asked to step in and present the show. I had, by this time, had plenty of experience of presenting, but as for broadcasting to a mainstream audience on a national network during the day, this was a first. I agreed to fill the breach but as I put the phone down, I wondered just what I had let myself in for. The show started and ended on time, though my recall of the important bit in the middle is, to say the least, hazy. As my star guests, I welcomed the actor James Fox and the best-selling author Ken Follett to the studio. After the show, I received a nice memo from David Vercoe who was editor programs, Radio 2 music department.

He said: "May I congratulate you for your extremely competent and professional performance as Gloria Hunniford's last-minute replacement last week. Considering that you were given very little notice to prepare for the unexpected we were all delighted with the way you presented the program. The voice was lower, and the legs less shapely but otherwise we couldn't tell the difference!"

Also listening to the programme, in his office in the BBC's Light Entertainment department across the road from Broadcasting House was a young producer of a regular weekly evening show on Radio 2 called "Nightcap," presented by Jeremy Beadle. Beadle had two days previously given notice of his intention to not renew his contract. He wanted the time to develop some of his ideas for television, 'You've been Framed' which went on to popular success, being one of them. The producer was consequently on the lookout for a replacement and as luck would have it, he had his eye or rather ear, on me. I was called to a meeting with him and the head of Light Entertainment, a genial man called Martin Fisher and they put the proposal to me. Would I present 'Nightcap'? How could I refuse? It was the first big break I had received since joining the BBC. I agreed on the spot (I would worry about it later, as I always did) and we scheduled a date to record a pilot show. My memory of that pilot is hazy, but it must have gone well because the first series was commissioned shortly afterwards. Friday nights, between 11pm and 1am, would never be the same again!

"Peter Dickson's Nightcap" as it was to be known, was conceived to be a comedy sketch, star guest and music show. We had an unusually large budget and a mission to entertain. The programme also planned to showcase and give exposure to new, up and coming talent in both music and comedy. We also planned to invite onto the show the biggest named guests we could find. I was to anchor the programme and participate in the sketches, like a kind of latter-day Kenneth Horne on 'Round the Horne'. Every Wednesday, our little troupe of actors including Brian Bowles, Jon Glover, Sarah Thomas, Phil Nice, David Baddiel, Rob Newman, Arthur Smith, Johnathan Kydd and Phil Cornwell; would convene at the famous Paris studio, on London's Lower Regent Street for the sketch pre-record session. It was nothing short of thrilling for me to be performing, albeit not in front of an audience but in this most well-known and historic of radio theatres.

'The Paris' studio theatre was located several floors underground beneath a building at 12 Lower Regent Street, just above the Bakerloo line and a stone's throw from the world-famous Piccadilly Circus, overseen by its equally famous statue of the God of love, Eros. Not the quietest location for a radio studio I have to admit! We frequently had to pause mid-recording to allow the deep rumble of underground trains subside as they rattled and rolled their way between Charing Cross to the south and Oxford Circus to the north. Nonetheless, this was a place not just steeped but dripping in radio history. This was the very studio that was home to 'The Goon Show', 'Round the Horne', 'Beyond Our Ken', 'The Clitheroe Kid', 'Educating Archie', 'Hancocks' Half Hour', 'ITMA', 'Much Binding in the Marsh', 'The Navy Lark', 'Take it from Here', 'I'm Sorry I'll Read That Again', 'Just a Minute', 'The Hitchhiker's Guide to The Galaxy' and a hundred other classic and much-loved radio light entertainment shows in the history of the BBC, that have been beamed across the airwaves and around the planet since the beginning of the last century. Its twelve-inch-high, blue carpeted stage was also graced by stellar music artists such as The Beatles, David Bowie, Led Zepplin, Joni Mitchell, Queen, Pink Floyd and Rod Stewart. It was the most intimate of venues. I use the past tense here, as sadly it hosted its final recording in 1995 when the BBC Radio Theatre opened its doors at Broadcasting House and replaced it. The Paris was built at a time when clearly, money was no object. The wainscotted walls were finished in elaborate mahogany and rich rosewood veneer. The upholstery of the seating in the stalls – plush deep red velvet with contrasting piped rope edges. There were elaborate burnished brass fittings everywhere and the actors' green room was like the officers' mess on a Royal Naval warship, complete with a circular brass edged porthole window in the door! It was a real jewel in the BBC's crown and one of the nicest, most unique studios I have ever had the pleasure of working in. On one of those Wednesday recording sessions for 'Nightcap', I arrived early and decided to wait in the green room. I opened the door and to my utter amazement, came face to face with comedy legend Kenneth Williams.

"Oh 'Ello!" He said. In that exaggerated camp voice, he reserved for comedic effect.

He was facing me as I opened the door and he remained at a jaunty angle on the arm of the green velvet chaise longue. Those infamous nostrils of his were flaring like Concorde, on its final approach on runway twenty-seven into Heathrow.

"Sorry, I shouldn't be here, I'm just about to go!" he said, as he looked me up and down.

"No, no, it's alright," I said, as I settled down into the large green leather sofa, which was lining the wall on the left-hand side of the room opposite where he was now standing.

He slowly sat back down again, on the chaise longue and began to write with a fountain pen in what looked like a battered, brown leather-bound diary which was perched on his lap. He pursed his lips and blew gently on the words and when he was satisfied that the ink had dried, he snapped the book shut, set it down on a small table by his side, removed his pince-nez and looked over at me, quizzically.

"So, what are you here for?" he said suddenly and rather abruptly.

"Oh, umm… Yes… I'm presenting a new comedy show, called Nightcap," I said, rather embarrassed.

"Oh, what fun," he replied. "Well, enjoy it. It'll never last!"

I knew what he meant, but it seemed a little insensitive considering we hadn't even begun! This was turning into a scene from a 'Carry On' movie! He then launched into a bitter diatribe about the BBC and like any other actor I have ever known, complained about everything under the sun. I couldn't quite believe it. Here I was, in this small airtight room, deep underground with Kenneth Williams – wit, raconteur, star of the "Carry On" movies and a national treasure to boot! Over the next half an hour or so, he recounted the most wonderful, largely unrepeatable stories about his life, barely stopping to draw breath. It was mesmerising. Then as quickly as he had started, he stopped. There was a moments pause. Silence.

"And what about you?" He said.

I remember feeling a distinct sense of panic because unlike him I didn't have anywhere close to his wealth of anecdotes or, his waspish razor-sharp wit, fine comedy timing and well… life experience. I was a twenty-something nobody. I remember blurting out some pathetic story – which by contrast to his spellbinding performance, paled into painful silence-inducing insignificance. I remember the moment like it was yesterday. The sudden excruciating embarrassment. Desperately fishing for a punch line, but none forthcoming. It seemed like an eternity. He was sitting on the edge of his seat now, his eyes alight and a devious smile playing across his lips. His nostrils, flaring in a way that has raised a million laughs over the years. A distant tube train, clattering its way north to Oxford Circus rumbled beneath us, shaking the very foundations of the building above.

Then, silence. Utter bloody silence.

His face crumpled. There was to be no climax. No dénouement. No happy ending. He sank back into his chair, crestfallen.

"Is that it?" he exclaimed, struggling to his feet. *"Is that it?"*

"Err, yes... sorry," I said, apologetically, looking at the floor.

He breathed a huge sigh, shook his head, gathered up his belongings, buttoned his jacket, tossed a paisley-patterned silk scarf around his impossibly long neck and exited the room with a casual "Goodbye Sweetie" over his shoulder. That was the first and last time I saw him. I was drained and not a little humiliated. Kenneth Williams was undeniably a comedy genius and in his own mind at least, a serious, classically trained actor. He was one of the greats in the venerable pantheon of British comedy entertainers, but he was also a deeply troubled soul. He suffered, it seems from low self-esteem and a form of self-loathing which often manifested itself in his treatment of those around him. He had a cruel, waspish sense of humour, was known to use it injudiciously on those he encountered, and he did not tolerate fools lightly. After our brief encounter, there was no doubting he had me marked down as a fool. Meeting one's heroes can be disappointing. I don't recommend it.

Another of my comedy heroes also appeared at The Paris. In 1985, Radio 2 had scheduled a short series with the great Ernie Wise, the long time and now erstwhile comedy partner of the late Eric Morcambe. I was scheduled to be the announcer on the series. This involved me turning up to The Paris and introducing the turns, including Ernie himself. It pains me to tell you, dear reader, that without Eric, he just wasn't funny anymore. Less charitable observers might say that as Eric Morcambe's straight man, he never got the laughs but that would be unfair. Their relationship was symbiotic. The script Ernie held in his trembling hand today though, was devoid of any jokes and the cast struggled to raise the laughs. What was worse, during rehearsals and unknown to me, Ernie's wife was in the audience sitting alongside his manager. She went everywhere with him. During a break, I made a somewhat unguarded and less than charitable remark about Ernie to one of the cast, and it was unfortunately within earshot of Ernie's missus. The producer shot me a look as if to say, "shut up you fool," but the damage was done. Nothing came of it, perhaps because she too had concluded the show wasn't funny either. Needless to say, it wasn't re-commissioned. As Wogan used to say, it's really difficult to know when to leave the party. Like house guests, some of us occasionally hang around a little too long, beyond our welcome.

Anyway, back to 'Nightcap'. Several writers had been lined up, to pen episodic and stand-alone sketches for the series. Among these young buck wordsmiths were Ged Parsons, John O'Farrell, Mark Burton, David Baddiel and Nick Newman. David and Nick went on to form a stellar comedy partnership, eventually filling huge stadia with their double act and although commonplace today, David and Nick were the two who were the first to blaze that particular daring yet lucrative trail. Those who followed and made millions in the process, owe them a debt of gratitude. John O'Farrell is now a successful novelist and Mark Burton is now a Hollywood screenwriter. I love it when people I know become successful.

There were other freelance writers too, including Mike Coleman, Bill Matthews, Alison Renshaw, Simon Bullivant, Terry Johnson and Robert Linford, many of whom have carved out successful careers as professional joke-smiths and script editors on top-notch shows both in the UK and the USA. We met every Wednesday in The Paris, to record the raft of sketches that were to be incorporated in that week's show. Phil Cornwell, one of the actors, was a law onto himself. He would frequently turn up late and amuse us all with his high-speed antics and machine-gun fast delivery. Most of Phil's energy it appeared was fuelled by a cocktail of Night Nurse and Benadryl, but he delivered some blisteringly wonderful performances, even if they often ran to multiple takes and took forever to record. I remember the great John Glover comparing my role to that of Kenneth Horne in "Round the Horne." A maelstrom of chaos, whirling around the eye of a slightly imperfect storm!

The producer of the first series was a chap who was former Butlins redcoat, with a wealth of entertainment experience. He was great fun to work with and I formed an enduring friendship with him. In the week before the Friday night broadcast, he would commission the sketches, select the music and book the guests. Then on Thursday he would put the running order together and produce the scripts. When Friday came around, we would get into the studio at 8pm and do two 'dry runs' of the show with the 'tops and tails' of the music and check the ins and outs of the sketches. Then we would get together in the office to go through the questions for the guests. By the time we got to go on air at 11pm, I was well any truly sick of the whole bloody thing, having heard the music and sketches multiple times! Some weeks I had to muster all my energy to do the show. The producer though kept things interesting. When he sensed that I was flagging, he would go into one of his routines, which more often than not would conclude with him unzipping his trouser fly and waving his penis at me through the control room window! His long-suffering PA just looked the other way, shook her head and sighed the deepest of sighs. We nick-named him: 'The Old Wrinkled Retainer'! It's difficult to imagine any producer doing that nowadays and not being subject to instant and terminal disciplinary proceedings, but this was the '80s and many people as we now subsequently know, were getting up to all kinds of appalling things for which they would later have to pay. All of them but one, as it turned out. My producer though, was a good egg and his behaviour, though in questionable taste was as innocent as it comes.

One of the regular elements of 'Nightcap' was 'Dial a Sketch'. This involved the audience at home having input into the show and was a precursor to today's highly interactive, red button and app-driven media world. At the start of the show, I would invite listeners to phone-in with a topical sketch idea. The writers on hand would then select the best one and disappear off into a back-office behind the studio, write the sketch, and then we would perform it live at the end of the show. It must have been quite a nerve-wracking experience for the guys because forty-five minutes or so is not a long time to select, write and hone a fully polished sketch, complete with stage directions and sound effects! In the most part though they pulled it off with a certain measure of confidence, even if the performances were not all they might have been. At least I laughed!

The first series of *'Peter Dickson's Nightcap'* must have gone down well with the suits on the fourth floor. The audience figures and satisfaction surveys were equally encouraging. The weekly senior management meeting minutes presided over by the Controller of Radio 2, Bryant Marriott recorded what they all thought of the new show. The head of light entertainment radio said:

"This series is the way forward in comedy broadcasting and took full advantage of fresh, young writing talent."

The controller, Bryant Marriott also expressed his appreciation. Subsequently, they commissioned another series. Sadly though, my original producer and his amazing dancing bell-end weren't on board. I was assigned, two new producers – Mark Robson and Dan Patterson. On one of these shows in the new series, the guests included Stephen Fry and Hugh Laurie, whose stars were in the ascendant and their new comedy sketch show "A Bit of Fry and Laurie" was airing on BBC1 TV. Dan, Mark and I concocted a couple of sketch routines involving them and me, and they were gracious enough to perform them live on the show that week. Stephen and Hugh are two of the nicest people you could ever wish to meet. After the show as we were packing up to leave, Stephen invited us both to a house party he and Hugh were holding at their place the following Saturday night. It was a generous gesture, considering we had only just met.

A week later, on the night in question, I picked Dan up in my car and we headed off in search of Fry's house in North London, using my trusty A to Z map. His home, when we eventually located it, turned out to be a towering Georgian townhouse on a street in achingly trendy Islington, North London. Stephen, it seemed, even at this nascent stage in his career wasn't short of cash. It transpired that several years earlier he had amassed a small fortune from penning the libretto to the musical 'Me and my Girl' and this large pile of bricks, was just one of his judicious investments. Dan and I were greeted by Fry at the front door and shown into a rather grand, candle-lit, bay fronted drawing-room. To say the room contained the crème de la crème of British comedy talent, would be an understatement. Quite literally, anyone who was anyone was there. As I looked at Dan, I couldn't help noticing that his jaw had dropped to the floor. I quietly picked it up and put it back where it belonged, next to mine. Looking around the room, I could tell that he was also wondering what on earth we were doing there. We were the only people we hadn't heard of! In one corner was Rowan Atkinson chatting with Hugh Laurie and Mel Smith, in another Jennifer Saunders and Dawn French were engaged in animated conversation with Ben Elton. At that point, someone tapped me on the shoulder. I turned around.

"Hi, I'm Jools Holland. I don't think we've met."

I had been a fan of Jools Holland for many years and to meet him in a social setting was a bit of a treat. He is one of the most down to earth, well centred and balanced people you could ever hope to meet. Our conversation ranged from Boogie Woogie, Fats Waller, Squeeze and Paula Yates to the exorbitant cost of owning one of those new-fangled mobile phones! Magnums of vintage Bollinger champagne were being hefted around the room like they were going out of fashion and the party had now truly ignited. At one point, I became separated from Dan and found myself in the hall, next to the front door. The doorbell rang so I opened the door to let whoever it was in. A woman appeared from out of the gloom of the November night on Islington's Upper Street, backlit and silhouetted by the orange glow from the streetlights outside. Her face was in shadow. She was around five feet three inches tall, wearing a dark green fur hooded parka overcoat and an oversized multicoloured striped woollen scarf around her neck and lower face, like the type Dr Who used to favour.

She extended her hand and said "Hi."

As she began to unwind the scarf from around her neck. I didn't immediately recognise her, but there was something vaguely familiar about her appearance and her voice. My alcohol addled brain was of no use at all.

"I'm sorry," I said. Stumbling forwards like Hugh Bonneville's character in 'Notting Hill'. "I don't think we've met."

"Oh, sorry," she said, extending her hand again, "I'm Kate Bush."

Ah yes, of course, you are. It truly was one of *those* parties! Dawn French and Emma Thompson bounced up, covering my obvious and rather clumsy recovery and we got into conversation about God only knows what. That's the beauty of Krug. You know you had a good time, but you can't remember why or how!

Shortly after 1am, I headed upstairs in search of the bathroom. I needn't have concerned myself about finding it. There was a long line of celebrities, winding down the wide Georgian staircase. The reason for the delay became all too apparent. I overheard one very famous guest, who shall remain nameless, announce that she was just popping upstairs to "powder her nose." I hadn't appreciated at the time, quite how literally she had meant it! I was such an innocent soul.

'Peter Dickson's Nightcap' ran for three years and one year aired on both Christmas night and New Year's Eve. We even had a Bank Holiday special called 'Peter Dickson's Happy Hour and A Half'. I had wanted to call it 'Peter Dickson's Happy Ending' but it was roundly rejected by the executives on the fourth floor without explanation. The show, however, received quite an accolade from 'Time Out' magazine who praised our successful attempt at producing a long overdue comedy and music show. This almost universal praise was shattered by the comments of the then head of Radio 3 music, Christine Hardwick who, at a management meeting said:

"I really like Peter Dickson, but some parts of this programme were truly awful and that "I would not wish to listen to it again!"

The incredibly posh Piers Burton-Page, the Radio 3 Presentation Editor countered her however and said:

"I found the programme absolutely exhilarating, particularly the show's air of frenzy and the fact that it was packed full of the zaniest ingredients."

And the Editor of "Woman's Hour," Claire Selerie-Grey (most members of management had double-barrelled names back then) said:

"I loved the show and I've become a member of the club!"

All of which just goes to prove that you can't please all of the people all of the time, though God knows we tried.

Towards the end of 1987, I had a call from my good pal Gavin McCoy alias 'Sid the Manager' from The Steve Wright in the Afternoon show on BBC Radio 1. Gavin is one of those people who always calls you – *in character*. It's great fun when you have the time for it but incredibly annoying when you are busy. This time it was Sid the Manager, enquiring about my colostomy bag! This bizarre conversation continued for three or four minutes and ended with him or rather Sid saying,

"Yes boy, look I can't stop now – cheerio – hello?"

He hung up and so did I. Seconds later the phone rang again and this time it was Gavin as himself, with no reference whatsoever to the previous call!

At around this time, Gavin was presenting on BBC Radio Bedfordshire, from its studios in glamorous downtown Luton, in the fair county of Bedfordshire. He was on air six days a week including Saturdays, and on that day, he fronted a show called 'The Weekend Warm Up'. He told me he was on the move and had been offered a job presenting a show on Radio Essex, in Southend. Quite why Gavin continued to dick about in the provinces is anyone's guess. He is one of those rare radio naturals. Gifted in so many ways that many less able, yet nationally known radio personalities, sadly are not. He deserved a bigger audience. Anyhow, I digress. The point of the conversation was that he wanted to put my name in the frame, to take over his Saturday morning show on Radio Bedfordshire and invited me up to Luton

Backstage with Joan Rivers – 1995 – BBC TV Centre, London.

the following Saturday to see the show go out live. This way at least I could see first-hand what I was letting myself in for. The only slight reservation I had, was that I was on air on Radio 2 with "Nightcap" until 1am on Saturday and would have to be at Radio Beds in Luton thirty-five miles away by 09.30 later that morning. This would only give me about four hours of sleep at most. Against my better judgement, I relented and agreed to meet up with him the following weekend. And so, I found myself a week later careering up a rain soaked M1 Motorway to Luton, bleary-eyed and robbed of sleep, looking for the studios in a one-way hell hole of a gyratory system in Luton, going round and round in circles. I must have spent a good hour searching for the bloody place, but all was not in vain. While driving around I almost crashed the car twice while listening to Gavin's show on the radio. It was one long piss-take, relentless in its ferocity and waspish wit. Gavin was accompanied by his posse and mercilessly yet subtly toyed with one hapless telephone caller after another, like a Lion playing with its prey before the kill.

I eventually located the studios but found it incredibly difficult to get out of the car, as the show was just so dammed entertaining. Eventually, I joined Gavin and his posse in the studio. During a break for music, I was introduced to Ian Brown, his producer and Tony, Dave and Mary his assistants. What I hadn't quite appreciated was that these four were not on the BBC payroll. They were enthusiastic amateurs who helped out each weekend for the love of radio – and of course, they loved Gavin! This was music to my ears. I have always regarded myself as an enthusiastic radio amateur – who just happened to get paid. I sat through the rest of the show, mesmerised and mentally placed myself in the driving seat, assessing whether or not I could and should take on this show. At the end of it, as we chatted in the office, Gavin said that he could see no reason why I shouldn't do it. I've always been a bit of a yes man, so I agreed. What on earth is wrong with me?

Three weeks later I took my place at the microphone of 'The Weekend Warm Up' on BBC Three Counties Radio in beautiful downtown Luton and began what was for me, a very happy but somewhat brief association with BBC local radio. What appealed to me most was the unfettered freedom of the whole exercise. There was no one breathing down your neck like there was in London and as it was a weekend, the suits were all at home pruning the roses and fiddling in their allotments or whatever is they do when they're not getting in the way demanding unnecessary meetings, sharpening pencils and shuffling papers!

The show was a mix of music, competitions, phone calls and whatever else we could think of. We made full use of the very limited facilities and I brought my collection of idents, sweepers and stings that I had accumulated during my time on 'Nightcap'. These were all contained on blue Sonifex carts (rather like the old eight track cartridges we all used to play music on) and were packed into three large BBC travel cases that took the best part of twenty minutes to arrange on the desk above the mixer, before the show. It looked like a mountain of blue plastic and would today probably set alarm bells ringing at Greenpeace and the UN. As there were so many of the damned things, I came up with the ingenious idea of colour coding the labels on them. Pink for spoken idents, yellow for sound effects and blue for music beds. This way I had a better chance of locating the right one – in time. There were three cart machines, rather like the ones I had played with on that Radio One console in Belfast all those years ago. I had watched and studied Steve Wright for years and now it was my turn to try and be an audio alchemist!

The team and I were getting on like a proverbial supermarket on fire.

Each of us sparring and bouncing off one another like some crazed verbal pinball machine. The chemistry, as they say, was just right. Tony, who had a waspish and slightly dark sense of humour, I christened 'Terrible Tony', Dave I called 'Donkey', don't ask why! My wife Barbara who had never been in front of a microphone in her life also joined in and Mary, for obvious reasons was called 'Mouthy'. Mary was rumoured to have come from a family of travellers and had an opinion on absolutely everything, which is what makes great radio. She had a voice like a foghorn and sounded like one of those harridans you encounter outside Harrods in Knightsbridge selling lucky heather, around Christmas time! The words, common and muck spring to mind, but she had a heart of gold and took the relentless ribbing we dished out in her direction with good grace. Why she came back week after week for more punishment, is anybody's guess.

During one Saturday broadcast of 'The Weekend Warm-Up', Tony suggested we make use of the radio outside broadcast vehicle and mount what is known as an O.B from Mary's house. I have no idea why I agreed, but it seemed like a good idea at the time. It was the 'agent provocateur' in me, knocking on the door again. As the show on that particular Saturday began, Tony and Dave fired up the old O.B car in the yard outside and headed off for Mary's house in nearby Houghton Regis. Forty-five minutes later, the signal from the O.B vehicle crackled into life, appearing as a sound source on one of the spare channels on my desk. Lights began to flash. Good, they were inside the house. Let in by a kindly neighbour, and they were ready to begin. For the next thirty minutes, both Tony and Dave performed a side-splitting room by room commentary, painting a detailed picture of the inside of Mary's house, including the contents her kitchen cupboards. Increasingly horrified, Mary sat in the studio providing additional explanations and apologies for what they found. Every minute detail was picked over, analysed and commented upon. I have to say it was riveting stuff. The detritus of life and individual personal domestic arrangements and what it reveals about people are fascinating. This was an early and very unstructured 'Through the Keyhole'. I should have copyrighted it. Come to think of it, my own cupboards have the potential to be a tad embarrassing. That fifteen-year-old spice rack, for instance, should probably go! Her embarrassment though was palpable and when the duo moved upstairs to the bedrooms, I sensed that she was getting way out of her comfort zone.

How many people do you know have had the minutiae of their private life picked over in such a public manner? It was mundane stuff I grant you that, but fascinating, nonetheless. From the colour of her wallpaper and carpets to the things in her fridge, no stone was left unturned. This was *true* local radio and an example of why radio is so much better than TV. It's all in the mind, though exactly what was in the mind of the listener to this particular broadcast is anyone's guess!

Our team of intrepid investigative reporters had now reached the marital bedroom and I paused proceedings there to play a record and to allow the listeners to hold their breath. When the music stopped, like some giant game of musical chairs, we resumed our tour. Pulling back the purple velour duvet, we were treated to a detailed description of Mary's lurid synthetic satin sheets and mid-century authentic shag pile rug. Meanwhile, Mary's husband who was an eighteen stone hairy arsed Luton taxi driver was listening to all this on his car radio with punters in the back and was not a happy bunny! I decided to pull the plug and ordered the hapless pair to head straight back to the studio. It was the right thing to have done. Ten minutes after they left, her husband arrived home and called me at the studio to give me a right verbal ear bashing. I dread to think what would have happened had he arrived home sooner. We might have had a double murder on our hands – live on air. Mary thought the whole episode amusing and not surprisingly separated from her husband soon afterwards. I can't say for sure if 'The Weekend Warm Up' episode hastened her divorce, but it can't have helped. The things some people will do to chase ratings, I don't know!

As the weeks progressed, 'The Weekend Warm Up' went from bad to worse. It became a huge self-indulgent social occasion held purely for our selfish amusement and gratification. The listeners, if there were any left, (we had long since stopped worrying about ratings) were carried along on a tidal wave of in-jokes and juvenile innuendo. We were winging it, taking risks and chances and delivering a show that was entertaining, though entertaining us, mostly. That point was crossed on more than several occasions. We were certainly having fun, but the BBC's charter was being abused like a tramp's dog. We had even resorted to breaking into the station's technical area and adjusting the output levels to the transmitter, pumping more volume to the Optimod processors so that our signal would have seemed louder to anyone casually scanning the dial on a normal FM radio within a forty mile radius! Eventually and not unsurprisingly, the management stepped in as I knew they surely would. Local BBC radio, like a three-legged stool, had a remit to inform, entertain and educate. This particular stool wasn't just wonky, it had lost all three of its legs, completely fallen over was now in bits on the floor like some cheap, uncompleted IKEA coffee table. I can't say I was surprised to receive a rather sheepish call at home from the station editor, to tell me that after three years the show was being rested. 'Rested' in this case was a euphemism for 'axed'. And so, with a heavy heart, I had to tell the rest of the happy gang that their Saturday mornings would be a little less fun-filled from now on. They all took it in good form and thanked me for the time we had. It wasn't as if any of us were out of work. It was just as though an enjoyable hobby had come to a premature end. I for one was not too disappointed either. The death of that Saturday show came as a blessed relief. Combining the late night on *'Peter Dickson's Nightcap'* on Radio 2 with the early start on BBC Radio Beds was beginning to take its toll. I was knackered! I needed all my strength because over at BBC Radio 1, things were about to turn distinctly sour.

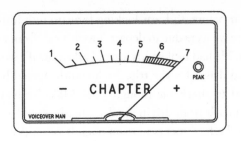

I'VE BEEN STANDING OUT THERE
LIKE A PRICK FOR THREE MINUTES

⊢————⊣

T he BBC Radio 1 Roadshow was a great British institution. Every summer, the station would de-camp from its rarefied London base in a huge vehicular convoy and sally forth with gay abandon into the British countryside like a mad, uninvited travelling circus on a grand tour of the UK's major seaside resorts. For many people, a holiday in Bognor or Brighton was not complete, unless you had sat for at least four hours on damp grass and licked an ice-cream in front of the Radio 1 Roadshow, sung along to your favourite tunes and laughed uproariously at the juvenile antics of your favourite 'Smashy and Nicey' DJs. Given the fact that otherwise sane people actually did this, was an indication of the paucity of other local attractions. The Road Show was hugely popular but more importantly, it was completely free! The show, which was broadcast live each morning to the nation, regularly attracted a live and largely captive audience of 20,000 to 30,000 people! During the summer of 1986, at the height of Steve Wright's popularity on the afternoon show on Radio 1, we were scheduled to perform on the south-western leg of this great British tour. Cornwall was our destination. I had never been to Cornwall never mind on a roadshow, apart from that brief heart-stopping encounter with John Craven in

Brighton the year before, so I was looking forward to it immensely.

A week before we were due to depart, I took a call from Malcolm Brown, Steve's producer. He had broken his leg and asked me if I would mind acting as the designated driver for the trip. I reluctantly agreed but couldn't help the niggling and uncharitable thought that Malcolm had engineered his fall, to excuse himself from driving and so that he could avail himself fully to whatever liquid refreshments were on offer. It was indeed an uncharitable thought. Malcolm had, while very drunk, fallen off a barstool the week before, and was in obvious and considerable discomfort.

One bright sunny July Sunday afternoon, we set off from Broadcasting House, London in a rented silver Ford Granada, Malcolm in the front seat, acting as navigator and Steve in the back seat acting like a hyperactive child who had consumed too many Haribos. We headed westwards out of London, cleared the Hammersmith and Hogarth Roundabouts and I squeezed the accelerator on the big 2.5-litre engine and gunned the Mark II, 160 brake horsepower Ford Granada down the outside lane of the M4 and hoped for the best. The journey was largely uneventful, apart from an incident at Gordano Services when Steve was spotted by a coachload of school kids on an outing. Leaving the squealing and screaming behind and with Gordano, in the rear-view mirror (possibly the best view you will ever have of it) I pointed the nose of the big lumbering Granada westwards towards Newquay, the first stop on our week-long tour of the south-west holiday towns along the Cornish Riviera.

Being part of the Radio 1 Roadshow, was the next best thing to running away with the circus, you will have to take my word for it, but it was so perversely entertaining and is the most fun you will ever have with your clothes on! Accompanying the roadshow was a cavalcade of jalopies, juggernauts, articulated wotnots and assorted trailers and wagons containing, among other things, the stage, lighting, PA system, sound desks, records, a thousand miles of cables, the technical vehicles, the production HQ, and the ubiquitous goodie-mobiles. The latter vehicles were under the control of the infamous Smiley Miley. Smiley, or Tony Miles to give him his actual name, was a real character. A Bristol businessman with a larger than life personality, he had aligned himself so closely with the roadshow that he practically owned it. He and Johnny Beerling, Radio 1's controller dreamt up the idea all those years ago and made it a reality. And so I found myself careering down the M4 Motorway behind several lorries containing over a million tacky Chinese plastic key-fobs in the shape of the number '1', bottle openers, water pistols, Blue and white striped lighters, Smiley pen sets, bath sponges, lurid fridge magnets, bottle openers and pencil top erasers. As we approached Newquay, the sun was beginning to dip into the horizon. Hordes of singlet wearing teenagers, tattooed ladies and happy families were swarming around the town enjoying the final moments of what had evidently been a perfect day by the seaside. We followed the great British smell of fish and chips, candy floss and beer, located our hotel and met up with the rest of the crew. They were a motley bunch. There were the hairy arsed rigger drivers, man-mountain security personnel, Smiley's assistants, the audio guys from Broadcasting House control room and an assortment of PA's, assistant producers and various hangers-on. All of them were seasoned roadshow veterans. Every single one of them, living the brand by wearing Radio 1 t-shirts and tighty-whitey, shorter than short shorts – well, it was the '80s love and we all have George Michael to thank for that! You only live once, or YOLO, as we used to say back in the day.

Steve, despite his outward sunny persona, has never been one for socialising en masse, so he took himself off to his room which was, being the star's privilege, the main suite of the hotel. I, meanwhile, settled into a comfortable corner of the hotel bar with Malcolm, Smiley and a few of the technical guys and ordered up the first round of drinks. We discussed what we were going to do during the week and ran through a couple of scenarios for games and how we were going to introduce the characters. Steve joined us briefly around 7 o'clock and sat nursing a single Drambuie and lemonade on ice. Steve is many things, but a serious drinker he most definitely isn't. That fact though didn't deter us, we more than made up for his share. As the night wore on and the drink flowed, life took on a new more agreeable hue. It was what Malcolm called: 'positive attitude adjustment'. Steve had excused himself and gone to bed and after a few more pints, Malcolm commandeered the hotel's piano for a good old-fashioned sing-along. This was a tradition and one that Malcolm was obliged to follow, despite his lame protestations. Hours of fabulous drunken Les Dawson style piano playing, accompanied by the even more inebriated voices of a bunch of tuneless half-wits, wafted out of the French windows and onto the promenade below. It was 2am and the roadshow was unmistakably in town. If there was anyone within a five hundred-yard radius of the hotel who had journeyed here for a spot of silent contemplation by the seaside, they were probably checking out right now.

The morning alarm on the bedside table slammed into my skull like a jackhammer. My mouth felt like the floor of an Egyptian Souk and my brain was complaining, in no uncertain terms, about the two hundred monkeys who were still partying as dawn broke inside my head. The strident screech of a flock of hungry seagulls circling overhead and the bright sunlight piercing the curtains brought me to my senses and reminded me where I was. It was 7am, we were in Newquay and would be on air to the nation and in front of a crowd of thousands of expectant holidaymakers and six million more listening at home in less than three hours. If the rest of the week was to continue like this, I thought, I'd better update my will. Down at the roadshow site, Smiley and his posse had circled the wagons spaghetti western style, in preparation for the assault they knew was coming. There was a definite siege mentality like a latter-day Rorke's Drift. The stage was set, we were positioned facing up a large grassy escarpment. A kind of natural amphitheatre, with us as the bait. Steve was busy with Malcolm preparing the running order for the show. I was due to come on during the second half of the show and scare the children as – 'Mr Mad', my alter ego at the time. This really was becoming a circus. As I sat in the cramped green-room, next to the chemical toilet nursing a cup of BBC coffee and a king-sized hangover, Steve breezed in, wearing a pair of white trousers and a red and white striped blazer that made him look like Dick Van Dyke or Super Mario's long lost brother. Sartorial and elegant were never going to be words used in the crafting of his obituary. Not that he cared.

"I know this looks ridiculous love, but we've got to showbiz this lot up!"

Steve was terrified, that unless he went over the top and infected everyone else in the vicinity with his enthusiasm the whole show would deflate and sound dull. This was and always has been his modus operandi. Though who was kidding who, I'm not so sure. We were all too terrified and some of us possibly still too hungover from the night before to perform even the briefest, perfunctory analysis. The clock was ticking down to transmission time, Simon Bates' 'Our Tune' was blasting out of the large array of speakers in front of the stage and I could see the great man in my mind's eye back in London, a Cuban cigar nestled between the thick fingers of his right hand barking at his producer, trying to hold it all together.

A massive crowd had gathered on the grassy banks on three sides of the stage. It's hard to put a figure on the size of a crowd. After you've counted up to a hundred, things go a bit pear-shaped. That morning, as I gazed out through a small chink in the door which led onto the stage, there were more people than I had ever seen gathered together in one place before. As far as the eye could see – there were bodies everywhere. The security guys had erected a waist-high metal barrier about six feet from the edge of the stage, so we felt some degree of separation, but crowds are unpredictable and can behave in ways you don't expect. It was a good turnout alright. We only hoped we could live up to their expectations. Still, what did I care, my name wasn't on the programme. Steve, who had also been looking at the crowd unobserved, turned away and laughed nervously. Performing in front of a microphone albeit to a radio audience of millions is one thing but facing an audience and seeing the whites of their eyes is another matter altogether.

As the smell of the candy floss, damp clothing, fish and chips, ozone, freshly mown grass, toffee apples and municipal drainage wafted uninvited into our nostrils, I could tell he was way out of his comfort zone but as any performer will tell you, even the most seasoned ones, the moment before you walk out on stage is the worst. Once out there, provided you don't trip and fall over on your entrance, appear with your trouser flies undone or soil yourself before your introduction, things invariably calm down considerably quickly. At ten minutes to eleven, Malcolm, who was also battling with nerves and a lack of blood in his alcohol stream went out onto the stage to warm up the crowd. The trouble was, this crowd was hotter than a pole dancer's G-String. That five-foot-high security barrier in front of the stage was a blessing. Had the crowd been any closer, I feel sure Malcolm would have knocked them out. Not with his carefully honed comedy routine, but by the beer, whisky and tobacco fumes on his breath. Quite who the crowd thought Malcolm was is anyone's guess. The sight of a fifty-three-year-old man wearing tight white shorts out of which were protruding a pair of equally white hairy legs like stalks of rhubarb, talking at you like a comprehensive school headmaster, must have caused considerable confusion as the crowd immediately went quiet; except for one lone teenage boy on a BMX bike, next to the public toilets who screamed "WANKER!" at the top of his voice before cycling off up the promenade at speed. Back in the wings, Steve and I nearly passed out trying to suppress our laughter. We needn't

'Generation Game' aftershow party with Paul O'Grady
2003 – BBC TV Centre, London.

have worried though, as Malcolm had them all eating out of his hand within seconds. He is after all, though with no intention on his part, one of life's natural comedians.

The moment had arrived. It was three minutes to eleven. Malcolm, who by now was drenched in sweat, wrapped up on the stage and introduced Steve. The noise that followed was like a small nuclear explosion as Steve walked out, took the microphone from a grateful Malcolm and immediately went into his Radio 1 DJ routine. It was a well-honed act which I know Steve viewed with detachment. Bizarrely, in conversation he would often refer to himself in the third person. 'Steve Wright' would never say that or 'Wrighty' would always do this as if he were talking about someone else. It was all very odd indeed! Steve Wright, the DJ, 'the personality' was his alter ego, his public persona. A persona that had slowly over time, merged with his own. Quite who the *real* Steve Wright was, I never truly discovered. I'm not even sure if he knew either. Once or twice, in quieter moments I think I got fairly close to meeting the real man, but those fleeting glimpses were rare. He was and is an enigma with more layers to his complex personality than a Vidalia onion. Above all though, he always needed to be in control and that in part explains his reluctance to socialise with alcohol. Steve can't bear the thought of being out of control. This character trait, combined with an evident reluctance to suppress strong underlying emotions of jealousy and feelings of insecurity, led in part to the eventual destruction of more than one of his relationships – about which, more later.

Meanwhile, back in the wings, I was getting ready for my big moment in the spotlight. The question of how we would portray Mr Mad visually was one which had vexed us for some considerable time. Steve's driver, John Farr had helpfully brought along some props. These consisted of a pair of large plastic joke feet in hideous clown shoes and a pair of rubber hand shackles, which he'd bought in a joke shop in Reading. I had provided a blue denim straight jacket on which I had crudely painted "Mr Mad #1142" in white paint, a pair of oversize green corduroy trousers tied with string and a wild-looking shoulder-length black wig! The look was completed with a latex prosthetic nose and a handful of white, red and black make up which I had applied to my face. I looked like a latter-day 'JOKER'.

The idea was simply for me to go out on stage to scare the horses and frighten the children. There was however a subliminal message. If you're not kind to your parents and don't work hard at school, you too could end up like this! An additional surprise feature further enhanced the mad image. No, make that two features. In the first instance, I came up with the idea of making the character foam at the mouth. To achieve this, I had the idea of putting to good creative use an item of confectionery that has been around for years – a humble 'Bassett's' Sherbet Fountain. Moments before I was due on stage, I would chew the small liquorice stick that it came with until it became a paste and hold the contents in my mouth. Then, just as I went on, I tipped the entire contents of the sherbet tube into my mouth. Mount Vesuvius has nothing on the resultant explosion! It really was quite spectacularly gross. I would lurch onto the stage and open my mouth slowly, releasing a seemingly never-ending stream of brown sherbet and liquorice foam down my chin and onto my chest. It went on for ages, spewing this foul looking, brown oral emanation onto the stage, over me and Steve with the desired effect on the first six rows of the audience, who were close enough to see it and recoil in horror. The other effect was even more disgusting. In my trousers, I carefully placed a knotted balloon, which I had previously filled with water that I had dyed yellow. In my right hand, I hid a small pin. At the desired moment, usually, when the audience was giving me a hard time, I would burst the balloon with the pin and shower the front two or three rows with the yellow water. That always got a big laugh. And with no explanation for the audience listening on the radio, it made it all the funnier. You have to remember; these were simpler times!

Over the years, on many of these roadshows, we invented special road-show only characters, in addition to the regulars who appeared on the radio show each day. One year I played a character called 'Reg Ramsey–Street', a double-glazing salesman with extreme seborrheic dermatitis and even more severe personal hygiene issues. Reg was to be the host of a brand-new game we had devised. It was pretty straightforward. Two hapless contestants would be plucked from the audience and made to go head to head in a three-question quiz. The loser would then have to go into a small telephone-box sized double glazed booth with me and stay there for sixty seconds, while I tried to sell them double glazing! For the character, I wore an ill-fitting suit, the collar of which was liberally dusted with salt, to resemble dandruff, a top breast pocket filled with cheap pens, a pair of trousers which were short on the leg revealing a pair of un-coordinated socks and a rather conspicuous badly fitted wig! For additional authenticity, I also wore a pair of yellow false teeth. I have to say, even I was repulsed. As this was summer, the temperature in the glass box was over 30°C with very little breathable oxygen. It was unbearable enough for me, but I did feel sorry for the bemused contestant who only wanted to get out as quickly as possible. To make matters worse, on one of the weeks, I was joined by my good friend Adrian Juste, himself a veteran Radio 1 DJ. Adrian, who needs very little encouragement to get into character at the best of times, played the part of a rival double-glazing salesman, with pyorrhoea laden gums and equally disgusting habits, constant farting being the least offensive. When we both entered the booth with the contestant, there was barely enough room to turn around never mind breathe the hot, thin fetid air. When we launched into our sales patter, it was difficult to keep a straight face. The sight of Adrian gesticulating wildly, salivating and going red in the face was just too much. Like the great Shakespearian actor, Sir Lawrence Olivier he would insist beforehand that I shouldn't "look him in the eye," because if I did, he would surely go to pieces! And indeed, on several occasions he almost did. I am indebted to Adrian for not just for the laughs, friendship and advice but also for his tireless efforts helping me create my first commercial demo show-reel. I had 2,000 CD's pressed. I still have a garage full of them in case anyone's interested. Does anyone actually own a CD player these days?

On another show, we were joined by Richard Easter who had come down from London to showcase his new character 'Dr Fish Filleter'. This was the grossest thing I think have ever seen in the name of public entertainment. Smiley Miley had persuaded one of his pals to construct a large aquarium sized glass tank, which he had filled with seawater and... an assortment of dead fish, which were well past their sell-by date. Richard would come on stage wearing a pair of white fish mongers' overalls, white Wellington boots and a white coat and hat. He would then proceed to enter the tank and while the specially composed or should that be de-composed 'filleting fish' song was playing, reach down into the tank, pick out a dead Halibut or Octopus and casually toss it into the audience. The sound of confused and frightened teenage girls squealing and crying with the trauma of it all, still rings in my ears to this day. Quite what the radio audience thought was going on, is anyone's guess. As Kenny Everett would say, "It was all done in the best possible taste."

'Voiceover Man' rebranding publicity postcard No.1
2005 – Creative: Damon Hutson-Flynn.

John Farr, Steve's driver would also accompany us on these roadshows. John is fearless and has a cast iron, Teflon lined stomach to boot. I swear that what I am about to tell you is one hundred percent true. I personally witnessed him picking fish and Octopus tentacles out of the tank and eating them raw. I can't think of anything more disgusting and I have a feeling that the sight of that must have given Ant and Dec, who were guests on the show that day in their former guise as PJ and Duncan, the inspiration for the bush tucker trial on "I'm a Celebrity – Get Me Out Of Here," all those years later. John's 'human dustbin' act was also the main feature on the many personal appearances that Steve and I made at various tawdry nightclubs up and down the country. Again, hand on heart, I have seen John consume neat Castrol GTX engine oil, washed down with raw eggs, talcum powder, self-raising flour, toothpaste, paint thinners and a tin of Pedigree Chum. Quite how the man is still alive, is anyone's guess. Still, it goes a long way to explain why his man boobs are bigger than Marge Simpson's and his Vorderman-proportioned arse resembles an overstuffed string bag full of Italian Buffalo Mozzarella. Apart from that, the man has a heart of gold, possibly from a wedding ring that he accidentally consumed one night at Raquel's in Basildon. These personal appearances in nightclubs were hilarious. Not so much for what occurred on the stage, but more for what occurred backstage and on the journey to and from the venue – more of which in a moment. The live gigs were planned by Steve's agent Jo Gurnett, to take place on a Friday night. Steve would remorselessly plug the fact that he would be showing up at the club in question, on his radio show that afternoon, thereby guaranteeing a good turnout for the nightclub appearance later. Something that would be frowned upon nowadays in the current BBC.

After these shows, we would set off in Farr's gleaming red E-class Mercedes down some God-forsaken motorway, stopping on the way for refreshments at the various motorway service stations. Arriving at the venue, we'd be met by the club's security people and escorted, more often than not up a dingy backyard fire escape to the equally dilapidated manager's office. Once there, we would order up drinks. Orange juice for Steve and Orange juice (liberally doused with vodka) for John and me. Steve thought we were all-consuming Orange juice of course, but John's order, telephoned in advance of the trip to forewarn the bar staff made sure we were properly catered for! It was an amusing private joke that John and I shared to our obvious mutual delight! "Cheers" he would say. "Down the hatch my lover!" Then we would get on with the business of organising ourselves for the show in a slightly better frame of mind than when we had arrived.

I invariably played two characters on stage at these gigs. Dickie the Exec, a pompous twit of a man, dressed in white bow tie and tails and Mr Mad, the slavering, foaming at the mouth, incontinent maniac. Dickie was first on and after a brief routine, I introduced Steve. I would then make my exit, change costumes and apply the many layers of face paint and latex prosthetics to complete the hideous transformation into Mr Mad. Most of these clubs were not designed for theatrical presentation and so often lacked an obvious stage area. Often, we would find ourselves, escorted by John to the dance floor at the centre of the club through an ugly crowd of drunken, Friday night club goers. My only concern was that my wig didn't come off as we traipsed and bounced awkwardly through the crowd, so I made sure that I held tightly onto it as we made our way in. It's amazing, but the Mr Mad character had an army of adoring young female fans. I was propositioned on more than one occasion and once in Norwich, I was assaulted by a particularly enthusiastic gaggle of very drunk travel agents!

At one of these personal appearances, I was scheduled to make my entrance through a set of thick steel fire doors. Radio 1 DJ, Adrian Juste was with me and he was dressed in a Gorilla costume (I have no idea why). In the 30°C of heat, inside must have smelled like the actual Gorilla cage on a hot August day at London Zoo! The only problem was that behind these doors and underneath the wig and bear costume, neither of us could hear what was going on inside the club. As the time for our cue approached, I sent a club security guard out to listen for our pre-arranged audio signal – the song: 'Come on Eileen' by Dexys Midnight Runners. Foolishly, I thought that the security man had understood the instruction, but I had overestimated his comprehension skills. The minutes ticked by. Nothing. Just the faint thud of the bass, from the club below. Suddenly, without warning the doors burst open and in stormed a furious Wrighty, sweating and puce with rage.

"Where the fuck have you been?" He bellowed. "I've been standing out there like a prick for the last three minutes introducing you!"

The Gorilla looked at Mr Mad, Mr Mad looked at the Gorilla, both looked at Wrighty and all three of us dashed out into the club to a deafening roar. Wrighty did eventually see the funny side once he had calmed down and the show had been a success. Back in the manager's office, as we were changing back into to what passed for normality and downing another flagon of orange juice, the manager appeared out of the back office clutching the biggest wad of £20 notes I have ever seen – it was pay time! John invariably took charge of this. If there was to be any funny business, he, rather than Wrighty, would be best placed to deal with it. There and then on the table, several thousand pounds in grubby £20 notes were counted out and stuffed into a large brown envelope. Then it was back outside, down the fire escape to side-step a bunch of club-goers who by now, were being sick over their shoes and stuffing chips into their fat faces beside the bins at the rear of the club. It was a quick dash across stony open ground and into the back of the Mercedes for the long trip through the night, back to London.

The journey home was preoccupied with an analysis of the gig and there was much discussion about the various characters we had met and things that had been said and done. During our return trips from all of these personal appearances, Steve took the curious view that his stage clothes were largely disposable. Most of the time he ended up covered in egg yolk, dog food, engine oil, brown sherbet, tomato ketchup and talcum powder, so rather than taking the clothes home to wash and face an inquisition from his wife Cindy, he used to simply chuck his jacket and trousers out of the speeding car window, including a pair of brand new 'Green Flash' tennis shoes – his preferred stage footwear. This was invariably performed at high speed on the M1, just after Watford Gap. It struck me then and indeed strikes me now that in a field somewhere north of Milton Keynes someone, at some time will stumble across hundreds of pairs of white trousers liberally dusted with an unidentified white powder, a large selection of brightly coloured size thirty-six jackets, smeared with a substance that resembles dried blood and four hundred Green Flash tennis shoes covered in engine oil. It will either trigger a murder enquiry, a search for an elusive Bedfordshire drugs cartel or an immediate national immigration service investigation.

Another of Steve's quirky behavioural traits was performing acts of random kindness. Often, he would order John to stop the car whereupon he would jump out and accost some poor old dear, struggling with her shopping along the street. After the briefest of introductions, he would seize her arm, press a crisp £50 into her hand, jump back into the car and drive off. In the rear-view mirror as we drove away, John would describe the utterly befuddled scene. I'm sure it brightened many a pensioner's day and gave them something to talk about back at the care home, over that evening's mug of Horlicks.

As soon as we were within striking distance of the twinkling lights of London, Steve would ask John to tune the radio to London's LBC. Many insomniacs in the capital had long since discovered Clive Bull's late-night radio phone-in show and Steve, John and I among others, were three of his biggest fans. We were in good company. The late Peter Cook had been an anonymous phone-in contributor for several years, calling in as 'Per', a retired Norwegian fisherman. His calls were always worth listening to. They were relentlessly funny. An unscripted, flow of consciousness, from the mind of one of the 20th century's greatest comedians. Always bizarre and always hilarious. To ease the boredom of the long drives from these gigs, we would frequently pull off the road into a Motorway services area and call Clive's show ourselves. One evening I called up and was immediately put on air as 'Charles from Kensington'. I was complaining about late-night

Shouting "Come On Down!" on 'Bruce's Price is Right' – 1998 – YTV, Leeds.

revellers in London who were urinating in the street, outside my house. I struck out on this contentious theme in my best pompous voice, calling it a filthy practice and Clive, who knew my real identity, egged me on. As soon as the call had finished, we switched the radio back on and were amazed to hear that every second legitimate caller to the show for the next hour and a half, wanted to engage Clive on the subject of public street urination. Several miles down the road, we were laughing so much that we began to think that we too might have to do the same. Those late-night phone calls brightened up many dull journeys back from some God-forsaken place in the wee small hours of the morning.

Towards the end of 1989, I was travelling back home from central London on a train. Sitting opposite me in the carriage was a guy I had met once briefly at the BBC Club. He was the husband of one of the PAs in the BBC Radio Light Entertainment Department. His job was altogether more interesting. He was the engineer in charge of Mike Oldfield's recording studio, based at Oldfield's home in Little Chalfont, Buckinghamshire, not far from where I lived at the time. I was a fan of Oldfield's work and so during the conversation, I expressed an interest in coming over to take a look at the studio. This was duly arranged. So, several weeks later I found myself in Mike Oldfield's house having a chat with him over a cup of coffee. It was a fascinating couple of hours, and it ended with me agreeing to help Mike promote his forthcoming album 'Amarok', which was due for release in a few months. There you go, I told you I was a 'Yes' man. I mean, what in the name of God did I know about record promotion? I need to get help!

Mike Oldfield had recently ended a long and bitter contractual dispute with Virgin Records. Richard Branson, who had discovered him all those years ago and who had given him his first recording deal in 1973 as an impressionable newcomer, had tied him to a draconian, punitive fifteen-year contract. The jaw-dropping deal was heavily skewed in Branson's favour and the proceeds of Oldfield's multimillion selling albums over the years, including Tubular Bells 1 and 2, had largely helped to fund Branson's fledgling Airline business – Virgin Atlantic. Having said that, Oldfield judging by the mansion I was sitting in with an indoor swimming pool, ten acres of manicured lawns and a garage full of expensive and exotic supercars, wasn't doing all that badly himself! I convinced Mike that, rather than utilise traditional record label publicity and PR, he should fund a guerrilla-style marketing blitz, that I had devised. The album was what you might loosely call a 'concept' album. Though quite what the concept was, was anyone's guess! It was liberally sprinkled with a cacophony of sound effects. Mike's producer, the brilliant Tom Newman, had been a huge fan of the '50s American bandleader Spike Jones, as indeed was I. He and Mike had recorded the sounds of everyday household objects and had arranged them into an impressive soundscape in one of the album's jauntier passages. This gave me the idea of printing a set of four postcards. The first three would pose various questions, 'What has: a coffee percolator, a squeaky pair of leather Gucci loafers, a dustbin, a cheese grater and a Ferrari 355 got in common?' The plan was to send these postcards to hundreds of radio DJ's up and down the country at the rate of one a week. The final and fourth card would then reveal all and be sent with a copy of the album. The idea was that this teaser campaign would stimulate some interest in the new album and hopefully, generate some airplay. The second prong of the attack was to be a direct approach to DJ's and producers on Radio 1 and Breakfast and Drive Time presenters on local radio stations in London and within the M25 and along the M4 corridor near London. I planned to invite them in small groups to Mike's studio for 'Krug and canapés' and the chance to listen to the album – in the studio where it was recorded. Quite a unique and exclusive invite, I thought.

All was going swimmingly. I contacted a local PR company to assist with the graphic design and the despatch of the teaser campaign and met with the managing director, a woman in her early thirties. Her name was Tracey and she had a penchant for fast cars, swearing and un-tipped cigarettes. Unusual for a woman, I thought, but her aggressive business attitude, energy and positive outlook impressed me. We got down to it. Mike too was impressed, and the campaign seemed to be going well. In the meantime, Tracey had discovered that I was behind the many characters on Steve Wright's radio show. In conversation, she came up with the idea of offering bespoke 'Mr Mad' telephone answering tapes to the public, by advertising in Private Eye. As I considered the character my invention and was not signed to the BBC on an exclusive deal, I agreed it was worth a punt. We placed the ad and were inundated with orders. The ad, of course, was spotted by Steve, who took complete exception to the whole affair. One evening while I was at work in one of the BBC Radio 2 continuity studios, I took a call from him. It was an instant, ill-natured rant about my abuse of privilege. He didn't actually stop to draw breath. He ended our relationship there and then, with the promise that he intended to put a stop to the offer and told me in no uncertain terms, that if I didn't do it voluntarily, he would set the BBC's lawyers onto me. Now that got my back up. Up until then, I was half considering if I should concede his point, that I perhaps should have consulted him before embarking on a commercial venture. But now, the gloves were off. Two days later, I received a rather perfunctory cease and desist letter from the BBC's legal department. Immediately, I went to see an acquaintance of mine, Mark Stephens who is unquestionably London's leading media lawyer and senior partner at top London law firm; Stephens Innocent. A great name for a firm of solicitors I think you'll agree! Mark's view was that the copyright in the character belonged to me as I had created it and the BBC had no right in law to require me to cease and desist. Remember that this was in the days before the BBC had really embraced the marketing potential of radio or indeed TV characters and formats. Nowadays, all BBC contracts have been tightened up with all the "i's" dotted and all the "t's" very firmly crossed. I instructed Mark to write back to the BBC in the most robust way and tell them, very politely – to fuck off. Mark is so much more eloquent than I could ever hope to be. I waited with bated breath for the BBC's response, but none came. The fracas, as we must now call it had not so much ended but fizzled out. As for my relationship with Steve, both professional and personal – that hit the rocks and sank beneath the waves without a trace.

The last straw to this annus horribilis was provided by a phone call I took from a bemused Mike Oldfield late in December 1989. After the successful launch of 'Amarok', Mike had continued his working relationship with Tracey, from the PR firm. She had been round at Mike's house discussing the next wheeze. Mike, his long-suffering assistant Jeremy and Tracey had, after a long meeting which was fuelled with whisky, decided to take a walk in the woods behind Mike's house. During this walk, it transpires that Tracey dropped a bit of a bombshell on these two hapless lads. Tracey, it turns out, was a HE and not a SHE! It hadn't occurred to me that she was trans but when I thought back on it, it began to make sense. There was the sports car, the un-tipped cigarettes, the swearing, the backslapping, the manly walk, the shots of whiskey, the size twelve shoes, the Adam's apple!

Hindsight is a wonderful thing. The day ended for both Mike and Jeremy with a proposition from Tracey in the woods, following which both of them ran for their lives, blindly and in a state of complete panic through thick undergrowth, being hotly pursued by a chick with a dick.

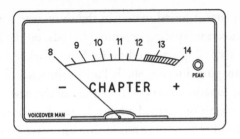

DON'T SUPPOSE YOU KNOW TOMORROW'S FOOTBALL RESULTS, DO YOU?

D espite my spat with the BBC and my regrettable, acrimonious parting with Steve Wright, the year ended on a high note. My agent had called with the news that the Industrialist Lord Hanson had won the most recently advertised radio licence in London. His company, the imaginatively titled Hanson PLC, had planned to open a radio station called *'Melody Radio'*, in Knightsbridge, London. The newly appointed programme director, a man called Peter Black, had enquired whether I would be interested in presenting the breakfast show. At this time, I was still contracted to the BBC as an announcer in the Radio 2 presentation department, a position I had held for almost eight years. While I enjoyed the job, I knew in my heart that it was the right time to move on. I spoke to my editor, Iain Purdon and told him about the approach from Hanson. He was entirely supportive from the get-go and offered to release me from my contract early and generously even went further than that. To provide a cushion for my newfound freelance status, he offered me occasional news reading and other announcery duties for the next six months. It was a kind gesture and one which I seized immediately. I wanted to hit the freelance deck running but a nice cushion to smooth the transition was especially welcome.

A week or so later, I found myself in the shiny new studios of Melody Radio, in a nondescript building opposite Harrods, on the Brompton Road in West London recording a demo show for Peter Black. Also, there, was the station's new managing director, Sheila Porritt, the sister of the well-known environmentalist Jonathan Porritt. The format of the new station was to be strictly MOR – middle of the road/adult-orientated music with a smattering of show tunes and light classical music thrown in for good measure. The new station's positioning statement plastered all over huge billboards around the city was *"Radio – without the DJ's."* This, I found somewhat confusing and not a little concerning. It transpired that Melody Radio was a virtual jukebox. Tunes were to be segued three or four in a row, with the briefest of introduction from the presenter. The presenter's contribution amounted to reading the news on the hour and half-hour, time checks, weather forecasts, back announcements for the music and generally driving the desk. I considered my position. The money on offer was good, too good to ignore. I'd be finished by 10am and could easily double my weekly earnings by freelancing as a voiceover artist during the day. It was worth a shot. The demo samples of all the prospective presenters were forwarded to Lord Hanson himself, and I was selected.

Leaving the BBC was a difficult decision for me. Working for any large organisation has its benefits. There's a certain amount of job security and in those days at least, a real feeling of being enveloped and protected. There was a structure, a solidity to the whole organisation with decent men at the top who had come up through the ranks and knew the broadcasting business inside out. However, I was beginning to feel institutionalised. The decision before me was, should I leave the bosom of Auntie Beeb and sail off into unchartered waters or should I stay and enjoy the somewhat predictable status quo and maybe a nice pension and a cottage by the sea to look forward to? I remembered the sage advice of veteran broadcaster Whispering Bob Harris, who once told me that: staying in your comfort zone was infinitely more dangerous than venturing out of it. I have always since tried to live outside it, as that is invariably where the magic happens. The freelance life is altogether more discomfiting. There's an edginess about it, it's a hand to mouth, dog-eat-dog, day to day existence where the only yardstick of success is the amount of cash flowing into your bank account on a monthly or in most cases, an annual basis. The freelance world is so uncertain and irregular, that one has to invariably take this longer-term view. Annual income rather than monthly is the more accurate window of measurement. Scary stuff indeed for the dutiful wage slave I had become. I took a long hard look at myself in the mirror the next morning. Later that day, I closed my eyes and jumped.

The first day of broadcasting on *Melody Radio* arrived. Launch day is always an exciting event at any new radio station. Despite all the planning and rehearsal, there is always the opportunity for abject failure and embarrassment, especially when the eyes and ears of the press and nervous investors are upon you. I'm pleased to say that day one at Melody went more smoothly than any of us could have hoped for. The Good Lord, that is to say, the good Lord Hanson, not the one on the very top floor, was in attendance. Though having said that, the one on the very top floor was probably there too, quietly enjoying a glass of Hanson PLC's vintage Bollinger in the big boardroom in the sky.

Lord Hanson had taken a deep and slightly obsessive personal interest in the station from day one. Privately, my fellow presenters and I likened his enthusiasm to that of a small boy who had just been given his first train set, at Christmas. He listened to the output from early morning to early evening. How he continued to run a multinational PLC at the same time, is anyone's guess. Melody Radio was his constant companion from day to night. He even resorted to recording the shows onto cassette tapes and taking them with him when he left the country on business! It was an unhealthy addiction, a kind of madness even. He even resorted to calling me most mornings on his specially reserved private bat phone which terminated in my studio, to request certain tunes. I often had this vision of him lying in his silk pyjamas on a massive four-poster with Lady Hanson at his side, in a flowing negligee, impressing her with his total mastery and control over the airwaves. Frank Sinatra was his favourite singer, ever since he had personally entertained ol' Blue Eyes at his Palm Springs home many years ago. The images of that fateful encounter adorned his office wall in a series of expensively framed vintage monochrome prints. One couldn't help form the impression that Lord Hanson considered himself to be an honorary member of the infamous 'Rat Pack'. Move over Sammy. Move over Deano – Jim's in town!

Most entrepreneurs have huge egos. Jimmy Hanson was no exception. In the basement of the Brompton Road office and studio complex, just along from Harrods, he kept a fleet of official cars. A selection of pristine, gloss black vintage Rolls Royce vehicles, maintained by his two full time uniformed chauffeurs. The front doors of each car, hand-painted with the Hanson coat of arms. Gleaming, they sat in air-conditioned comfort ready for the call from upstairs, to take him to his next big deal. I recall speaking one day in that basement to Barry, one of his drivers. We were reflecting on Lord Hanson's massive personal wealth. He listed the properties, the businesses, the cars, the yacht, the helicopters, the international investments. Barry had been a faithful servant for over thirty years, so knew the industrialist better than most. I asked him if he considered Hanson to be a happy man. Barry took a draw on his un-tipped, hand-rolled cigarette, thought for a moment, then shook his head and looked away – enveloped in a cloud of blue smoke. Great, I thought. Money doesn't buy you happiness, but it sure brings you misery in comfort!

Before too long, my days fell into some semblance of routine. Up at 4am, drive the thirty miles to the studios in Knightsbridge, broadcast between 6am and 10am followed by the occasional visit to Harrods for an early lunch and then off to earn a decent crust shouting into expensive microphones, selling dog food, second-hand cars, insurance, pizza, sofas or whatever. Several years of this passed and the mind-numbing routine of it all began to take its toll. I was called to see Peter Black who informed me that my on air performance had lost its sparkle. I had to agree. He suggested that I take a holiday and I readily agreed. It was during this holiday, in the USA in 1992, that I took a call from an old friend of mine, the radio presenter Simon Cummings. Simon was leaving his current job at a radio station in Surrey, to join a new station called Star FM. This new station was to be the latest in a raft of local radio station acquisitions for the UKRD Group, headed up by a guy called Mike Powell. Simons' call that day was not to tell me about his career move, but instead to sound out my interest in joining this new venture. I have to say that at first, I was not terribly enthusiastic, but he sold the idea to me of presenting the new breakfast show based on freedom of creative input. The management was looking for a presenter with a distinctive style. Someone who could take chances and push the boat out a little. In short, be different. I seemed to fit the bill. The job at Melody Radio was going nowhere fast and I was beginning to stagnate. I agreed to join Star FM in Slough as its first breakfast show presenter at the station's launch at the end of the summer. I fired off my resignation letter to Sheila Porritt at

*Sharing a joke with Bill Morton and Howard Huntridge on 'Bruce's Price is Right'
1998 – YTV, Leeds.*

Melody and offered to work out the remainder of my contract. Imagine my surprise when she fired one immediately back telling me not to bother. That was that. I never stepped foot inside that place ever again, and I have to say in retrospect, it hadn't come a moment too soon!

So, there I was, within a matter of three years, preparing to launch yet another radio station. Star FM was located within the glamorous Observatory Shopping Centre in Sir John Betjeman's favourite town – Slough! No sign of any bombs, friendly or otherwise… yet. All the way from the BBC in London's Portland Place, to Slough via Knightsbridge. I couldn't help but feel that my career had seriously gone into reverse – with the afterburners on. I kept reminding myself that often in a career, sideways and seemingly retrograde steps were sometimes required to move forwards. I needed to put some space between myself and the BBC. I needed to learn how to be more commercial. No matter how I tried to rationalise it though, this felt like a freefall, though in retrospect it was the right thing to do.

I have to say, that presenting the breakfast show on Star FM was great fun. The only downside, which I discovered pretty quickly was the programme director, a perfectly balanced man with a chip on both shoulders, called Paul Owens. Owens had been a DJ of sorts himself and had drunk from the poisoned Mike Powell chalice, to rise to the dizzying career-defining pinnacle of Programme Director on Star FM at the Observatory shopping mall in Slough. He is the original living, breathing embodiment of Ricky Gervais' fictional monster, David Brent from the hit show 'The Office'. What he lacked in charisma, he more than made up for in his inability to organise his way out of a brown paper bag. I'm not sure that analogy makes all that much sense, which is apt because... err... neither did he. In his nascent management role, Paul incorrectly assumed that the way to exert his authority was to hold endless meetings with his presenters.

Now, I don't know about you, but I have never been much of a fan of meetings. I much prefer the directness of a short phone call, a terse email or better still – a long lunch! What Paul failed to grasp, was that as the presenter of his breakfast show, I had risen at 3am and been on air until 10am. The last thing I wanted or needed at Midday was a bloody meeting. Most presenters and radio and TV turns abhor them. You should hear Howard Stern on the subject. My refusal to attend these meetings grew to be a point of conflict between us and I frequently exited the building, as the last record was playing, to avoid having to attend them. These occasions were often followed by an irate phone call from Paul, in my car, as I was on my way to my next more lucrative appointment.

Six months into the contract, in November of 1989, I took my annual holiday in the USA, as arranged. Upon my return to the UK, I had barely turned the key in the lock of my front door, when I received a phone call from Owens. He explained that in my absence, the station had run into financial difficulties and that they would be terminating my contract prematurely. He was clearly embarrassed at having to do his master's bidding and I felt, by the tone of his voice that he was not being entirely truthful. Aghast at the looming spectre of unemployment, I offered to work through the difficulty by charging a reduced fee for as long as the local difficulty remained. My offer was flatly rebuffed. Putting down the phone I considered my position. I was without a job for the first time in my professional career. The company I was working for and with whom I had a guaranteed signed contract for twelve months of work had reneged on the deal. What was I to do? Sue the bastards was my initial response. As it happens it was my only option although I have to say I did briefly consider bombing the place in accordance with Betjeman's advice. It was no less than they deserved. However, revenge is always a dish best served cold, so I decided to sleep on it.

The next morning, I called my old pal, Uncle Chris Underwood, the general secretary of the Chartered Institute of Journalists, who I knew from my time at the BBC when he was the BBC's Home Affairs Correspondent. Chris was somewhat of an expert in employment law and having listened to my account of the shabby underhand shenanigans in Slough, decided it was worth taking the bastards on. Statements were given to solicitors and legal letters were sent to Mike Powell at UKRD. There was no response. It seemed we were destined to have our day in court. My brief asked me to provide character witnesses for the trial. My pals, James Alexander Gordon, who is sadly no longer with us but was then the voice of the final score football results on the BBC and Simon Bates – the former BBC Radio 1 DJ, were issued with subpoenas to attend and the date was set for a Court hearing at Slough County Court in front of a district judge. It was all very grown-up and not a little terrifying. If it wasn't for the gravity of the situation and the potential losses, both financial and reputational that I faced should I lose the case, it would have been a hugely amusing affair and the trial did have its lighter moments. When James hobbled up to the witness box and dropped his walking stick for, I assumed dramatic effect, the judge leaned over to him and whispered:

"Don't suppose to know tomorrow's football results. Do you?"

Simon Bates, who isn't normally short on words was somewhat initially thrown when the defence counsel unexpectedly asked him to define the word 'Turn', as in performer. Thinking on his not insubstantial size thirteen feet, Bates immediately launched into a surprisingly well rounded and comprehensive definition of the history and definition of 'The Turn', recalling the great 19th Century actor-manager Charles Wyndham. His Stentorian and much loved, rich baritone voice reverberated quite comfortably around that inhospitable, cold, Slough county courtroom, as he adopted that very familiar 'Our Tune' vocal style that he reserved for situations of deep gravitas. My old willy-waving producer from Radio 2 who was also there to give evidence and provide moral support, began to hum the 'Our Tune' theme through clenched teeth and thankfully, much to everyone's relief kept his dick in his pants – for once. Bates concluded his seven-minute oration by describing me as the 20th Century equivalent of the 19th Century actor-manager or 'Turn'! When the boggle-eyed judge started to ask me about quantifying my actual loss as a result of the early termination of my contract, Chris Underwood looked across at me and gave me a wink. It seems that early on in the trial, the wise old judge had already made his mind up about whose evidence he preferred. Even the defence counsel's desperate attempts to persuade him otherwise, did little to convince him to alter his view. Owens, Powell and the station's news editor a vituperative woman called Val Handley made increasingly desperate pleadings, which fell on deaf ears up on the bench. They had tried to claim that I had been unprofessional and that I was a 'loose cannon'. My CV and the various character and professional witnesses shot that one down in flames and it was apparent that the judge was similarly unmoved. In his summing up, His Honour decided that he preferred my evidence to theirs, awarding me full damages and costs. The relief was immediate, and I was more than a little pleased when he announced his judgement.

Resorting to law to remedy a perceived wrong, is not something I would ever recommend. It's stressful, expensive, unpredictable and very time-consuming. The feeling though when you win, is incredible. It's exhilarating. I had been vindicated. Powell, Owens and Handley, with sheaves of dog-eared legal papers under their arms, scuttled awkwardly out of the court with their heads down and their tails tucked firmly between their legs. Powell had brazenly told the judge in a final, desperate plea that if I were to win, it would mean a sea-change in the way presenters in radio were contracted in future. That sealed his fate. If only he had kept his mouth shut. After costs and damages, his business balance sheet took a hefty dent to the value of almost £100,000.

To celebrate my pyrrhic victory and to say thank you to those who had given of their time so freely in my defence, I invited the main protagonists and witnesses to lunch at the splendidly posh Odin's restaurant in Marylebone. It was at this lunch that Simon Bates told me that on the day of the trial while on his way to Slough, he had been stuck on the M4 in heavy traffic. Not wishing to incur the wrath of His Honour the Judge, he slipped his big Audi A6 into first gear and rumbled onto the hard shoulder of the motorway gunning the car eastwards past a three mile tailback toward Slough. Almost immediately, he was seized by a traffic police motorcycle patrol cop.

Group hug with the models on 'Bruce's Price is Right' – 1998 – YTV, Leeds.

Winding down the window, the policeman was about to issue him with a fixed penalty ticket when Simon waved his subpoena at the officer. The policeman, realising the situation required urgent action, told Simon to follow him. For the next seven or eight miles along the hard shoulder of an almost stationary M4, Simon had the pleasure of an open road accompanied by a police outrider from Her Majesty's Constabulary, complete with two-tone siren and blue flashing lights!

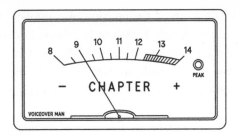

ASSAULTING A NATIONAL
TREASURE ON LIVE TV

I n 1994, I took a call out of the blue from a guy called Arch Dyson, who was a producer in the TV Light Entertainment department at the BBC. Arch had been given the job of cobbling together a series over the Summer for Saturday nights on BBC1, featuring Steve Wright. The show had been given the imaginative and snappy title: 'Steve Wright's People Show.' It had been scheduled, to be a big-budget prime time extravaganza with star guests, live music and comedy. Arch wanted me to be a part of the new show. My initial reaction was one of apprehension, as Steve and I had last parted company several years ago on poor terms. But Arch, it seemed was now acting as a go-between as Steve wanted me on board. Arch and I decided not to go with the established radio characters but instead develop some new ones. After some deliberation, I came up with the idea of an irritating floor manager character, who was always interrupting the show and accidentally getting in-shot. We gave him a name: Stuart Cosworth – a paunchy, tank top wearing, abomination of a man with a wig, poor personal hygiene, a locker full of miniature bottles of whiskey and fiddled expenses claim forms. Pre-production for the series was going well, until a week before the first show, Arch announced his resignation from the BBC! He had been offered and had accepted the position of controller of entertainment at the ITV regional broadcaster Yorkshire Television, in Leeds in the North of England. It was a blow to everyone, especially me, as I had liked and respected him enormously. In truth, we had got on like the proverbial house on fire. I didn't know it then, but Arch and I were to cross paths again at a later date.

The powers that be, had to act fast and so immediately assigned the series to an experienced live TV director called Julia Knowles. As there was no time to find a producer, Julia took on the onerous responsibility of both roles. We needn't have worried. Julia was a supremely confident and able professional and took to it like George Best at a wine and cheese party – without the cheese! Steve though, the veteran radio performer, was not so comfortable. TV is an altogether less forgiving medium. In the recent past, he had notched up some TV experience as the occasional host on BBC's Top of the Pops, but this big Saturday night extravaganza was an entirely different kettle of fish. A big, shiny floor prime time show where the focus is entirely on the host for the best part of an hour, is not for the inexperienced or indeed the faint-hearted. The rehearsals, in the BBC's Acton rehearsal rooms, were a fraught affair. Attended by Steve, me, Richard Easter and the show's *real* floor manager, a BBC veteran by the name of Quentin Mann, who was Terry Wogan's floor manager. When Quentin discovered that I was to play his alter ego on the show, he was at the same time both horrified and excited. During the lunch hour, he would often take me to one side and instruct me in the black art of floor managing a big TV show with a live studio audience. Floor managers are the director's eyes, ears and voice on the studio floor. They are responsible for positioning the turns, relaying the director's instructions and coordinating the action. Quentin was one of the very best. From Parkinson to Wogan and everything else in between for over thirty years, he has been there, done it and worn the extra-large T-Shirt! A professional television floor manager should never be seen in-shot. He or she operates on the dark side of the studio, behind the lens. My character, however, Stuart, was to buck this age-old convention. The idea was that at various pre-arranged points in the show, Stuart would pop up onto the set in the middle of one of Steve's guest interviews shouting, "Hold it! Hold it! Hold it right there chief!" Interrupting the turn is something that just shouldn't happen, but in this case, as Steve was to be the butt of the joke, it was more than alright with me. Steve had been mucking around in rehearsals, not taking the process at all seriously and getting on everyone's nerves. It seemed to me that this was an opportunity he was simply throwing away. Quentin came up with the brilliant idea that after my interruption I should give him the old five-fingered count down and instead of cueing him with a downward swish of the index finger and hand, I should make a reverse lateral movement and smack him firmly in the mouth instead! It was universally agreed (though not by Steve) that this would get us a sure-fire laugh.

Ever since that episode, where I was almost dragged through the courts by Steve and the BBC for copyright infringement, I had been waiting for my opportunity to get even. This was it; retribution was about to be served. Unbelievably, I was being permitted to fake an assault on a nationally known star, on a live entertainment show on BBC1 TV on a Saturday night, in front of millions of witnesses. See I told you, revenge is a dish best served cold. This particular dish was about to be taken out of the freezer. John Farr, who by this time had also grown weary of Steve's antics, pleaded with me to wear a knuckle duster.

The show eventually stumbled onto the air in the summer of 1994. Wright was his usual sweaty, nervous self. Constantly complaining that the studio was too hot and cooling himself with one of those cheap battery-operated fans, while on set. My character Stuart Cosworth, the booze-fuelled floor manager went down well with the audience, who were clearly relishing the joke and when I gently smacked him in the mouth, it practically brought the house down. As the weeks went on, the production team encouraged me to hit him harder. I remember on one of the shows, flicking my hand, a little too enthusiastically. I misjudged the distance and accidentally smacked him softly yet squarely on his not unsubstantial nose. Out of the corner of my eye, I saw him reeling backwards in his chair. The recording was halted temporarily as he regained his composure. Turning his back to the audience and while his microphone was muted, he asked me if I could possibly manage to not to hit him like that in future!

One of the biggest guests on the show was the legendary Hollywood superstar, Dennis Hopper. The plan was that during Steve's interview with him, I was to interrupt in the usual way and lumber onto the set carrying a dirty looking brown coat and pork pie hat, tell Hopper that his taxi had arrived and that if he didn't get a move on, he would be paying for the waiting time himself! I bundled him into this threadbare coat, plonked the hat on his head and manhandled him off the stage. He clearly didn't have a clue what was going on but went along with it anyway. The audience loved it and gave him an extra big cheer, as he left. He probably thought it was our quirky British humour. After the show, the production manager confided in me that Hopper had insisted on his fee being paid to him in cash. A grubby brown BBC envelope containing £3,000 in £50 notes, was pressed into his hand as he left the building and was bundled into a waiting S class to take him to the airport. Now that's showbiz! On a subsequent episode, I got to act with and man-handle off the stage another entertainment legend – Joan Rivers. She was so much fun and up for anything we wanted to do. All she cared about were laughs. She was quite elderly at this point and I was terrified that she might fall off the set and die. I didn't want to be the guy who killed Joan Rivers! Anyway, she did manage to get off the set and get the biggest laugh and cheer I have ever heard from a TV audience. Incredibly, the first series of 'Steve Wright's People Show' went down well with the suits upstairs and much to our amazement they commissioned a second series. It was scheduled for the same time next year and the same team would be back again, for more

In character as Stuart Cosworth on 'Steve Wright's People Show' – 1994 – BBC TV Centre.

fun and casual violence.

In the meantime, things at Radio 1 were in a state of flux. Simon Mayo, the incumbent presenter on breakfast, had decided to throw in the towel and move to BBC Radio 5 live. Matthew Bannister, the Controller at Radio 1 needed a big hitter to fill his shoes and as Steve had done wonders for the afternoon figures, he concluded that to put him in the breakfast slot was the right – and possibly the only thing to do. Our recent collaboration on the TV series had thawed our relationship to the point where we were once again on speaking terms. And so, when Steve took over the reins of BBC Radio 1's breakfast show, his producer Mick Wilkoijc, called me to see if I would be interested in providing character voices for the show. After some discussion, Mick and I came up with the idea of an announcer, who would appear on the show each morning and run through that evening's TV highlights in that singsong, extreme prosody voiceover style, so beloved by regional radio and TV announcers. For the sake of simplicity and without too much thought, we called him 'Voiceover Man'!

Before long, the character developed a life all of his own. I was contracted to supply two spots each morning. One, just after 7.30am and again, one after 8.30am. The best thing about it was that he was a telephone character and so I could literally phone it in from home. Consequently, each evening before I went to bed, I wrote the two scripts and put them on the bedside table. I would then get my early morning call from Steve at about 7.20am. During this first call, he would typically ask me to read to him the first script – off-air. He was paranoid about being sued for libel, obsessed with being on the right side of the law, terrified of authority. So, while carefully conveying the impression that his show was edgy, spontaneous and at times dangerous, it was about as conservative and ultra-cautious as you could imagine. On many occasions, he 'blue-pencilled' whole sections of my script, for very little reason. Naturally, this irked me somewhat so like the agent provocateur that I am, I decided to throw a spanner in the works. It's just the way I am, I can't help myself sometimes. One morning just after 7.30am, just after our script review and before I was due to go on air live to eight million listeners, I swapped the scripts without telling him. As I launched into my piece, I could palpably hear the tension rising in his voice as he listened to this entirely new and un-vetted delivery I was now giving.

Eventually, he could stand it no longer and gave me both barrels live on air.

"Err... this isn't what we agreed at rehearsals!"

Regardless I ploughed on, with the guffaws and cheers of his posse who were in on the joke ringing loudly in the background. I could barely keep a straight face myself. The thought of him, not knowing what was going on or what I was going to say next was hilarious. For a control freak like Steve, it must have been truly unbearable. My feeling of guilt at my unprofessionalism must have lasted all of oh... two seconds!

It was around this time in mid-1994, that I had a call from my old Radio 2 'Nightcap' producer Harry Thompson. Harry had moved into TV production and was currently working with a production company called Tiger Aspect, headed up by Peter Bennett-Jones. Tiger Aspect also ran an artist management company, looking after the careers of some of the country's finest comedy talent. The company was in pre-production for a new series of 'Harry Enfield and Chums', and Harry wanted to know if I would be interested in playing a variety of small character parts in the series. I was a fan of both Harry Enfield and Paul Whitehouse, so I jumped at the chance. I have never acted on a TV show before but, come on – how hard could it be? There I go again – what an idiot! Consequently, several weeks later I found myself back at the BBC TV rehearsal rooms to work on the new show. Also appearing in the series were, Martin Clunes and Kathy Burke who are both a total joy to be around. In makeup on the first day of filming, Harry and his comedy partner Paul both began doing 'Voiceover Man' impressions. It was apparent that they were fans of the character. They were avid radio listeners themselves and both were responsible for some of the most enduring characters on TV, including the redoubtable radio DJ creations 'Mike Smash' and Dave Nice'. These two larger than life monsters lampooned some of the older DJ's on Radio 1 whose outmoded styles were potentially forgiven, by the thin excuse that they also did a lot of 'Chari-dee' work. The characters referenced Tony Blackburn, Dave Lee Travis, Noel Edmunds, Alan Freeman and Mike Read. Many cultural commentators at the time, attributed Enfield and Whitehouse's parody, to Radio 1's increasing irrelevance to the youth audience and it is not too much of an exaggeration to say that it was almost entirely responsible for the massive cull that followed. Controller, Matthew Bannister wielded a pair of long knives to the senior DJ cadre in the middle of that decade. The writing was undoubtedly on the wall for many of these dinosaurs of the airwaves, Enfield and Whitehouse simply hastened their demise.

The first sketch I was to appear in was with Harry, who was playing one of his favourite creations, 'Tim Nice But Dim'. I was to play an old public-school friend, who was now a chief underwriter at Lloyds of London. The story went like this: Nice but Dim had been persuaded by some pals in the City including Martin Clunes, who was playing the heartless city broker to buy into a syndicate called 'Earthquake, Flood, Tidal Wave'. Clunes' character had convinced Tim that it was a sure-fire investment bet. The next scene began in my office where I was playing the head of the syndicate, with a big close up of a newspaper I was supposedly reading. The headline screamed: "Earthquake, Flood, Tidal Wave Hits Britain!" Tim enters the office, takes one look at the newspaper and gasps;

"Gosh! That's bad news. I see that England is losing in the test!"

Looking up from my paper, I tell him not to be so stupid and that to cover his losses I will have to repossess his house, his parent's house and their parent's houses. I then get him to empty his pockets and hand over all his money and assorted bits of string, pencils, old hankies and marbles. Big laughs all round. It was all I could do to keep a straight face, because every time I looked up at Harry, all I could see was him grinning back at me wearing his character's ridiculous set of prosthetic teeth. It took multiple takes to get the scene in the can as we were all laughing so much. The studio audience, of course, loved it, as they do every time anything goes wrong.

In early January 1995, Radio 1 suffered a bit of a setback with the unexpected resignation of Steve Wright, after almost fourteen years at the station. When I say unexpected, I mean genuinely unexpected. He told no one in advance. I found out when I saw the headline in the Sun newspaper at a newsagent in London. In a report the next day the 14th of January in the Independent newspaper, Matthew Bannister the Controller of Radio 1 stated that:

"Steve Wright, who was recently voted the nation's most popular DJ by readers of 'Smash Hits' magazine, was leaving Radio 1 to pursue his burgeoning television career. Steve has made a great contribution to Radio and we wish him every success on TV."

He clearly hadn't been watching his recent performances on TV! Steve spent a whole year away from BBC Radio. Instead, he worked on various radio stations and as a consultant for Global Radio – floundering in the wilderness and eventually returning to BBC Radio 2 in April 1996, where he presented 'Steve Wright's Saturday Show'. Despite the fall in his fortunes, The BBC kept its promise and ordered up Series two of 'Steve Wright's People Show', the following year. All I can conclude from this is that the ideas cupboard in the Entertainment Department must have been pretty well damned near empty. This time around, the show had both a producer and a director. The producer was a fresh-faced young man called Mark Wells. The show was to be directed by veteran TV director – Alisdair McMillan a fearsome, take no prisoners, chain-smoking Scot, who dressed entirely in white, including pristine white tennis shoes and white starched laces. Anyone encountering him in a corridor at BBC Television Centre would have assumed he was an actor in the long-running medical drama 'Casualty'. For all his eccentricities and his bluff and bluster, Alisdair's bark was far worse than his bite and once you got to know him, he was indeed very agreeable company.

Series two of 'Steve Wright's People Show' showed no marked improvement on series one. Wrighty was his usual nervous, sweaty, edgy self. All over the place, like the proverbial mad woman's shite. Again, I was to perform Stuart the floor manager and additionally, the out of vision character 'Voiceover Man'. During the recordings, when I was not required on the floor, I hid in the comforting darkness of the studio voice booth behind the main gallery, where I was joined by the show's writer, Richard Easter. There we would sit unheard and unseen, viewing Wrighty's performance on the monitor and cackling like hyenas and smoking cigars. Appallingly unprofessional I know, but by this point, we were long past caring.

Several shows into the series, one of the assistant producers came to my dressing room in a bit of a panic. One of the star guests to be interviewed that night was Ivana Trump, the ex-wife of US President Donald Trump. After the interview, the producers had scheduled an item that was designed to test Ivana's legendary, finely tuned personal money-radar. The idea was that four unidentified men would walk onto the set in an identity parade line-up and Ivana would then be invited to guess which one of them was a real-life millionaire. Each man in the line-up would have around fifteen to twenty seconds to tell his brief story, outlining how he made his millions. Only one though was a real millionaire, the other three were complete charlatans. The problem though, was that the *real* millionaire had developed cold feet, was having genuine reservations about appearing on the show and

In character with Tim Nice But Dim on 'Harry Enfield and Chums'
1994 – Tiger Aspect / BBC TV.

had locked himself in his dressing room. The proposal from the associate producer was that I should be the fourth man and spin some yarn about my past. Was it duplicitous – yes but it wasn't exactly 'Newsnight' and this was, after all, a bit of a TV light entertainment comedy crisis. Why can you never find a real millionaire when you need one? Several minutes later I was in the BBC wardrobe department, selected an outfit to wear and then headed for the BBC's wig department to look for a wig that would disguise my identity. Suitably togged and bewigged, I headed to the BBC Club with Richard for a swift half and to concoct some cock and bull story about how I had made my money. What kind of way is this to earn a ruddy living?

The Berlin wall had recently been torn down, so while blowing the froth of a half-pint of London Pride, we came up with the idea of portraying myself as an entrepreneur who had sold certified bits of it at $500 a time, to gullible collectors around the world. Genius! Standing backstage that night in TC1 at Television Centre with three other actors, who were also wondering what was about to happen, we listened to Steve conclude his interview with Ivana on the sofa. The audience applauded and I knew that the point of no return had arrived. We were introduced, so out we walked into the full glare of the studio lights and I joined the other three guys on set with Steve and Ivana and in front of the cold unblinking eyes of six cameras and watched by six million people, began to lie my socks off in the name of entertainment. Amazingly, after the item, when we had all recounted our cock and bull stories, Steve asked Ivana which one of us was the real millionaire. To my utter astonishment, she picked me. Neither she nor the crowd was in on the joke, so as the end credits were rolling and the audience was applauding, she began to engage me in conversation. She leaned over and asked me what my next entrepreneurial project was going to be. I sidestepped the question and we exchanged a few pleasantries while maintaining our rictus grins for the cameras. Then, out of the blue, she told me that she was getting married again later that year in Palm Beach, Florida to Riccardo Mazzucchelli, a suave, attentive Italian with a Rolls-Royce, a moneyed aura and a showy townhouse in London. He had, I later learned appeared in Ivana's life at a time when she was very much the bounced Czech, following her divorce from 'The Donald'.

"Would you like to come and join me and Riccardo as a guest at the wedding?"

It was too ridiculous for words. Over the riotous applause of the audience in Studio TC1, I, of course, said I'd be delighted to come and gave her my phone number. Actually, it was Wright's home phone number I gave her. I have no idea if she ever called, but it would be nice to think that she did and that the long-distance call from Palm Beach back at the Wright household in Henley in Oxfordshire, was answered by Cyndi, Steve's Wife. He must have had some explaining to do at teatime!

Other memorable guests on series two of 'Steve Wright's People Show' were Vic Reeves (aka Jim Moir) and his comedy sidekick, Bob Mortimer. In between rehearsals and recording, I nipped into the BBC club for something to eat. Sitting at the table next to me were Vic and Bob. I had been a huge fan of the pair, ever since their ground-breaking 'Big Night Out' series, which first aired in the early '90s on Channel 4 television. I found Jim to be extremely good company. Both he and Bob, it transpired, were about to go into production on a new series for the BBC, called 'The Smell of Reeves and Mortimer'. They had written some spoof TV commercials featuring bizarre products, such as – a glossy, coffee table picture book called: 'Dogs and their Hats' and the sister volume, 'Cats in Bomber Jackets'. There was also the: 'How to build your own scale model replica Peter Stringfellow pole dancing club'! Charlie Higson, who was the associate producer on the series under Executive producer, Alan Marke asked me if I would join legendary veteran voice actor Patrick Allen and provide a voiceover for these spoof commercials. It was one of those beautiful serendipitous moments and I was thrilled at being cast. I have worked with both Jim and Bob on various shows and projects since. I finished my sandwich and headed back to TC1, for more TV light entertainment shenanigans.

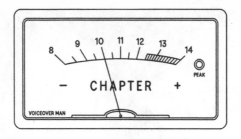

THE STINKING BISHOP
WAS ON THE TABLE

I n early 1995, I took a call out of the blue from Arch Dyson, the new controller of entertainment at ITV's Yorkshire TV. I had worked with him, albeit very fleetingly you will remember, on series one of Steve Wright's People Show at the BBC. I liked Arch enormously. He is a very direct, no-nonsense Yorkshireman so when he asked if I would join him for lunch, as he had an idea he wanted to discuss, I immediately agreed. A week later we met in a Pizza Express in Dulwich, of all places! After a couple of thin-crust pizzas washed down with a bottle of Valpolicella Superiore Ripasso like a couple of high ballers, Arch got to the point of our meeting. Would I be interested in joining Bruce Forsyth on a revival of the old game show format, 'The Price is Right'? I hesitated for what seemed like an eternity, but in truth was only 0.1 of a second and agreed to the idea, while trying not to look too excited. To get to work with a showbiz legend like Bruce, was an experience not to be missed. The intention was to use 'The Price is Right' game show vehicle to replace 'Play your Cards Right', which had been rested and that only one series was planned so that the suits at ITV could gauge the audience's appetite for its return. Early the following year in 1995, a rehearsal room briefing and run through was planned in London.

Posing as a 'millionaire' with Ivana Trump
1995 – Studio TC1 BBC TV Centre, London.

I drove down to Acton from my home in Buckinghamshire. Around a large table was Arch, Howard Huntridge, the executive producer, an assortment of production people from Fremantle who were the format owners, Bruce's gag writer Wally Malston, who had also written for The Two Ronnies, Little and Large, Keith Harris and Ted Rogers and of course, Brucie himself. I was in the presence of true showbiz royalty.

"Come and sit over here beside me, Peter." boomed Brucie, immediately making me feel welcome.

I briefly closed my eyes and his instantly recognisable voice transported me back to my childhood all those years ago. I had watched him on a tiny black and white telly in the living room of my parent's house in Belfast when he hosted The Generation Game and before that, 'Live at the London Palladium'. 'Good game, good game'. We ordered cups of tea and chocolate digestives and soon got down to business. The business of 'show'! Arch opened the meeting by welcoming everyone and thanked us all for attending. Howard explained the history of the format and why ITV thought it worthy of a revival. Out of the corner of my eye, I saw Bruce, dip half a digestive biscuit into his steaming mug of tea, raise it to his lips and suck at it, appreciatively. I also couldn't help noticing that while we were all in scruff order, Bruce was immaculately turned out. Polished leather tasselled loafers, slacks, open-necked shirt and a tailored blue blazer under which he wore a finely knitted cardigan with plaid leather buttons. His well-publicised toupee was firmly anchored to the top of his head. Through the window, as I looked into the adjacent rehearsal room, I could see the TV illusionist Paul Daniels wielding a four-foot-long saw, about to cut his wife, Debbie McGee in half. This was turning out to be no ordinary day. I bloody love my job!

Three weeks later, in the summer of 1995 with a very pregnant wife at home, I boarded the train at London Euston, bound for Leeds in Yorkshire. Series one of 'Bruce's Price is Right', was to be made at the studios of Yorkshire Television, located in an unprepossessing conglomeration of dull grey concrete buildings on the equally unprepossessing Kirkstall Road. Yorkshire's TV HQ was conveniently located on the outskirts of the city right across the road from Kwik Fit, a 24-hour massage parlour and adjacent to a Halal butcher. Hollywood or Burbank, it most certainly wasn't. The entire cast and crew were being accommodated in the Marriott Hotel in the city centre and Bruce, being the star had the top floor penthouse suite, complete with a fluffy dressing gown, nightly pillow chocolate and the obligatory bowl of exotic fruit accompanied by a selection of international cheeses, presented, alongside Muscat grapes on the ubiquitous Welsh roofing slate. More on the cheese later. You'll have to wait but believe me, it'll be worth it.

On day one of the three days of camera rehearsals, we all met in Studio 1 at Yorkshire Television. Studio 1 had an impressive TV entertainment history. From '3-2-1' to 'Wire in the Blood', A Touch of Frost, The League of Gentlemen and Mastermind; all were shot inside those four walls. Now, it was our turn. Accompanying Bruce on set were the show's models. Three girls and one poor hapless lad, whose job it was to demonstrate and lovingly caress the prizes as they were revealed on camera. These prizes were the real stars of the show and ranged from food mixers to toasters, to speedboats and Jacuzzis! It was like a branch of Argos backstage! One afternoon, when ITV was shooting an edition of 'The Jeremy Kyle Show' in the studio next to ours, the props guys quickly moved the smaller, easily portable prize items into locked steel cages, so that the pilfering by Kyle's audience, that had occurred the day before, didn't happen again! Apparently, we lost a Teas-Maid, a chocolate fountain and a pair of faux pearl earrings that day. The audience for our show was conveyed to the studio on a fleet of coaches from Leeds, Manchester and outlying towns and villages with the occasional party venturing south from Scotland – and was made up largely of retired gentlefolk and the great unwashed and unemployed, who were looking for somewhere to go, off the streets and out of the relentless rain for a few hours. The funniest cultural audience clash I think I ever saw was when two very different shows were being recorded at the same time at Yorkshire TV. Coming in one door, dressed in shell suits, head to toe in Lycra and what you might call – loungewear, was the audience for 'The Jeremy Kyle Show' and entering via the adjacent door, wearing cardigans, cavalry twills, tweed jackets, ties and blazers was the audience for 'University Challenge'!

The director of our show was an urbane stalwart called Bill Morton. Bill was a TV veteran. Very old school and a thoroughly likeable man. He began his career as a vision mixer at the BBC and worked his way up the ladder. He was the vision mixer for the legendary TV comedy series 'Fawlty Towers' and his claim to fame, he once told me, was when John Cleese borrowed his name and used it in the script, as one of the hotel guests in the show. Anyway, Bill had been Bruce's director of choice for as long as anyone could remember. He was the only person Bruce truly trusted to both shoot and edit his shows, which was quite an accolade. Bill had the appearance of a 1960s public school classics teacher, all cardigans, tweed and corduroys and had the most richly round, sonorous voice. During the day, he would sit in the production gallery and talk, almost continuously, for ten hours, I have no idea how he did it, day in day out. It was quite a feat. Bruce himself was also no spring chicken. He was approaching his seventieth year but had the energy and enthusiasm of a twenty-year-old. Both men were a complete inspiration to me. During the taping of the show, I sat in the softly lit voice booth, across the corridor from the production gallery upstairs on the first floor. I had a couple of video monitors positioned in front of me, so I could see what was going on down on the set below. Before each episode was recorded, Bruce would go on set and give the excited audience a little pep talk. Actually, it was so much more than a pep talk, it was a full-blown scripted and rehearsed audience warm-up!

One of my favourite things in the whole world is being backstage watching performers, in the moments before they go on stage. That period, just

With Brucie and the cast and crew of 'Price is Right' – 1996 – YTV, Leeds.

before they cross the line from the dark anonymity of the wings and into the glare of the spotlight, is a magical one. Watching Bruce in this intensely personal moment was fascinating. He was generally a very affable person to be around, but he insisted on being left alone during the fifteen minutes immediately before his performance. He would stand in the stygian gloom of the wings out of sight, among the lighting and camera cables deep in thought, listening to the audience, like it was his rightful prey. Then at the appointed time, when the producer introduced him, he would pause, tilt his head back, give a very odd little skip, rocking from toe to heel and back again on his patent leather shoes, transform into Bruce Forsyth the entertainer, open his arms wide, palms forward and march confidently, chin first onto the set, with his eyes ablaze and within seconds, he would totally own that crowd. In all my forty plus years of watching performers do this, I have yet to see anyone else create such a palpable and immediate positive rapport with an audience, in quite the same way as Bruce did. He was a genius and to watch him do it, was a complete masterclass.

'The Price is Right' was a total joy to work on. It was three weeks of hard work and hard play. All of us were away from home and enjoying each other's company. After work each day, we would all jump into cabs back to the hotel and then reconvene in the hotel bar before heading out to dinner. These restaurant dinners I particularly looked forward to, not just for the food but I always enjoyed the look on the faces of the other male diners when I walked in, arm in arm with two beautiful models either side of me! The girls found it incredibly amusing and used to play up to the crowd as we made our champagne-fuelled entrance through the restaurant. Bruce generally didn't join us on these nights out, but he did very generously take the entire cast and crew out for a slap-up, Sake wine charged Chinese dinner at the conclusion of each series. Those were riotous evenings, which would invariably end up with all of us having far too much to drink at the restaurant and then ending back at the executive lounge at the hotel ordering more drinks, while we listened to Bruce regaling us with stories of his showbiz past. On one of these nights, I remember hearing about his early exploits in the 1940s when he was touring the music halls in the UK. He would travel from town to town on trains at night and sleep on the luggage racks to save the cost of an overnight hotel. If anyone deserved the title 'Mr Showbusiness', it was Mr Bruce Forsyth.

The first series of 'Bruce's Price is Right' seemed to go down well with the public and the suits at ITV – so much so that ITV offered Fremantle a second series. So, in the spring of 1996, off we traipsed again on the train from London to Leeds for more fun and games. And what fun we had! All of the prizes on offer on the show required prize descriptions that I had to readout. The writer of these was a veteran stand-up comedian from London called John Maloney. John had a laconic demeanour and a sense of humour that was darker than the black hole of Calcutta. About three shows in on series two, I sensed John had become rather bored of writing the same old, overly flowery descriptions of food mixers and hair straighteners and the ton of other tawdry tat the show paraded in front of the boggle-eyed, cooing audience. In conversation with him in the pub that night, I revealed that I was also getting weary of reading them. So, between us, we decided to liven things up a little. Chancing our arm, the following day, we concocted a paragraph describing an item of jewellery that began with the sentence:

"Yes… every woman loves a pearl necklace!"

When the time came, Bruce threw to me and said;

"So, Peter, tell us what Ethel from Barnsley is in with a chance of winning tonight."

I could barely get the words out. About half the audience (the depraved half) began to titter and snort. The other half were cooing and clucking over the pearl necklace that was now in crisp, iridescent close up on the big studio monitors. Over the open talkback in my headphones, I could hear the gales of laughter from the show's PA and the vision mixer. Bruce, who had nor forewarning had to look away momentarily and regain his composure. Amazingly, this moment and many other risqué double entendres like it made it past the edit and into the final show and are being repeatedly broadcast ad infinitum on Challenge TV, in front of a family audience! One person did subsequently complain. The producer, Dave Morley took the call after the show had aired and among much-stifled laughter and tittering in the 'Price is Right' Office, managed to deftly sidestep the complainer by feigning innocence and eventually dispatching the caller by asking him to explain exactly what he meant. He never called again.

One day, at the end of filming, I was sitting on a sofa in the reception at Yorkshire television waiting for a cab, to take me back to the hotel. Suddenly, to my right through a set of swing doors that led to the dressing room corridor, Bruce made his entrance and we got into a conversation about the days filming. He was also rushing back to the hotel as he wanted to catch the first of a brand-new chat show with Richard and Judy. Richard Madeley and Judy Finnegan were at the time, the most famous married couple double-act on television. They rose to fame as the co-hosts of a show called 'This Morning' on ITV daytime but tonight was their very first venture into prime-time TV. Bruce was intrigued to see how they would cope, so he asked me if I would like to watch it with him back at the hotel. I told the receptionist to cancel the cab and jumped with him into the back of his chauffeur-driven Lexus. Back at the hotel we took the lift to the top floor and entered the fabulously appointed penthouse master suite, that ITV had generously provided for him. Once through the door, he dropped his briefcase and scripts on the coffee table and headed into the bathroom saying he was going to get into something a little more comfortable. I immediately began scanning the room, searching for where I might sit in an effort to cause the least amount of social awkwardness. But there was no avoiding it. There it was – looming large in the room, a vast super king-size bed with a chocolate on each pillow and a what looked like a grey Welsh roofing slate on the bedside table, on which was surely the biggest international cheese selection I have ever seen. A wedge of Auriccio Provolone, a wheel of Dutch Leerdammer, a Colston Basset Stilton and a 9oz log of Sainte-Maure Caprifeuille which explained the slightly musty, aroma that assailed us as we came through the door. Five minutes later, he was still in the bathroom. I could hear things being moved around, the unmistakable clink of a toothbrush, distant tinkling, the flushing of water. I began to panic. Surveying the room, I could see only one chair, beside the right-hand side of the bed. Uneasily, I sat down and waited.

"Ahh... that's better!" He said.

The words were uttered as he emerged from the marble tiled en-suite bathroom. I looked up and to my utter horror, there was Bruce Forsyth, national treasure and cultural icon, wearing a knee-length, fluffy white hotel dressing gown and sporting a pair of dark blue socks held up on his surprisingly thin hairless legs, by a pair of bright red suspenders. I immediately got up, out of the chair and stumbled away from him towards a small coffee table and reached for the TV remote control.

"So, Bruce. Err... Shall we watch this Richard and Judy thing?" I said, as I gingerly walked backwards across the room and slowly sat down.

Dinner with Bruce Forsyth – 1997 – Maxi's.

"Yes, yes that would be good. Let me just get comfortable. This is going to be fun!"

And with that, while letting out an audible sigh of pleasure, rubbed his hands together, leapt up onto the bed and crawled on all fours before settling himself amongst a pile of premium feather pillows that he had neatly arranged against the oversized, studded leather headboard.

The TV flickered into life.

'ASS VENTURA – CRACK DETECTIVE, with Kaitlyn Ashley', was the graphic that screamed from the screen. Ass Ventura?

The previous occupant of the room clearly had; shall we say exotic tastes. Looking up and ignoring the pair of impossibly large breasts that accompanied the graphic, Bruce quickly grabbed the remote and changed channels. Just when I was thinking that this couldn't get any more bizarre, he turned away from me on the bed and gesturing at the large selection of international cheese on the bedside table said:

"Would you like some cheese, Peter?"

I glanced at the huge Welsh roof slate on the side table, that was groaning under the weight of not only the largest selection of cheese I have ever seen but accompanied by a fine selection of Brazil nuts and Walnuts still in their shells and several bowls of satsumas, grapes and extra-large Costa Rican bananas. They must have thought he appeared undernourished when he checked in. There was enough food here to feed a family of four for a week!

"Err… Yes. Why not." I said.

He ripped the thin layer of cling film off the slate, with the speed and aggression of a man who hadn't seen food in weeks.

"Oh! They forgot to bring a knife! Oh! Oh dear," he sighed. "Can I spoon you some Cheese, Peter?"

As requests go, it probably ranks at the very top of my personal 'Things I Never Thought I'd Hear', list. As he gently popped a creamy spoonful of Stinking Bishop onto a tissue on my lap, Richard and Judy announced their arrival on the telly in the corner of the room. I remember thinking to myself, this will go down as probably one of my favourite moments of all time. Richard and Judy on the telly and Bruce Forsyth spooning cheese off a Welsh roof slate, wearing a dressing gown and socks held up with suspenders. Not your normal Saturday night in!

'Bruce's Price Is Right' ran for an amazing seven years in primetime on

ITV1. It was and still is universally loved for its deliciously gaudy fairground style, ridiculously big physical games and bizarre prizes such as – his 'n' hers matching go-carts, facial steamers, bread makers, faux gold and onyx drinks trolleys, Swiss fondue sets, wooden saucepans, cut glass cruet sets, home saunas and pearl necklaces. I will never forget a 'Showcase Showdown' in series two, when a woman who lived on the twenty-fifth floor of Cottingly Towers, a residential high rise block in Leeds, won £86,000 worth of gear, including a Mazda 323 Sedan, a twenty-six-foot long Commander speedboat with a 220 horsepower Mercury 5.0 engine, complete with dual axle trailer and a six-berth Bailey Pageant caravan with extendable awning! As I write this, an episode from 1998 is running on Challenge TV and is bringing back so many happy memories. I don't think there will ever be a time when it's not on TV somewhere, which is why I am as sick as a proverbial parrot that I am not earning royalties from it as I did on 'Family Fortunes'. Ah well, that's showbiz. The money-grabbing bastards!

'The Price Is Right' afforded me one final very amusing and unrepeatable experience. Emma Noble, who was one of the models on the first series of the show, met the then Prime Minister's son, James Major, at a dinner at London's Café Royal in February 1998. The couple became engaged that May and were married in May the following year, in the beautiful undercroft in the Palace of Westminster, in London. My wife and I were fortunate enough to be invited to both the service and the reception at The Dorchester, which reputably earned them a £400,000 deal from Hello! It was evident that we were among the last people to leave. A fleet of waiting cars and taxis had ferried the majority of the guests to Park Lane. We emerged through an ancient doorway and into the bright light of an early summer afternoon, to be met by a formally dressed John Major, in morning suit complete with waistcoat, grey pinstripe trousers and top hat. Major, who was until recently the Prime Minister, walked briskly over to where we stood.

"I am most terribly sorry," He said. "Until recently, I used to be able to order a nuclear war. Now, it appears that I can't even order a bloody cab!"

In 1996, my agent took a call from an old friend of mine, Stephen Stewart. Stephen is a television director of some repute, who I knew from my days on the telly in Northern Ireland. Like me, he had relocated to England and was making a name for himself in light entertainment TV. His higher-profile projects included; The British Comedy Awards, TFI Friday, and

Robot Wars. He had recently returned from Los Angeles where he had been directing the Keenan Ivory Wayans TV show. No, I had never heard of him either, but he is apparently, a big shot on the west coast! The reason for Stephen's call? He wanted me to be the voice of a new show on Channel 4 hosted by Patrick Kielty, a comedian who was also from Northern Ireland. There's a kind of McMurphia thread developing here! The show's name was 'Last Chance Lottery' and its basic premise was that members of the audience, in the studio and at home could use their losing national lottery tickets one more time, to win prizes on the show. Because the show was to be transmitted on Saturday evening after the lottery, it by necessity had to be one hundred percent live. Now, I love live TV both as a viewer and a performer because basically anything can happen. I have always found that the added pressure of being on live TV always brings the best out in people. I also like it because there are no retakes and the show has to start and end on time, regardless of what happens in the middle and crucially, there is no opportunity for post-production. There really is nothing quite like live TV to deliver that pure rush of adrenalin. Kielty is a natural live performer and also relishes the live TV environment, so he was in his element. Although by his admission, he pebble-dashed the inside of his pants at least once every series. Also, on the show was a band of musicians called 'The Pontiffs', which included among its members two of the funniest men I know. Keith Law and John Campbell, the brother of Vivian Campbell the lead guitarist with Def Leppard. Like me, both have an extremely dark sense of humour. To stave off the boredom during rehearsals, they would often write devastatingly hilarious, uncomplimentary songs about the host and the guests on the show and play them for the amusement of the crew, during the breaks.

There were many key moments from this ridiculous series – too many to mention, but three stand out in my memory. On one occasion a racing greyhound called 'Gorgeous the Dog' appeared on the show, live at a dog track in Essex. Gorgeous had never won a race in her life, but this particular evening when having a £1000 prize jackpot placed on her to win a race she won, giving each member of the audience a sizeable wad of cash to go home with. There were regular star guests too. On one occasion Alvin Stardust murdered the Pulp Hit 'Common People', a British TV moment that will never be forgotten. Well not by me anyway. The series also had its fair share of controversy. On one show we had a pig racing team. A bizarre item where pigs would race through the studio and out into the scene dock behind the set, around a very vague obstacle course and back into the studio. Members of the audience would bet on which one came first and money would be added to the final prize pot. I was tasked with providing the live commentary, something I never thought in a month of Sundays I would ever find myself doing! Not unsurprisingly the show attracted many complaints from animal lovers, so the next week they used penguins! Go figure! 'Last Chance Lottery', despite drawing a healthy audience of over three million, which was pretty respectable for Channel 4, was not re-commissioned for a second series. I for one wasn't surprised.

In April of 1996, Steve Wright called and asked me to join his merry band over on BBC Radio 2. He had just signed a contract to be a presenter on the afternoon show. I did give it serious consideration but decided that both he and I would only be repeating ourselves, so I politely declined the offer. In any case, radio and TV commercial voiceover work and work in the corporate voiceover world were now placing huge demands on my time. Every week, I was travelling up and down the length and breadth of the UK in my trusty red Audi Quattro, visiting independent radio stations, like an itinerant door to door salesman. Once through the doors of whichever radio station I was visiting that day, I would be warmly greeted by the station producer who would put a cup of coffee in one hand and a sheath of fifteen to twenty commercial scripts for me to read in the other. The scripts more often than not demanded not only straight narration but often character voices. This intense, pressurized experience was the most fantastically steep learning curve and was invaluable practice for what I was eventually to become – a fully freelance voiceover artist. The sessions themselves were often hilarious. One station I visited frequently, Radio Mercury in deepest Surrey was manned by a couple of writer-producers called; Jon Atkinson and Neil Fairburn. Those sessions often took three times as long as they should have because we were laughing so much. They were happy days.

While every week was undoubtedly different, I was nonetheless covering hundreds of miles each week, driving between radio stations as far apart as Devon in the South West of England and Newcastle upon Tyne in the North East. The long hours and the constant, relentless pounding up and down Her Majesty's finest motorways, were beginning to take its toll on my health. It was, not to put too fine a point on it, bloody knackering! Some of my other voiceover pals had begun to invest not only in home-recording studios but also in equipment that enabled them to connect their studios to the British Telecom ISDN network. This meant that a home-based studio could be linked, by two very high quality 64-Kilobit per second dedicated phone lines, to a remote studio anywhere in the world – in sparkling high fidelity.

Tony Aitken, who is a pal of mine and a fine voice actor himself, had taken the plunge so I drove down to East Sheen in London to check out his new ISDN studio for myself. As with any new and disruptive technology, many of my colleagues viewed ISDN with deep suspicion. They saw it as the work of the devil – something to be feared and avoided at all cost. After all, they reasoned, part of the fun of the job was to be able to get out of the house and enjoy social interaction and live direction from a producer in a professional working studio, even if it happened to be two hundred and fifty miles away from where you lived. I had a feeling that the ability to work from a home studio over ISDN lines, would signal the end of this cosy cadre and break up what was a rather happy band of travelling voices in the UK, known as 'The Circuit'. I saw it as an exciting new opportunity. As Heraclitus once said: 'Change is the only constant', and he knew a thing or two. I learned early on that if someone moves your cheese, you have to move with it. ISDN, I considered could open up so many more new markets for my services. No longer would I have to travel vast distances just to read a handful of scripts. With ISDN, I could be in Devon one minute, Scotland the next and Australia or New York soon after. ISDN was remarkable in that it transformed the way that I and many voice actors work and continue to work to this day. We now have the ability to be ruddy time lords!

Tony Aitken lives in a beautiful Edwardian house on a leafy road in East Sheen in south west London. In what I thought was a bold and brave move, he converted his front room, which was formerly his living room into an office and home studio. His long-suffering wife Adrienne had given up all hope of ever entertaining friends and family in that room ever again. Along with fellow voice-over artists; Lois Lane, John McGuinn and Jacky Davis we would meet at Tony's house once a week. We were a troupe of voice actors that we rather grandly titled: 'The East Sheen Repertory Company'. We informed every single commercial radio station in the UK and Europe that we would all be together around one rather expensive Neumann U87 microphone, every Thursday. The East Sheen Repertory Company was born and for a good six years, it was a massive hit with producers both in the UK and beyond. Radio stations all over the country were clamouring to buy our vocal services. Hour after hour, Tony's fax machine which sat in his hallway was in a constant state of flux, whirring and spewing out scripts at such a rate that poor Adrienne had to be dispatched most weeks to find more rolls of replacement fax paper, at the local office supplies store. This was voice-over production on an industrial scale, and it was, of course, more fun than anyone had a right to be paid for. When we broke for lunch, we would regale ourselves with stories of when we used to drive ourselves literally round the bend, by visiting radio stations all over the country. Impressed with all this new-fangled tech and its rapid adoption by broadcasters and sound studios around the world, in 1999 I set about installing ISDN lines into my home and building a rudimentary studio in a spare room. This arrangement, how-ever, was clearly never going to work as the room was not soundproofed sufficiently, and we had a young child at the time. Hearing the sound of a child screaming on a commercial for Pampers is one thing, but on a BMW commercial, it just doesn't cut the mustard. Mustard commercials weren't keen on kids either as it turned out, so with the help of a former BBC engi-neer called Andy Bantock and one of his ex-BBC colleagues, I bit the bullet and built a purpose-built recording studio in the grounds of our house in deepest Buckinghamshire. It was the best thing I ever did, and I am still working remotely in it, to this very day. For those of us who adopted ISDN, it was revolutionary. I could work around the globe from the comfort of my own home, frequently wearing my pyjamas! What other job affords you that level of delicious informality and comfort. The digital revolution was in its infancy, email was the new way to communicate but the internet it-self was still cumbersome and slow. High-speed fibre-optic broadband was some years off yet. Digital recording equipment and software, however, had reduced in price quite dramatically. The barriers to entry into the home studio game had come down and the prospect of running a studio from home was now within reach of most people. Quarter-inch reel to reel tape recorders, which were notoriously expensive to buy and maintain and were frequently unreliable, were a thing of the past. An all-new digital future was now blazing a fast, forward trail. No longer did I have to slice the tips of my fingers while editing tapes with razor blades. Now, I could easily remove all the imperfections in a vocal recording. Inappropriately loud breathing, lip

'Voiceover Man' rebranding publicity postcard No.2
2005 – Creative: Damon Hutson-Flynn.

smacks, microphone pops, spurious tummy rumbles, squeaky chairs and paper rustling – all disappeared with the flick of a wrist and the click of a mouse. Using my new ISDN connectivity, I could either be directed live in real-time or send my recordings anywhere in the world, at the touch of a button. It was a total game-changer.

What I and others hadn't bargained for, however, was that this was about as far from a sociable way of working as you could imagine. In practice, it was exactly the opposite. I now found myself spending whole days in the studio – often not seeing or speaking to anyone, with only myself for company. Now, I don't have an issue with this because I am by nature a fairly private individual and like my own company, but some of my colleagues, however, have found it difficult to adapt – and struggle with the long hours in isolation. It was this very issue that led me, Tony Aitken, Lois Lane, Jacky Davis and John McGuinn to found VOX, the world's first social network for voice talent and much later, *'gravyforthebrain.com'* – a global training and networking organisation – about which, more later.

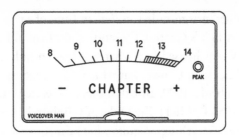

I LOOKED LIKE A BLOODY
CAR PARK ATTENDANT!

As the '90s ticked over into the noughties, and all our computers, microchips, radios and digital gizmos and thing-a-me-jigs failed to explode – courtesy of the much anticipated zero-day millennium bug, light entertainment television began to raise it's not so ugly head again. Since 1987, ITV had been constantly re-commissioning a show which began life in the United States as 'Family Feud' but which in the UK was called: 'Family Fortunes'. The year is now 2000, and the show is in its thirteenth year with Les Dennis at the helm, who took over from Max "You've Got Hands" Bygraves. The show back then employed a live in-show announcer who had to interject and announce the spot prizes and introduce the families and Les himself. This role had been very expertly filled by two men. For Les' predecessors, Bob Monkhouse and Max it was Andrew Lodge while Stephen Rhodes, a talented Sony award-winning radio presenter, was the voice of the show for twelve years from 1987. For reasons best known to ITV, they asked me to replace Stephen on the show. I always feel awkward when that happens, but change is something we all have to accept, regardless of which side of the deal it falls, and I have and will continue to experience both.

'Family Fortunes' was recorded '*as live*', in front of a two hundred strong studio audience at ITV's Central TV studios, on Lenton Lane in Nottingham. Central TV was housed in a what was known rather grandly as The East Midlands Television Centre, but which was in reality, a grey concrete shithole that resembled a 1970s British motorway service station. It was officially opened in 1984 by HRH The Duke of Edinburgh, who has forthright opinions on almost everything, so quite what he made of it is anyone's guess, though I think we can all imagine. The entire production team, who were London based had to travel north to Nottingham and stay at a local hotel in the town. At the time, Les was married to the actress Amanda Holden and most weeks, she and their two dogs would join him at the hotel for a night or two. On those occasions, Amanda, Les, the show's producer and I would have dinner. Amanda has an incredibly mischievous personality and is such a dreadful flirt. There is nothing she likes more than a story containing oodles of filth and innuendo and once she starts, there's no stopping her. She's my kind of girl! Unfortunately, though, things were going from bad to worse in their marriage and in the middle of recording 'Family Fortunes' that year, her alleged affair with actor Neil Morrissey was exposed in the press. Poor Les, I felt incredibly sorry for him as I do for any celebrity who lives their life in the constant glare of the spotlight. He battled on, finishing the series by putting on a brave face, despite the huge press intrusion and his life falling down around him. He and Amanda tried to rekindle their relationship but sadly, eventually separated in December 2002 and were later divorced in the following year. I have fond memories of working on 'Family Fortunes', not least because I had to work in what was essentially a small caravan on the studio floor. This was positioned just out of sight of the cameras but in plain view of the audience, which they found endlessly amusing as they could see me through the window! I looked, to all intents and purposes like a bloody car park attendant.

The two series in which I appeared, were directed by a most fabulously camp director called Peter Harris. Peter was one of those larger-than-life characters. A TV veteran, with huge hits like 'The Muppet Show', 'The Muppet Movies', 'Bull's-Eye', 'Fraggle Rock', 'Spitting Image', 'New Faces', 'Celebrity Squares', 'The Jim Henson Hour' and '15 to 1' – under his not inconsiderable belt! He is the only director that I have ever worked with who had a rider in his contract for every show, which demanded that the production gallery must at all times have pink lighting and several vases of fresh pink lilies! He was quite a character, but he was a hard taskmaster and was not afraid of cracking the whip when he sensed people were losing focus, which we frequently did. On one show, Les asked a hapless contestant to name a bird with a long neck. The response – "Naomi Campbell" – completely floored not only Les but all the cameramen, the floor manager, the audience and me so much so, that no one could speak for several minutes afterwards.

Later that year, I gave the keys to my apartment in Naples, on the beautiful Gulf of Mexico in Florida, to my then good pal Mark Wells. Mark, you will remember, was the producer of the ill-fated 'Steve Wright's People Show' on the BBC but was now the recently appointed Controller of entertainment at Carlton Productions, an independent offshoot of Carlton TV. On his return from the USA, Mark told me that he had been spending time in my apartment watching a guy on TV, by the name of Jerry Springer. Springer, a former politician had a show which was the most heavily syndicated tabloid-style 'freak show' in America. By 1998, it was beating 'The Oprah Winfrey Show' in many cities and was reaching more than 6.7 million viewers. Springer was a TV tour de force. Most people in the UK think Jeremy Kyle pioneered the format, but Springer had been mining this particularly rich, low-life vein since 1991. Mark was convinced he could bring Jerry to the UK and so invited him over for discussions. Jerry has a great deal of affection for the UK. Unknown to many people, he is British. Born to exiled German-Jewish parents in London towards the end of the war. So, when Mark asked him if he would be interested in coming to the UK, he jumped at the chance. And so, in May 2000, he burst onto UK screens on the ITV network. Springer wanted to be taken seriously as an entertainer and interviewer instead of the host of a show that paraded dysfunctional families and individuals for entertainment. In the US, the talk show market was sewn up by Letterman and Leno, so Springer hoped to make the transition here and become the new late-night chat show Grand Fromage in the UK, eventually transitioning back to the USA in a new guise. Earlier in that year, his reputation in the US had suffered a serious blow when a guest, Nancy Campbell-Panitz, was beaten to death shortly after the broadcast of a Springer show in which she appeared. The woman's husband had announced on air that he wanted to divorce and re-marry. As a result of this

With Les Dennis and cast and crew celebrating
21 seasons of Family Fortunes – 2000 – Central TV.

negative publicity, Springer's image in the US had been indelibly tarnished. Ironically, a similar fate lay in store for Jeremy Kyle nineteen years later after a participant on one of his shows took his own life. Kyle's show was permanently, abruptly and unceremoniously taken off air and buried deep in that section of the Mariana Trench, reserved for very dead formats. The move to the UK looked like it might give Jerry some timely separation from the USA and possibly even, save his career in the long run. Sadly, ITV did not renew the series, but poor old Jerry was picked up by channel controller Dawn Airey over at Channel 5 and his new series for that channel was renamed 'Late Night with Jerry Springer'. Only two series were made, and Jerry's late-night TV chat show dreams crashed and burned, kamikaze style, ending in 2001 after just sixteen episodes. I liked Jerry a lot. Late one evening I was sitting with him and the producer of the doomed show on the roof terrace of Thames TV in Teddington to the West of London. We were overlooking the river, gazing into the dark swirling water of the lock, smoking cigars and chugging at a bottle of Jack Daniels, late into the night and listening to Jerry trying to explain the US college electoral system. He might as well

Shooting the breeze with Jerry Springer – 2000 – Teddington Studios, London.

have been speaking in Swahili, but I remember nodding to him as though I understood every word!

Jerry's sojourn into British television had hit the buffers. My TV entertainment career, on the other hand, had just slipped into fifth gear and was cruising down the fast lane. Stephen Stewart, my old producer/director pal from 'Last Chance Lottery' had asked me to be the voice of a new ITV daytime Quiz show called 'It's Not The Answer', an impossibly complicated and convoluted format that he had somehow managed to sell to an ITV daytime commissioner, during a long lunch. The show was to be hosted by Nadia Sawalha, the sister of the actress Julia Sawalha who was making a name for herself, playing Saffron the daughter of Jennifer Saunders character Edina Monsoon in the award-winning and much-loved TV comedy, 'Absolutely Fabulous'. The format of 'It's Not the Answer' required three members of the public to answer general knowledge questions with multiple-choice answers. Each question had five possible answers but only one of them was correct. Nadia gave me the moniker: 'Pete The Penaliser' because I had to penalise people if they hesitated after buzzing to answer. I also had to shout out useful advice for each question such as "It's NOT Duck a l'Orange! It's

On Chris Moyles' Breakfast Show – 2006 – BBC Radio 1, London.

NOT Spaghetti Bolognaise!" and for each answer eliminated in this way, the points value of the question would go down. I couldn't understand it at all, but I wasn't alone. On one show, Nadia was reading aloud the contest rules off autocue, to a hapless contestant who happened to be a solicitor from Bromsgrove. Following her impossibly complicated explanation she turned to the contestant and asked, "Now, do you understand how the game works?" Well, we all knew what was coming next. There was a moments pause, then clear as a bell he said "Err… actually no I don't!" Nadia collapsed in a heap and the studio audience was in stitches. None of us understood the rules either! It took a good ten minutes for the producer, who had made his way onto the studio floor to explain to him what he had to do. There were five rounds like this, all with increasing complexity and at the end, the winner walked away with a holiday abroad – but as this show was being made on an ITV daytime budget, it was never too far abroad! At the end of a week of this torture, Nadia, the vision mixer Naomi Neufeld and I had taken to the bottle and were frequently hungover from the night before by the time we got to the studio for the next day's recording. This of course, only made matters worse with me giggling and she, practically wetting herself with laughter as she read the rules to each contestant, in the knowledge that no one had a ruddy clue what was going on. Needless to say, 'It's Not the Answer' and 'Pete the Penaliser' were not the answers to ITV daytime's prayers and quite rightly the show was handed down a life sentence with no parole, put on death row, shot by firing squad at dawn, buried in the trench and never saw the light of day again. Good riddance. But it was fun!

Between 2002 and 2007, two shows dominated my schedule. 'Today with Des and Mel' for ITV and 'Test the Nation' for BBC TV. 'Today with Des and Mel' was an ITV daytime staple, and not only launched the TV presenting career of former model Melanie Sykes, who is now married to the actor Daniel Caltagirone but revived the flagging career of living TV entertainment legend Des O'Connor, who had just celebrated his seventieth birthday the year before it launched! The format of 'Today with Des and Mel' was loosely based on the format of the popular American TV chat show, 'Live with Regis and Kelly'. My role on the UK version was to announce who the guests were and then introduce Des and Mel onto the set. Because I had my ISDN studio set up at home by this time, I was able to phone-in my contribution each morning from the comfort of my own home. The only slight downside to this arrangement was on the two occa-

Back to back with Nadia Sawala on set – 2001 – Central TV.

sions that I went to our home in Florida USA and I was forced to get up at 5am every morning, go into my home studio and shout very loudly for thirty-five minutes. God only knows what my neighbours must have thought! It was and continues to be, a dream job – for most of the time!

'Test the Nation' is a show that I hold in the fondest regard, as it became the gateway for something much bigger in my life. There's more on that, later. Made by Talent Television for the BBC, 'Test the Nation' was originally presented by Anne 'You are the weakest link' Robinson and Phillip Schofield. It ran for seventeen editions between 2002 and 2007. The tests were devised and standardised by the academic, Colin Cooper from the psychology department at my alma mater Queen's University in Belfast. He was referred to on the programme as 'Superman Cooperman'. During the show, viewers could play along and answer questions on the BBC website, or just use an old-fashioned pen and paper to keep score. We all played along in the studio and I was always worse than useless. The first show, which aired in primetime in May 2002, was an IQ test and the six groups of fifty studio participants included blondes, brunettes, teachers and students. They were pitted against a group of ten celebrities including 'EastEnders' star Adam Woodyatt, broadcaster Fearne Cotton, Olympic athlete Jonathan Edwards and former Sunday Times editor and broadcaster – the brilliant Andrew Neil. Not surprisingly, the teachers came out on top. The last 'Test the Nation' show in the UK was shown on 27th August 2007. It took six years, 2,750 questions and hundreds of millions of pounds in fees and production costs to discover that we were largely a nation of thickos after all!

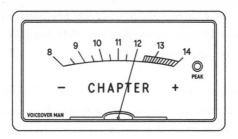

AFTER THREE MINUTES
YOU HAVE TO STEP OUTSIDE
AND TAKE A TYLENOL

U p to this point in my career, I had confined myself mainly to voicing radio commercials, corporate videos, and in-show narration for broadcast television. It's now 2003 and I'm about to get my first taste of character acting, in the world of animation. It was a baptism of fire. I was about to be cast in quite possibly the most important and now, most critically acclaimed and revered animated TV series to ever be produced in the UK – 'Monkey Dust'. Harry Thompson, who had been my producer on 'Peter Dickson's Nightcap' on BBC Radio 2 back in the late 1980s, had co-written with Shaun Pye, a satirical animated sketch show for the brand-new TV channel BBC3. The two had locked themselves away for months to write sketches for the show that would include: 'The Failed Chatroom Pervert', 'Ivan Dobsky: The Meatsafe Murderer', the adventures of 'The Classically Trained Actor', played by yours truly and a compulsive liar named 'Clive Pringle', who hid his depraved antics from his wife by trying to pass off the plots of movies and otherwise generally well-known folk stories, as the truth. 'Monkey Dust' was, in the opinion of esteemed columnist Dan Wilkinson:

"The best animated satirical sketch show ever produced in the UK, which sadly, only lasted for three seasons between 2003 and 2005." Its themes were uncompromising, hard-hitting and real."

Shining its light on the dark, disturbing underbelly of Britain. 'Monkey Dust' took no prisoners and left no topic unturned, no matter how uncomfortable it was to view. From Big Societal Themes, like murder, paedophilia and terrorism, to more singular, ideas such as a young girl giving her dad all of her birthday presents to help him feed his gambling addiction – it managed to both completely lampoon its target and find that all-important human angle that allowed the viewer into a world that was closed to most. It was in short, a work of genius. The cast read like a who's who in voice acting. Enn Reitel, Brian Bowles, Morwenna Banks, Rebecca Front, David Baddiel, Sharon Horgan, Frances Barber, Kate Robbins, Simon Greenall and me! It was a wonderful experience and to this day I can't quite believe my good fortune to be cast in such an influential show. It ran for just three series, with a total of eighteen episodes produced. More were planned but the future but 'Monkey Dust' was to be no more. The life of its producer and principal author Harry Thompson was so tragically cut short in November 2005 by lung cancer.

Writing in the Guardian at the time, media commentator Maggie Brown described Thompson as:

"One of the most successful television comedy producers of the last twenty years, delighting millions of viewers with such enduring hits as 'Have I Got News for You', 'They Think it's All Over' and 'Never Mind the Buzzcocks'. He was regarded within the industry as one of those rare, clever, creative producers who could make a key impact on a show – the difference between a hit and an also-ran – such as the first series of Channel 4's 11 O'Clock Show (1998), which he produced and helped write, spawned Ali G and later 'Da Ali G Show'."

I was devastated at losing a friend and someone I admired so greatly and adored working with. I was lucky to have known him and I was grateful that we had lunch together, a few months before he died. That afternoon in the Charlotte Street Hotel, over a glass or three of wine after lunch, we reminisced about some of the great shows we had worked on together.

'Nightcap', 'Have I Got News for You', 'Never Mind the Buzzcocks', 'Harry Enfield and Chums' and 'Monkey Dust'. I was grateful to have had the opportunity to thank him for his friendship and support over the years. We cheerfully parted company that day, not knowing that it would be the last time I would see him. I miss him greatly, as does the world of television. It was also not the last similar parting from someone who had significantly influenced me. More on that later.

In the summer of 2003, my agent called to let me know that I had been cast for several parts in a new video game called 'Fable'. I didn't know at the time, just what a big deal this was, one never does. I have been cast in over thirty 'triple-A' game titles but this one was to be one of the biggest ever made. 'Fable' was to go on to break records in the world of gaming, not just with phenomenal international sales but also with the sheer scale of its production and technical complexity. A cast of over forty actors took part and the game makers, Lionhead/Microsoft Games assembled a team of over a hundred and fifty specialists under legendary games director Peter Molyneaux. They broke all records for the amount of data they squeezed onto a single disc and the game took just over four years to develop. The brilliant Danny Elfman, whose previous credits read like an Oscar-night award nomination, wrote the score. This was a game produced on a vast new scale and on a feature film sized budget. The combined efforts of all cast and crew were well rewarded, however. Following its release in September 2004, 'Fable' went on to become a huge worldwide commercial success, selling 375,000 copies during its first week alone, and 600,000 copies in the first month. Sales rose to 1.4 million copies by March 2005 and by July 2006, the Xbox version had sold 1.5 million copies and earned $58 million in the United States alone. To date, the game has sold around three million copies worldwide! I was re-cast to appear in the sequel, Fable 2, in October 2008.

To anyone not in the business, voice acting in a major video game may seem like a rather glamorous and exciting thing to do. I hate to disabuse you of this view because it absolutely, most definitely is not – unless you enjoy reading random phrases from Microsoft Excel spreadsheets and grunting and shouting a lot, first thing in the morning! Let me explain – videogame makers take their intellectual property rights very seriously indeed. They guard all pre and post-production elements of the game like they were state secrets. Before you can even get a whiff of a script or plotline, you have to sign not only your own life away under NDA but also those of your children… and your children's children… and your children's children's children. Once all the legal formalities are dispensed with, and you have agreed to be shot and buried in the trench, if you even dare mention one word of your involvement in their precious project, you then wait for the script to drop through your letterbox several months in advance, so that you may prepare for your role. Except that doesn't happen either. Incredibly, the first you know about the part you are to play is when you walk through the studio door on the day of the session. At this point, you are presented with a sheaf of spreadsheets containing lines of various length in numbered cells and if you are lucky, a teensy weensy, poorly reproduced monochrome drawing of your character, together with the briefest of brief character description. This is typically something like:

"The Minotaur is a passive-aggressive character. Sometimes good, but mostly bad. He speaks with authority and confidence, but with a soft voice, which he sometimes raises in anger. He also has an alter ego – an unforgiving, homicidal maniac."

Great! So, with that information and a quick glance at a grainy black and white photocopied image the size of a postage stamp, I have two minutes to create a character for a $60M game, that will sell to millions all around the world. On many occasions I have been cast for multiple roles within a game, all at the last minute, all requiring different voices. No pressure! It's madness. I have met and worked with many famous actors over the years and of those who have appeared in video games, all of them bar none have told me that it was one of the most difficult genres of voice acting they had ever worked in – most of them principally citing this lack of preparation time. Liam Neeson, with whom I appeared in several plays at the Lyric Theatre back in Belfast many years ago, credits his experience doing radio plays for the BBC in London and RTE in Ireland, as the most helpful precedent to his video game voiceover work. He identified the shift of focus you need to make as an actor, to convey something through your voice and the rhythm of the words. Something that you wouldn't have to worry about so much if the camera was on you. Elijah Wood provided the voice for his most famous role, Frodo, in multiple video game versions of *'The Lord of the Rings'*. In addition to Frodo, he voiced Mumble in the animated film *'Happy Feet'* and the accompanying video game.

Wood's interest in video games makes sense – he's a gamer himself, and his older brother produces video games. He also enjoys the unique acting challenge that they provide. Gaming actors frequently find that the characters they play are often in situations that are not really that commonplace and so they have to vocally make the character sound like he or she is going through what can sometimes be some pretty intense experiences. In 2012, Gary Oldman was a guest on US late-night chat show *'Conan'* and talked about his video game voice acting. He described voice acting in games as particularly challenging, especially the difficulty of recording really loud and often violent battle scenes. Having been there myself many times, it's easy for me to understand his observation that:

"After about three minutes of it, you have to step outside, walk around, and take a Tylenol!"

It wrecks your voice, not to mention what it does to your blood pressure and heart rate! The one thing that will drag a game's meta-critic score south is predictable and repetitive dialogue. This can occur when game players replay a scene over and over again. To overcome this potential problem, game

Working with Harry Shearer on 'Not Today, Thank You' – 2006 – BBC Radio 4, London.

producers often ask the actors to record what are known as non-scripted vocals or NSVs. These are essentially human noises like verbal grunts, huffs and puffs that accompany the action when your character does something strenuous in the game, like climbing a high wall for instance. To prevent this vocal repetition, gaming actors need to be able to produce hundreds of these noises in one sitting. Easier said than done. I challenge you to go ahead and try it now. Imagine you are in a battle scene and have just been punched hard in the guts by an adversary. Now, verbalise that sound and give me fifty variations, all of them subtly different. See? It's not easy, particularly when you next have to do this all over again three more times (mild, medium and intense) with increasing projection. It doesn't stop there though. Add to that, another hour of heavy breathing, yelling, drowning, bleeding to death, vomiting and grunting in a session that to the casual observer has all the audio qualities a porn movie! I know of some voice talent who have quite literally passed out in front of the microphone, foaming at the mouth as a result of systemic hyperoxia and others who literally could not speak for days afterwards. I told you it wasn't glamorous.

To be a truly great video games actor, you need to either innately have or be able to develop a strong sense of visualization. The key is to acutely sense and mentally visualize, in almost infinite detail not only your character and the environment that the scene is taking place in but all the other characters as well. Through my business, '*gravyforthebrain.com*' (at the time of writing, the world's largest on-line voice acting school) that I founded with gaming voice director Hugh Edwards, we now teach actors to, among other things become video game actors. The techniques and skill sets that are needed to succeed in this genre of voice acting aren't taught in all drama schools. I learned it myself through trial and error – mostly error if I'm being honest. Hugh often talks about voice sessions that he has directed, with otherwise perfectly talented actors, who simply couldn't deliver their lines consistently and quickly enough. He frequently found himself training actors, in the subtleties of video game acting in the presence of clients and producers, which is not good. My forte in gaming is playing, WW2 pilots, army officers or zombies! If I were to choose one, it would be zombies! There's nothing like getting your teeth stuck into a good zombie although, in reality, it's traditionally the other way around! I also do a mean bloodcurdling yell and once took over forty-seven seconds to die in a well-known AAA titled blockbuster! In one game, I played a psychotic pink Octopus with a freakish multiple personality disorder. I swear some of these game designers need to lay off the magic mushrooms. Towards the end of the game, I had to read a one hundred twenty word long paragraph super-fast, while switching between eleven different accents and then flip in the air and drown in the sea! Recording it took forever and I almost actually did drown in my own blood, sweat and tears. It's a performance I have absolutely no desire to repeat ever again.

I have always been and still am an avid consumer of TV entertainment. I love a well-executed shiny floor TV show with a proper host and scintillating guests. One of my earliest memories of watching TV light entertainment was back in the days when the flickering images on our cathode-ray set in Belfast were on 625 lines and in black and white. If I close my eyes and listen, I can still hear the now distant voices of Bob Monkhouse on 'The Golden Shot' – "Bernie the Bolt." John Benson on 'Sale of the Century' – "Live from Norwich," Hughie Green on 'Take Your Pick' – "Open the box," and 'Opportunity Knocks' – "OK folks, let's look at the Clapometer," and of course Bruce Forsyth on 'The Generation Game' – "Didn't he do well?" All of them were enduring; popular British TV formats that were brilliantly executed by the most consummate hosts of the day. It's hard to imagine it now but 'The Generation Game' with Brucie, for all its family-friendly innocence, became the number one game show on British television during the 1970s, regularly attracting over 21 million viewers and at one-point peaking at an astonishing 25 million. Put in context, that was over half the population of the United Kingdom back then. Those heady numbers are unheard of these days. You are lucky if you can muster 6 million in today's multi-channel environment. 'The Generation Game', because of its undoubted popularity, is still held in great affection by many people in the UK, even to this day. Someone who was making in-roads as a host in TV light entertainment in the new millennium was Dale Winton. Dale had come to the attention of producers, when he was cast, by a friend of mine called Howard Huntridge at Fremantle, as the host of a little-known afternoon show called 'Supermarket Sweep', which slowly developed a cult following mainly among undergraduate students. Supermarket Sweep returned to TV in 2020, hosted by X Factor finalist turned TV presenter, the brilliant Rylan Clark-Neal. Which just goes to prove that while they may come and go, really great formats never actually die. They just have a cup of tea and lie low for a while and then reappear – rising phoenix-like, transformed and dusted down for a whole new generation to enjoy. I do not doubt that in time this will happen to many other TV entertainment behemoths. Anyway, in 2003, the BBC was planning a revival of 'The Generation Game' and had been casting around for a suitable host. The show had revived the careers of Brucie, Larry Grayson and Jim Davidson. The question on everyone's lips was, who was next? Under great secrecy, a pilot show was filmed at BBC TV Centre in the spring of 2003 and somehow, I ended up being drafted in as the voice-over. From my point of view, whether this ended up being commissioned or not, this was quite a thrill. Having watched the show on TV as a child, here I was in the legendary studio TC1 at BBC TV Centre where it was originally made, about to take part in this legendary format, hosted by Mr Paul O'Grady. The interesting thing about the 'Generation Game' is that it looks beguilingly simple. In reality, it is fantastically complex to pull off. There are so many moving parts and physical props. It's like a Swiss watch. Experts demonstrating their skills on Live TV and asking members of the public to have a go, is asking for trouble! The recording started on time and got underway in front of a live audience. Then, slowly and surely it began to unravel. Beset with technical difficulties, props failures, mechanical faults and multiple retakes. Before too long, Paul began to lose the will to live. He much prefers live telly and actively dislikes the process of recording. The dénouement of the show was the appearance of Dame Barbara Windsor, who was to be revealed to the audience on a revolving, high-backed, purple gilded throne but by the time we got to that point, it was just after 11pm. As the weary stage-crew activated the mechanism to rotate Barbara's chair, I watched her, in full fairy Godmother costume complete with a wand in hand, turn to face an audience of... five people. Everyone else had left to get the last train home! Her face was a picture. As O'Grady and I left the studios that night, we exited Studio TC1 into the fresh night air. We walked past Dale Winton's brand new, pristine V8 Bentley Continental GT, which was cheekily parked right outside the stage door at Television Centre. Paul was in a foul mood. Staring at this gleaming new vehicle he turned to me and said:

"Is that Dale's new car?"

"Yes." I said. "Isn't it beautiful?" It was.

"I hope the fucking wheels fall off," was his parting comment as he slipped into his Toyota Prius and disappeared down Wood Lane to the near-est pub.

Towards the end of 2003, I was invited to be the voice of a new science show on Sky One TV, called 'Brainiac'. It was a quasi-science-entertainment show where numerous experiments were carried out by the show's boffins to verify whether commonly held ideas about the physical world, are ver-ifiable. Important 'sciencey' things we all need to know such as; whether it's possible to run across a swimming pool full of custard or whether it is easy to create ear-bustingly loud explosions using only a bicycle pump, some cling-film, talcum powder, an aerosol deodorant and a baked bean tin. The white-coated human scientists on the show were referred to as 'Brainiacs', though 'Lunatics' might have been more apt, as each episode ended with the destruction of a caravan either through fire or explosion or more often than not – both. No, I have no idea why either! The original presenters were Richard 'Hamster' Hammond from 'Top Gear', a known caravan hater and Jon Tickle, a known explosion lover. The clue to the answer to the afore-mentioned question is in there somewhere. I was the voiceover on the series for six seasons and in season five in 2007, I had the chance of working once again with Jim Moir, aka Vic Reeves who stepped into the presenter role. Any opportunity to work with Jim is one I have no hesitation in accepting, as he is such an utterly lovely chap to be around. Jim is a true surrealist and a keen artist. He and his comedy partner, Bob Mortimer were a breath of fresh air when they first appeared on our screens on Channel 4 in 1990. Who could forget; 'Les, The Man With The Stick', 'Novelty Island' and 'Morrissey The Consumer Monkey'? All of it was deliciously daft and utterly bonkers. I worked on 'Brainiac' on and off for six years. It's a show that my kids grew up with. I have fond memories of taking my eldest son Connor to a location shoot, to watch them blow up a caravan or two. I think it quite possibly scarred him for life and put him off caravanning and camping for-ever, which let's face it, is no bad thing.

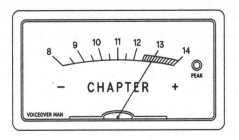

KEEP YOUR FILTHY HANDS
OFF THE UNION, SON!

In 2004, I was in Florida and I took a call from a TV sound supervisor friend of mine called Robert Edwards. I had worked with Robert on 'Test the Nation' and he was now working with Thames TV, Fremantle and a production company called Syco on a pilot of a new talent show series for ITV. The purpose of his call was to tell me that the producers were on the hunt for a voice for the show and he had very kindly put me in the frame. He gave me the production manager's number and told me to call as soon as I could. Well, in this business, it doesn't pay to sit around so as soon as I had ended the call with Robert, I dialled the number. Within ten minutes, I was viewing a QuickTime video of a pilot show of this proposed new series, in my home in Florida. I instantly knew that this was a show I wanted to be involved in so I called the production manager back and told her. Luckily, I have an audio production studio in the USA, so I arranged to send a voiceover audition across to them the very next day. Twenty-four hours later, I took a call from the executive producer who told me I had landed the job as the voice of 'The X Factor'. And that was how it happened. Serendipitously, I had just unwittingly boarded a behemoth of a TV entertainment format that would change not only the landscape of entertainment television around the world for the next fifteen years but would launch more international superstar careers than any other TV show, including multi-million selling global artists; One Direction, Little Mix, Olly Murs, James Arthur and Leona Lewis. Of course, back then, no one had any idea how big this show was going to become, nor indeed how long that last sentence was going to turn out. The show completed fifteen seasons and was syndicated around the world to over one hundred fifty countries! 'The X Factor' will remain a cultural and ratings phenomenon and has now entered the pantheon of the most successful TV entertainment shows in the entire history of television. Since its launch in 2004, the British format has been watched by almost 400 million people around the world and can be seen in almost every country on earth. The show has discovered more international breakout artists than any other singing competition in the world, with more than 180 million record sales by 'X Factor' artists globally. Those statistics I think you'll agree are pretty phenomenal.

The other day I came across a clip on the internet of me introducing the show in 2004. I was astonished by not only how different the show looked back then but by how I sounded. The trademark deep-throated roar was not yet fully developed, and the ridiculously self-important intentionally portentous delivery had yet to appear. We were all feeling our way with this new format. Nobody, least of all me knew initially whether this show was a serious talent show or a pantomime… or quite possibly something in between. By series two, I was beginning to get an idea that it was most certainly both. So, I took the bold decision to push the boat out a little further on my vocal delivery. It was still a long way off from where it ended up, but we were headed in the right direction as far as I was concerned and in the absence of any direction or otherwise from the producers, I pushed on. It dawned on me just how popular this show was when in 2007, I was doing a spot of Christmas shopping one Saturday on London's Oxford Street. I was constantly hearing people saying things like "Get a move on Chardonnay! We have got to get home, 'The X Factor' in on in an hour." I was also amused to hear a couple of young lads impersonating me on the street, as I walked behind them down The Strand, just outside Charing Cross station. I was sorely tempted to break cover but decided against it. I'm not a fan of a public kerfuffle ever since the scourge of the 'cheeky selfie video' emerged.

As the years rolled on, 'The X Factor' grew in popularity – 12 million people were now tuning in each week. Kate Thornton, the show's presenter was riding the crest of a wave and was seen everywhere; premieres, parties and openings of every sort. Then suddenly and without warning after three years at the helm, the production unceremoniously dropped her. A decision, which for her, must have been a crushing blow. I can only wonder that at the time, people must have questioned why they would change such a key element of a format that was clearly working. It was eventually revealed that a relative unknown was to take the reins of TV's biggest show. Dermot O'Leary. Or "MISTER – DERRMOT – OHH – LEEARRRY" as he must now, regretfully for him perhaps, now be known. Dermot was a natural fit for the show, this was apparent from the get-go. His sharp-suited style and youthful easy patter complimented the slick and hugely expensive production values that were fast becoming the show's hallmark. Over 50,000 people auditioned on the very first series but by series six in 2009, over 200,000 hopefuls auditioned. The lure of a £1M recording contract and the resultant fame and fortune was proving difficult for many to resist. The viewing public was lapping it up too. By 2010, at the glittering Wembley final show of series seven, over 19.5 million people witnessed Matt Cardle beat Rebecca Ferguson and One Direction to win the coveted title. Who the real winners were that season, I'll leave you to decide!

The desire to be famous that so many people appear to have is incredibly difficult for me to comprehend. Frankly, I wouldn't wish it on my worst enemies. Fame once attained, invariably ends in tears. No good ultimately comes of it. As the great 19th Century American poet Emily Dickinson once observed:

"Fame is a fickle food upon the shifting plate, at whose table once a guest, but not the second time, he sat. Whose crumbs the crows inspect, and with ironic caw flap past it to the farmer's corn; men eat of it and die."

Even back then, before TV, radio, electricity, the telephone and the gramophone, old Emily knew a thing or two about the damaging effects of fame on the human psyche. Fame corrupts, distorts and destroys. If anyone promised me fame and fortune, I would ask them if I could possibly just try the fortune first, to see if that would perhaps cover it. Nothing good ultimately comes of fame. Don't even go there. Trust me, I have seen what it does to some people, up close and it's not pretty. It's partly the reason why I have chosen to lead my professional life out of the glare of the spotlight.

That, and the undeniable fact that I have the perfect face for radio!

I recall going out to dinner a few years back with Bruce Forsyth. Our first course had just been delivered and Bruce, with a primed fork in hand was just about to put the initial delicious morsel of a bit of prime beef into his moustachioed mouth, when a bloke came up and asked for an autograph and a 'cheeky selfie'. Bruce, as ever the true pro that he was said he would be pleased to do both but politely asked him if he could wait until after he had eaten. The bloke readily agreed, much to Bruce's relief but then proceeded to stand six inches away from the table hovering over us, as if he was in a queue at the post office! This is a fairly benign example of the intrusive nature of having a prominent public profile. The history of showbiz is of course littered with thousands of other more extreme examples of fan worship, stalking and obsession that did not end so well. A-list celebrities at least have the means to protect themselves from intrusion. But who wants to live their life in a claustrophobic security bubble? Blacked out limousines, baseball caps and disguises, personal protection, men in dark suits wearing earpieces and carrying pieces, paparazzi decoys, two-way radios, elaborate home security and for those with children, the horrific, unthinkable, unimaginable spectre of kidnap. It's the Z-list crowd though, who I feel truly sorry for. The minor soap stars, the reality-show stars, the daytime TV and home shopping crowd and dare I say it, potentially the talent-show finalists who have neither the means nor the money to create their own bubbles. Some deal with instant fame better than others and some use it as a springboard to even greater things. Rylan Clark-Neal, the blubbing, hysterical X Factor contestant who auditioned on the show at the age of twenty-three in 2012, is a perfect example of one who has done superbly well. He is such a nice person and incredibly hard-working. Plus, he knows how to play the game. But many of these transient supernovae burn brightly, then flicker and die. Fame can be a fickle mistress yet, at the time of writing, 'The X Factor' has been on TV in the UK for an incredible fifteen years. It has been singularly one of the most popular TV formats globally, in decades. It has won a grand total of sixteen National Television Awards. I was there, at the O2 for six of those years. I walked the red carpet and drank my own bodyweight in Champagne!

Fame is intoxicating, exhilarating and incredibly addictive. And rather like the feral crack addict, when the dealer switches off the supply, the withdrawal process is neither a pretty nor an easy one. As the poet and

Being positioned for a stunt for E4 TV Promo – 2008 – Pinewood Studios, Iver.

With Leona Lewis at 'The X Factor' after party – 2006 – London.

Nobel Laureate Seamus Heaney observed in his poem: 'From the Republic of Conscience':

"No porters. No interpreter. No taxi. You carried your own burden and very soon your symptoms of creeping privilege disappeared."

Fame? Pah! Who needs it? I rest my case. Tick the box for 'no publicity' every time. You'll thank me for it.

My vocal presence on the biggest show on the planet was generating quite a bit of press interest on its own. My agent was getting calls from TV chat shows, radio stations, newspapers and magazines, keen to run feature articles and interviews with, as the inestimable Heat magazine dubbed me in 2009 – *'The most famous voice in Britain'*, an accolade that made me chuckle for all it's fallacious guff and affectation. We turned down most requests but in a moment of madness, I did agree to appear on 'Daybreak', ITV's national breakfast TV show in the week before Christmas that year. The producers had very kindly agreed to put me up in a nearby hotel, such was the early call time – 6.15am! Imagine my surprise when my ringing mobile phone woke me from a deep sleep at 6.20am with a junior researcher on the other end in a mild state of hypoxic panic, asking where I was. I hurriedly jumped out of bed, packed, flew out of the hotel and into a waiting cab and got to the London Studios on the Southbank at 6.45am, un-shaven, un-washed and practically un-dressed. On arrival and in my bleary-eyed confused state I was bundled into a lift and pushed onto the set as the titles rolled, much to the consternation of the two presenters, the usually unflappable fellow Ulsterwoman, Christine Bleakley and the practically horizontal Adrian Chiles. As they introduced me, off-camera I was buttoning up my flies, tying my shoelaces and trying to generally make myself look like I hadn't just stumbled out of bed, which of course I had. The bright lights in the studio didn't exactly help and nor did the immediate barrage of questions as the dark cold, unblinking eyes of five, big Sony Super 21 studio cameras panned in unison and pointed in my direction. It was a horrendous experience. Goodness only knows what anyone viewing must have thought. Probably that they were watching a bloke who looks like he had just got out of bed with a face like a busted sofa and hair resembling an explosion in a mattress factory, rambling incoherently. They were right! Several years later I appeared on Sky News Breakfast, with my pal and fellow Northern Irishman, Eamonn Holmes. I was there to review the papers. That too didn't go well – far too early in the day to read the papers, never mind review them.

In the dressing room with Danni Minogue – 2008 – Fountain Studios, London.

I have no idea how I got through it or indeed how Eamonn did it every day.

My scarecrow appearance and startled demeanour on 'Daybreak' however, was knocked off the *'dazed and confused'* leader-board top spot some years later by a man called Guy Goma, who had been waiting in the reception of BBC TV Centre in west London for a job interview. The stage door reception at TV Centre was a busy, bustling space at the best of times but the chatter of excited voices that day was louder than usual. A cheery young, clipboard wielding researcher from BBC 'News-24' appeared and called out the name: "Guy Kewney," who was an internet expert and editor of the tech website 'News Wireless'. He was due to be interviewed live that day on the news channel about the relatively new phenomenon of music downloading. The hapless Guy Goma, our job applicant and a native French speaker misheard what the girl had said and assuming that she had called his name, raised his hand and unthinkingly followed her into the lift, which rapidly whisked them up to the 'News-24' studio. His cheery demeanour and rictus grin was maintained all the way, via make-up right to the hot seat on set. Except, it wasn't the interview hot seat that he was quite expecting. The bright lights and all the cameras in the studio that day swung in his direction. I know that feeling well. This was followed moments later by the first question from the news presenter asking for his views on the recent growth of online music distribution. The change in expression on his face, in that moment of realisation, was priceless and it's why the clip on You-Tube has become an internet sensation, with almost 1.7M views at the time of writing. History does not repeat what the real Guy Kewney must have thought as he watched the interview unfold with mounting horror, on the big Plasma TV screen pumping out 'News-24' while he waited in reception that day. The ersatz Mr Kewney, however, did a remarkable job of answering complex questions on technical issues without even a scintilla of knowledge in the subject. I hope he got the job he came for. I'd have employed him in a heartbeat. He is future BBC Director-General material in my opinion.

At the time of writing, 'The X Factor' has been on TV in the UK for an incredible fifteen years. It has just been announced that it is being rested. It has been singularly one of the most popular TV formats globally, in decades. What must be concerning for the TV planners, however, is that according to a 2017 study by Omnicom Media Group agency – 'Hearts & Science', almost half of adults between twenty-two to forty-five years old are watching absolutely no content whatsoever on traditional TV. This is an unthinkably terrifying doomsday scenario for both broadcasters and content makers alike. Their cheese is moving fast. If we follow the bell curve to the bottom and fast forward to a few years from now, we can all look forward to 'Celebrity Plane Crash' an exciting new, allegorical format where those lucky publicity seekers who survive the impact, get to live by eating the flesh of those who didn't. It has a beautiful Darwinian symmetry about it, don't you think? And the best bit is that by series seven, we will have expunged the entire planet of every single wannabe and talentless reality show undesirable and will be back to where we were in 1990 when only proper actors and stars were allowed on the tellybox. Hurrah!

Despite the rapid proliferation of talent-based TV entertainment shows at this time, in 2006 Granada Productions in Manchester and ITV productions, now headed up by Mark Wells, thought it would be a good idea to stage a new show called *Soapstar Superstar*. One can only surmise that the pitch to the bosses at ITV went something along the lines of: "Well, Ladies and Gentlemen, everyone loves a good Soap and everyone loves a good talent show, so why not combine them into one?"

Why not indeed? Well, for a start, it was a pretty rubbish idea that was never going to stand the test of time as it would be obvious, even to Jedward that before too long you would run out of Soap actors who could keep a tune in their head. And while I enjoyed shouting the names of Shobna Gulati and Hayley Tamaddon very much indeed, it was for a far more sinister and wholly shocking reason that the show was unceremoniously dropped from the ITV schedules a mere twelve months later. On 18th October 2007, after an in-depth investigation of all of ITV's 'vote by phone' shows by Deloitte, it was revealed that phone-in votes for songs and even votes for contestants to go through to the next round on *Soapstar Superstar* had been manipulated by the programme-makers. This involved some twenty percent of the viewers' votes for songs being ignored. As a result, ITV aired an OFCOM *'summary of findings'* announcement just before the final of the second series of 'Britain's Got Talent' on 31st May 2008. It was shown again on the 8th June 2008 before that night's episode of 'Coronation Street'. Granada Television was heavily fined for the breach. A thick veil was drawn across the shamed production and the show was unceremoniously dumped into a vault labelled 'Shows That Should Never Have Been Made' and the key was thrown into the by now familiar Trench, where it remains ten miles down to this day, rusting in the inky depths being curiously prodded by passing Lantern fish.

It was during the wrap party for the ill-fated series, in the rather unglamorous surroundings of the Granada Studios canteen, that I discussed with Mark Wells, then the controller of ITV Entertainment the imminent move of The Paul O'Grady Show from ITV to Channel 4. O'Grady had indicated that he wanted to leave ITV for Channel 4, following a dispute with Granada Television after Granada forgot to renew his contract, resulting in him not being paid on time. This was a grievance he had aired publicly on his show much to the chagrin of the executives at the channel. O'Grady also wanted to exercise more creative control over the show. His own television production company, Olga TV named after one of his dogs, subsequently took over the production and the programme began its run on Channel 4 in March 2006, in the same 5pm – 6pm early evening slot, alternating in this slot every three months or so with the eponymous 'Richard & Judy'. I had been the voice of Paul's show on ITV since 2004 and this imminent move to Channel 4 had not gone down well at ITV. I took it as a bit of light-hearted banter from a friend but in conversation with Mark Wells at the Granada canteen party that night over a convivial glass of warm Champagne, he told me that if I followed O'Grady to Channel 4, he would never speak to me again. Guess what? I did and he hasn't! The world of show business can be a savage and cruel mistress. It's not in my nature to knowingly upset people or to make enemies, so this sorry episode when I look back on it is a particularly sad one, as I valued Mark's long friendship very highly. I can only surmise that he must have placed professional loyalty before everything else. In my defence, my decision was purely a professional one. As a freelancer, you have to move with the cheese and this will inevitably, occasionally result in collateral damage.

My dampened spirits were soon lifted however when I took a call from my agent in August 2007, with the news that Sky TV was bringing back it's deliciously outré camp series; 'Cirque de Celebrité'. Now, as you will have gathered, I have very little time for celebrities or circuses but Sky TV was offering me the role of commentator on a weekly live show from a genuine real big top, situated on Greenwich Common, in London. I had seen the first series with Ruby Wax as ringmaster and had enjoyed its uber camp style and the genuine risk to the performers who were competing against each other, by demonstrating circus skills in the big top that they had only learned from the show's circus professionals in the preceding week! As you will have guessed, I know next to nothing about celebrities or circuses but during that phone call to my agent, I found myself responding with that by now all too familiar "yes" to the offer. When the call ended, I immediately began to wonder what the hell I had just done. But there's always that small voice in the back of my head that urges me on to do the daftest of things.

"Go on mate," it says. "Say yes, you know you want to. Go on! It'll be fun!"

But as fellow stateside voiceover, Joe Cipriano, once said to me:

"Staying in your comfort zone all your life will do you no good at all. It's over there, outside the circle of comfort where the magic happens."

Whether the magic he spoke about would happen in two months, once we were under canvas, only time would tell but for now I had some serious research to do. Celebrities? I scanned the cast list.

"Who in hell's name are these people?"

I needn't have bothered! As the production got underway, I soon realised that no one else knew who these 'celebrities' were either, nor indeed cared what the various high wire and trampoline moves were actually, technically called. So to liven things up a little, I decided to... yes, you've guessed it – make it all up as I went along. And so, six weeks later I was sitting in a makeshift hut for a voiceover booth outside the main big top. (It's outward appearance resembled the temporary migrant shacks you used to see next to the Eurostar railway line at Calais, built with carpet remnants and bits of old fabric and cardboard for a roof), with a Coles commentator microphone in one hand, and uttering complete bollocks phrases like:

"Ah yes! And there it is, the double vaulted and semi crested – Half Swan."

The audience at home was none the wiser of course, but the circus professionals who were the technical and safety advisors on the show thought it was hilarious and would pitch up each week outside my sad, makeshift booth, with a list of new faux, exotic-sounding names for the various circus disciplines. I was only dumbstruck once when an Australian swimsuit model called Emily Scott was on the Silks and happened to open her legs in a rotating mid-air split, just as one of the new high definition cameras had zoomed in on her graceful performance. You could practically see what the poor girl had eaten for breakfast!

Commentating on 'Cirque de Celebrité' – 2009 – Greenwich Park, London.

Ever since my time on the BBC Radio 1 Roadshow, I had held the rather romantic belief that maybe; just maybe life in the circus would be a good life. After 'Cirque de Celebrité', I will be happy if I never set foot in a big top ever again. It's a tough, demanding, uncomfortable existence that is both physically and mentally challenging and very nearly drove us all insane. One night, during the live broadcast, the area around Greenwich Park in London experienced one of the most violent thunderstorms of the year. It was so bad, that at one point as I was commentating I could feel my feet getting wet. I looked down and to my absolute horror, saw that my booth was quickly flooding. The cardboard roof, no match for the eight hundred litres of rainwater above it. Worse still, the floor beneath was crisscrossed by a variety of 24-Volt electricity and audio cables. Large droplets of rainwater were dripping onto my head and my script was getting soggy. Gingerly, while sprouting more bollocks about a 'Cantilevered Ostrich', I slowly lifted my feet off the floor, for fear of being fatally electrocuted, live on air. The *real* jeopardy wasn't in the big top. It was inside my Heath-Robinson commentary booth, which was about to explode, go on fire and be reduced to a pile of ash with me inside it. In the big top itself, a gaggle of twelve celebrities, I use the term somewhat loosely, were risking life and limb and what was left of their already questionable reputations, to entertain a dwindling, dumbfounded TV audience. The live audience in the big top had long since given up and were sheltering under umbrellas and raincoats, draped over their heads.

As the series progressed, I realised that while all safety considerations and precautions had been taken into account, there was a real risk that any one of these celebs could at some point fall, and badly injure themselves or at worst die, live on television. As the commentator, it would be up to me to cover the unfortunate incident as best I could. I have always been very keen on thorough preparation; there is no substitute for it. So, in the period between the first and second shows, I created a 'serious incident' script for myself and pinned it to the wall in front of me. In the event of something disastrous happening, I could easily tear it down and read from it, while all hell broke loose all around me. I colour coded them for ease of use. Pink for a fall from a height, red for a burning, blue for drowning and white for loss of reputation! As you can imagine, altogether there were more white scripts than pink, red or blue combined! When something goes wrong on TV, it can often quickly go very badly wrong. A combination of shock and adrenaline surging through your system, as something unexpected occurs, plays havoc with your breathing as your body initiates its primaeval fight or flight response. With a pre-prepared script and a series of 'what if' scenarios thought out and prepared for, however, when the unthinkable does happen, you are at least prepared and stand a more than fair chance of emerging from it with your own professional reputation intact. What is it that the army say? 'Train hard, fight easy'. It's as true in the trenches as it is on TV. Preparation is key. It was a valuable lesson, absorbed in my early BBC training and never forgotten.

One of the other professional considerations of working as a voice artist or commentator on live television is that you need to maintain good vocal health. You do this by ensuring that you are suitably warmed up and well hydrated at all times. Drinking plain old water is best but just occasionally I succumb to a cheeky can of diet soda. But as we all know, what goes in must come out and so before any big live TV show, there is always a last-minute stampede to the loo backstage for all performers, and production crew in the minutes before transmission. Unfortunately, because of an alteration to the running order on a particular Cirque show one evening, I was locked in my booth, hastily taking notes over the talkback from the director, the affable Stuart McDonald, who used to direct 'Parkinson'. Consequently, I had to forgo the customary last-minute pre-transmission comfort trip to the on-site loos. The show duly got underway. I introduced our presenter, the lovely Jenny Falconer who in turn introduced the first act – the impossible to pronounce real-life Princess Tamara Czartoryski-Borbon – who was first up, wearing a white silk bodice and taffeta tutu, juggling flaming skittles while simultaneously balancing on top of an over-sized neon coloured beach ball. You couldn't make this stuff up!

As the showground slowly and inexorably towards the first commercial break with me talking bollocks and my bladder extending almost to my actual bollocks, in desperation I considered simply letting nature take its course where I sat. It was drizzling outside and I thought I might just get away with it and the extra-unexpected warmth would be welcome. But then in a flash of inspiration, I spotted the empty soda can on the desk. Gingerly, and you will be pleased to hear unseen by anyone, I happily relieved myself with not inconsiderable difficulty. Not only was I pleased with my inventiveness but by the fact that my predicament had come to an end. All in all, a neat solution to a very pressing problem, except the problem hadn't entirely gone away. It was still sitting on the desk in front of me! So, during the commercial break, I had the bright idea of casually taking the can of 'soda' to the loo and discretely disposing of its contents there. Imagine if you will, my surprise when on my way to the backstage toilets, I encountered our glamorous hostess, Miss Jenny Falconer who popped out of a side door in the tent, just in front of me, to get a breath of fresh night air.

"Ah, Peter," she said airily. "How's it going?"

"Oh not too bad," I replied. Trying to sound nonchalant but with a mild sense of panic setting in.

"It's bloody boiling in there under those lights," she said.

She eased her feet out of her size eight Jimmy Choos and sighed, the way all women do when their feet come back to earth after a few hours in stillies.

"Here, give us a swig of your coke!" she said. "I'm bloody parched."

I don't think she saw the look of terror on my face as she reached for the familiar red and white can in my hand. I could still feel the warmth of its contents through the thin aluminium skin. I rapidly withdrew my hand so that the can was just out of her reach. She looked at me quizzically.

"Err… No!" I exclaimed. "It's… err… it's off." I said lamely.

Her face screwed up. "What do you mean it's off you daft bugger? Since when has a can of coke ever been off? C'mere, I only want a swig, I'm gasping!"

She lunged once more at the can with her perfectly manicured hand. A slight parry to the left was enough to keep her from making the unthinkable contact. She must have thought I was mad.

"Listen, it tastes rotten. I'm about to chuck it out. Gotta rush. See you at the next break."

And with that, I turned on my heels and ran, stumbling blindly through the mud, elephant droppings and sawdust – swerving wildly to avoid going arse over tit on the big top guide ropes and a couple of unicycles which had been carelessly tossed against them by one of the clowns. Eventually, I reached a pair of back-to-back portaloos, which had been thoughtfully provided by the production company. Once inside, I located a free cubicle, locked the door and with heart thumping and breathing heavily, disposed of, with some relief, the entire 330mls of its amber steaming contents down the loo in one swift, waterfall-like, ear-shattering movement. I flushed, counted to three and immediately stepped outside to see 'Cirque de Celebrité' judge, the flamboyant Louis Spence, wearing a cerise satin blouse and pink, rhinestone-studded trousers at the washbasins looking at me, open-mouthed, in the mirror. After the deluge he had evidently just heard and judging by the expression on his face, he was clearly thinking that one of the circus elephants was in there. Now, seeing me emerging from the cubicle, and judging by the startled expression on his face, I imagine he was simply thinking that I must be hung like a ruddy elephant! Without a word, or stopping to wash my own hands I hurriedly made my way back to my commentary box. Skirting around the outside of the big top, head down I once again hopped over the pesky guide ropes, swerved past the unicycles – there to trap the unwary. Carefully avoiding the various piles of mammalian excrement, I hoped that the elegant Miss Falconer was now safely back inside having her makeup retouched with an alternative form of refreshment in hand – one that wouldn't have almost certainly caused her to retch and gag and quite possibly upchuck her recently consumed lasagne all over her exquisite, couture diamante ball gown.

Despite all the spicy incidents and the utter discomfort of it all, looking back on it, my time on 'Cirque de Celebrité' was in truth a real career highlight. Few jobs provide the sheer variety of experiences that being a voiceover does. I had hugely enjoyed the challenge of improvising my commentary and making it all up as I went along. A skill that would stand me in good stead for a once in a lifetime job that was waiting for me in a few years to come. I will never forget the close bond that developed among the cast and crew but the looming, foreboding presence of the tent and the smell of sawdust and wet canvas, has put me off circuses for life. If I never see another bloody big top again, it will be too soon.

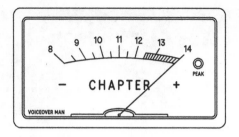

YOU AND YOUR FAMILY
MUST TAKE COVER

I n early spring 2006, my agent took an enquiry from Neil Gorringe, the creative director at Channel 4's presentation and promo department, asking me to audition for the role of promo voice for Channel 4's youth channel, E4. This role had been filled until recently by one of the UK's greatest voice actors, Patrick Allen. Sadly Patrick, who I knew and liked and had worked with many times, had fallen ill and was no longer able to work. His distinctive, rich voice was hugely familiar to millions of people across the United Kingdom, even amongst those who would never have recognised him as an actor. In the 1970s he had narrated the British Government's 'Protect and Survive' series of public information films. These chilling films, produced at the height of the Cold War, were designed to instruct the average person on what they should do, should this country ever be unfortunate enough come under a nuclear attack. "Put your head between your legs and kiss your arse goodbye," would have sufficed but these messages were supposed to inform and educate and above all provide a degree of comfort. Their dark, doomsday-laden content, however, married with Patrick's portentous vocal delivery, would have served to simply scare the crap out of the population at large causing them to panic, run outside,

Goofing around with Boy George backstage – 2010 – 'Isle of Man Festival'.

PETER DICKSON

stare blindly up and down the street and then freeze to the spot like helpless rabbits caught in the nuclear headlights, with tears of confusion running down their blubbing ashen cheeks. Had the unthinkable happened and nuclear Armageddon occurred, a subsequent search for survivors would have unearthed whole communities across Britain, whose faces would have been contorted in fear, Pompeii-style. Not from the explosion, that would have been too rapid and seismic an event to react to, but from the sheer cold drama and total bowel moving nature of Patrick's voice, heard on the wireless, seconds before impact.

When I was a young BBC radio announcer, I was shown a large reel of quarter-inch tape that was kept under lock and key in a box in the BBC Duty Manager's safe, just off the engineering control room at Broadcasting House in London. That reel of tape, on the instruction and correct codes being relayed from the Prime Minister or duty Government minister of the day, via an actual red telephone, was without delay to be removed from the safe and put onto a tape machine in one of the continuity suites and immediately played out nationally on all 4 BBC Radio networks. Thankfully, it never happened but in the '70s and '80s at the height of the Cold War, it occasionally felt as though it was never that remote a possibility. Those were dark times indeed. Some of Patrick's lines from that 'nuclear warning' production were re-recorded and sampled into the record 'Two Tribes' by the band Frankie Goes to Hollywood.

The most chilling phrase was:

"This country is under nuclear attack. You and your family must take cover."

Where exactly? Under the kitchen table? In the garage? On top of the wardrobe? Next door, at number 13? I think not! My own carefully considered plan was to pour myself a generous tumbler of Bushmills whiskey and Mrs Dickson a nice glass of suitably chilled Champagne, place a couple of deck chairs in the middle of the garden and sit down to enjoy the show. It's not every day you get to witness a nuclear holocaust – so you might as well try to enjoy it.

Anyway, Patrick had enjoyed this perfectly glittering, flawless career and in the twilight of his years, had been discovered by a whole new audience of young people as the voice of youth Channel – E4. His authoritative, very familiar and avuncular style of delivery allowed him to read the most outrageously risqué scripts that the Channel 4 promo writers could concoct, and somehow get away with it. Coming from anyone else, much of the stuff they were producing would have drawn heavy complaints from middle England but because it was Patrick saying it, well it must be OK because he sounded like one of them! Many of the lines they wrote for him have now passed into legend. My personal favourite being:

"Sit back and relax and allow us to pump oodles of thick, creamy audio loveliness – into your delicate earholes."

With Patrick now ill, the channel was desperately casting around for a replacement. My agent had put me up for it and so with a bunch of other voiceover artists, I took my place in line at a studio called Jungle, in London's Soho. When it came to my turn, I read the lines as best I could and when I had finished, I looked up to see the engineer and Neil looking through the glass at me open-mouthed. Eventually, the talkback flicked into life.

"Blimey. I think we have it." Said Neil.

"So, I've got the job then?" I said.

"Not quite." Came the reply. "We need to run it past Patrick first. We'll let you know."

It was a measure of the high regard in which they held Patrick that they wanted to consult with him on the question of who would replace him. I can't recall anything like that happening before or since. And so, before too long an enduring relationship with the E4 channel began almost fourteen years at the time of writing. We were all hopeful at the time that Patrick would return, and things would get back to normal. He was in his late seventies at this point, but voice acting is one of those careers that has no retirement age. It's a career in which you can keep going as long as the flesh is willing.

Sadly, for all of us, on the 28th July 2006 word reached me that Patrick had died. It was quite a blow because he was someone I had admired and respected for some time and I was grateful for the times we had spent working together. I had learned much from him. They don't make them like him anymore. His subsequent obituary, in the Guardian newspaper, recognised that he had not one but two careers when they observed:

"He always maintained that he was first and foremost an actor – for television and films, as well as for the Royal Shakespeare Company and the West End – Patrick Allen, who has died aged seventy-nine, spent the second half of his career primarily as the self-styled "grandfather of the voiceover" for TV commercials. This led him to the more profitable role of business-man, as part-owner of a Soho studio specialising in production services in that field."

He had starred on the stage at Stratford and in the West End of London and appeared in Alfred Hitchcock's 'Dial M for Murder', yet it is his for his commercial voiceover and broadcast promotion work that he will be best remembered and I hasten to say, greatly missed. They say we all stand on the shoulders of giants. Patrick Allen was one of the biggest of them all and the view that he afforded his many disciples from the lofty peak that was his rightful home was simply stunning. I was pleased and indeed honoured to have followed in his footsteps, not only by giving a new voice to the E4 channel's brand identity but to also make over a dozen short films, pro-moting the channel, in vision. My favourites being 'The E4 Party Political Broadcast', 'E4 Airways', 'The E4 Bunker' and one in which I played both HM Queen and Prince Phillip! ITV and Talkback made a short comedy film called 'The X Factor – The Voice Session' – a fictitious look behind the scenes at 'The X Factor'. The BBC got in on the action too, by writing and producing a short film with me entitled 'The X Husband', which features me at home in my dressing gown. They've all had thousands of views. You can see all of these and more on YouTube when you get bored!

Vernon Kay was a little-known TV presenter in 2005. He had hosted the odd show for ITV and Channel 4 here and there but in 2006, ITV handed him the host role on a new series of 'All Star Family Fortunes', a twist on the original format, where the guests were two celebrities accompanied by their respective families. Whether it was because I had been the voice of the show in its past incarnation or whether they couldn't be bothered looking for anyone else, I will never know but the job of being the voice of this new series came to me. I was delighted of course. Not just because I got the gig, but also because I could now voice it all from my home studio. The advance of digital recording technology now meant that I no longer had to travel to some far-flung studio and perform live. In this new series, my voiceover sec-tions would be added to the show in post-production, after the filming had taken place. Bingo! No more travelling, no more long days in a hot studio and no more inedible canteen food and no more dodgy hotel suite cheese incidents either!

This new way of working was such a radical sea change, not just for me but all voice actors. It was revolutionary. Between 2005 and 2015, the voice elements that made up each episode of 'Family Fortunes' were recorded in this way. The producers simply sent me the script by email, and I recorded it and sent it back. When these shows were on air, I am convinced that people thought I was working really long hours, when in reality an entire series only took me a couple of hours to complete! I didn't realise it at the time, but my exposure on 'The X Factor', 'E4', 'Soapstar Superstar', 'All Star Family Fortunes' and repeats of 'The Price is Right' on Challenge TV meant that I was now heard on TV more or less constantly, 24/7.

They say success breeds success. It's true. In 2007 my agent was getting all kinds of offers for me to participate in many different projects and shows. One of the weirdest projects that I agreed to join that year was a new show being made for the BBC, called 'HEDZ'. This was an odd, quirky, satirical show made by BBC Scotland for CBBC, the corporation's channel for children. The show was sketch-based and featured actors, who wore one-dimensional masks of the celebrities they were playing. The crude masks were strapped around their heads with string. I joined a cast of other voice actors whose job it was to provide the many voices. As the show was made in Scotland, the post-production was to be done in Glasgow. And so, in early summer in 2007, off I trundled to that fair city. With fellow actors, Kate O'Sullivan, Tim Dann, Rupert Degas and others, we set about bringing this new show to life. The producer of this pleasing bag of balderdash was a jovial man by the name of Nick Hopkin. We were recording the vocals in a turn of the century (that's 19th – not 20th Century) building, near the Gorbals on the South Bank of the Clyde, smack bang in the centre of Glasgow. I use the word 'smack' advisedly. Each morning as I arrived for work, I had to perform a little dance on my way up the street, to avoid inadvertently impaling my foot on a beach of carelessly discarded syringes. The building in which the studio was located had been the headquarters of the Scottish Co-operative Society and was one of those grand, Victorian red sandstone edifices, of the type which were built in huge numbers in the big industrial cities of the UK during the industrial revolution, when Britain truly was 'great'. Someone I'm sure will be along any minute to make it 'great' again. The studio was on the top floor and because it was in this ancient building, it didn't have the benefit of air conditioning. It was high summer in Glasgow, and temperatures were soaring outside, but not as much as they were inside the hell-hole-oven of a booth we were expected to work in. With three actors at a time in there and oxygen running out, the temperature frequently reached 35°C. We had to stop every five minutes and open to doors to allow some cooler air in and dry ourselves off with towels!

One evening after work, the others decided to go back to the hotel, but I was keen to see what culinary delights Glasgow had to offer. I sought advice from Nick, the producer on the nicer eateries in town, and the consensus was that a wee place called 'The Ubiquitous Chip' was worth a visit. So, I jumped into a cab, driven by the most disgruntled cabby I have ever encountered and headed off in search of it. The evening was still warm. People were spilling out from bars into the streets and on arrival at the restaurant; I was shown to a lovely table tucked into the corner, under a tree that bizarrely appeared to be growing through the restaurant's roof! The food indeed was delicious and afterwards, as I greedily tucked into a finger or two of a rare 1972 Invergordon single malt whisky, I became aware of a kerfuffle in the opposite corner of the restaurant. Someone of obvious importance had arrived. Waiters and managers were scurrying around, rearranging chairs and putting tables together. As the dust and tablecloths settled, I recognised, first the voice and then the unmistakable appearance of his ample girth and balding pate which was glinting in the gloom by the light of the candles on the table. It was none other than the nascent First Minister of the Scottish Parliament, Alex Salmond – accompanied by a raft of clucking party sycophants who were cooing over his every word. Under Salmond, the SNP had been pursuing their bonkers and deeply controversial ambition of securing the independence of Scotland from the Union, something I found utterly abhorrent. With the expensive whisky weaving its magic inside my head or 'heed' and it's known in these parts, I paid my bill and got up to leave. I don't know what came over me but as I swayed past his table and caught sight of his smug face in the antique mirror opposite, I reached out and gently rubbed the top of his head. He immediately spun around. The conversation at the table abruptly stopped and before I knew it, I said in a loud, calm very Scottish voice so everyone could hear:

"Keep yer filthy wee hands aff the Union, Son!"

And with that, I turned on my heels and left the scene, accompanied by the solitary sound of my footsteps on the stone flag floor, as the entire restaurant had now fallen silent. As I reached the exit, someone popped a bottle of Champagne and shouted 'Wanker!' This was immediately followed by some half-hearted booing and a polite round of applause. I had divided the audience and provided an unwelcome topic for heated after-dinner debate. Well, in the cab I laughed all the way back to the hotel and on getting to my room, immediately called my pal and fellow Scottish voice actor Lewis McLeod to tell him what I had done. He was cackling like a Hyena down the phone as I recounted the tale. He and has since repeated this story to everyone he knows in Scotland.

I am now very relieved that Salmond didn't get his way in the 2014 Scottish referendum because if he had, I would most certainly have had my passport marked, been turned back at the border on subsequent visits to Alba and made to walk the entire length of Hadrian's Wall, naked and quite possibly blindfolded while members of the Scottish National Party beat me with horny hiking staves and plumeless thistles.

With Nigel Heath at an ADR session for 'Ashes to Ashes' – 2011 – Hackenbacker, London.

PETER DICKSON

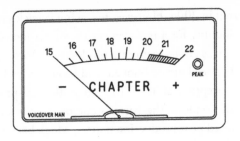

HE'S AT THE DOCTOR'S
GETTING A CHECK-UP
FROM THE NECK-UP

I n the year 2007, Harry Potter closed a billion-dollar chapter in publishing history. It was also the year that Apple unveiled the iPhone and it was the year that my career in television voiceover took off – big time.

Sitting in his study in his home in Islington, London in early January that year was a man called Addison Cresswell. Addison was, without doubt, one of the most influential people in British comedy and arguably the most powerful man in British entertainment for over forty years. As a talent manager, his client list included Sean Lock, Jonathan Ross, Lee Evans, Michael McIntyre, Alan Carr, Kevin Bridges and Rich Hall. Live comedy was the new rock 'n' roll. The TV perched on top of a bookcase across from his desk that night was tuned to E4, the youth and comedy channel, run by Britain's fourth TV network, Channel 4. He was keen to watch a brand new, hard-hitting series that was about to launch, called 'Skins'. Following the obligatory ad break and before the show began, E4 ran a promo for Dawson's Creek, featuring my voice. Addison looked up from his desk and made a note to himself to find out who I was. His BBC1 show: 'Live at the Apollo', which showcased many of his comedy acts had been introduced by Patrick

Allen since it started in 2004. However, following Patrick's untimely demise in 2006, he was looking for a replacement to voice a new series of 'Live at the Apollo,' which was about to go into production. Within days, my agent had received a call, a session was booked, and I found myself waiting for the great man in the reception of The Farm, an audio post-production facility on Soho Square in London. The Farm is one of the city's better and more luxuriously appointed post-production houses, which back then was located in a lovely fifth-floor Georgian townhouse. It was after lunchtime and I had just enjoyed a sandwich and a cup of coffee in a café close by. Outside, the coats of passers-by were being whipped and jinked around by a cold northerly wind that was blowing around the square. Fifteen minutes after the session was due to have started, the receptionist looked up from her desk and apologised for the delay. No sooner had she done this, than the door to the street, opposite the reception desk slammed open and in walked a man who was evidently in a hurry. It was Addison. On seeing me, he darted over, weaving around the glass coffee table on which was a bowl of fruit and copies of industry magazines and excitedly grabbed my hand and gave it an overly enthusiastic shake.

"Pete! Great to meet you! Amazing of you to do this! I have the script here!"

Whereupon, he produced from the pocket of his dark blue cashmere covet coat, a scrap of crumpled paper on which he had scribbled some names, in pencil. I also couldn't help but notice that his eyes were as wide as saucers and his cheeks were more than a little flushed. He continued to talk at me for a good five or six minutes, barely pausing to draw breath. It was like being hit by a forty-ton truck! Addison, I subsequently discovered, liked a good lunch. His regular table awaited him every day at the Club at the Ivy, on West Street in Covent Garden where he entertained clients, channel controllers and other showbiz grandees, surrounded by captains of entertainment and publishing, who lunched like gourmets and drank like fish. Lucrative deals were sealed by these grand fromages, in blood-red leather chairs at pristine white linen tables, surrounded by priceless artwork by Hirst and Emin, illuminated by the iconic, red, blue and green lead latticed, stained glass windows for which the club and its sister restaurant are famous.

For the next six years, this pantomime of a recording session for 'Live at the Apollo' was repeated and each time Addison was just as amusing and animated as the last. I loved working with him. In late December 2013, as the preparations for Christmas that year were well underway, I was preparing to go to Ireland to join the family for the festivities. As I sat down to write another batch of Christmas cards, I was looking forward to seeing him again in January for our next recording session. It was not to be. The day before Christmas Eve, I took a call from his PA who informed me that Addison had died the previous evening, at home. It was such a huge shock. He was only fifty-three. I still miss him to this day, as do countless others who owe their considerably successful careers to him and his genius. His talented team at 'Open Mike Productions', the TV production arm of his company, 'Off the Kerb', have been very loyal and supportive of me since. I have now completed thirteen years as the voice of the biggest stand-up comedy show on primetime British TV, though I now work with the equally nice but much calmer producer Anthony Caveney.

The year 2007 also saw the return to ITV of many of the old TV game shows of the past, all wrapped up into a whole week of shows entitled 'Gameshow Marathon'. The series first aired in 2005 with Ant and Dec at the helm. 'Ant and Dec's Gameshow Marathon' was such a success, ITV wanted to bring it back. But the pair were otherwise engaged that year with a much bigger project. There'll be more on that, later. The 2007 series was in equally good hands though with my good pal Vernon Kay as the host. Viewers were treated to a whole week of game-show classics such as 'The Price is Right', 'Blockbusters', 'Blankety Blank', 'Name That Tune', 'Mr and Mrs', 'Bullseye', 'Play Your Cards Right' and my favourite from my childhood; 'The Golden Shot'. While I had been the voice for years on 'The Price is Right', the opportunity for me to voice so many of these great TV classics, was a dream come true. The format has since been sold to many countries around the world.

My career, I sensed, was now really starting to take off. Life was good both personally and professionally and I was enjoying what you might call a purple patch, where my services were very much in demand. But how long would it last? That was the question no freelancer dare ask. On my way back home from a recording session in town in May that year, I stopped off at a bookstore on the Charing Cross Road. My eye had been drawn by a book, which I had seen displayed in the window. The title of the book was 'Yes Man', written the year before by an acquaintance of mine called Danny

Wallace. The book is a memoir based on a year in Danny's life, in which he chose to say, "yes" to any offers or invitations that came his way. The book has since been adapted into a movie starring Jim Carrey. For me, the book was an absolute revelation. Saying, "yes" to absolutely everything could get you into the most terrible trouble and impossibly deep water for sure, but it could also equally manifest into your life the most wonderful things. I decided to try it for myself. Now, I am not kidding here when I tell you what happened next. Within twenty-four hours of me making this decision, I took a call from a guy called Hugh Edwards. Hugh is a video games director and had called me directly on the recommendation of an audio drama specialist friend of his called Neil Gardner. Hugh's proposal was for me to narrate a film he had produced with Tony Jopia, the Creative Director in Western Europe of Sony Pictures Entertainment. I felt an instant frisson of excitement. Imagine my disappointment when I learned that there was no budget and that I would be working for... wait for it... no fee. Now, as a professional voice actor, this is contrary to the promise and standards I set for myself when I started out many years ago. I never work without compensation, unless it is for one of the charities I support or for a friend in

With Marcus Bentley on a commercial shoot for 'The Sun'
2014 – Elstree Studios, London.

need. However, I had embarked on the Danny Wallace 'Yes Man' crusade and here was an opportunity that had presented itself to me, as a test of my resolve. As you have probably guessed by now, I said yes! A week later I drove to Hugh's studio near Banbury in Oxfordshire. I say studio, it was a make-shift recording space set up in his Mum's garage! I did the voiceover, and all went well. I didn't so much as do that job for nothing. It actually cost me to do it, as I had to fill the car up with a tank of petrol to get there. This 'Yes Man' malarkey was turning out to be a costly exercise!

They say the universe loves balance and a thing called karma, we are led to believe, takes care of this. I used to be a bit sceptical of this philosophy, but the older I get, the more inclined I am to believe it to be true. A month after that garage recording, my agent called to say that National Geographic would like me to voice a new computer game for them. The director? Yes, you've guessed it – Mr Hugh Edwards. This time though, a very respectable fee was on the table. The National Geographic session passed without incident and was unremarkable, except for the conversation I had with Hugh as we wrapped up. He had told his girlfriend that he was going to be working with me that day and she had asked him if he could get me to record a bespoke voicemail message for her, in the vocal style I use for 'The X Factor'. On the way to the studio, he got thinking. If she wanted a voicemail message, then there must be others who would like the same. And so, was born our very first business venture together. An Internet enterprise called, 'MyRuddyVoice.com'. We designed and built a platform where anyone could download a bespoke voicemail message onto a mobile phone. It was pretty cool and at the time – unique. The user simply chose their name from a 5,000-name dropdown list and then chose the message it was to be inserted into, there were hundreds of them, ranging from simple ringtones to voicemail messages to birthday and anniversary wishes. For a payment of around £5.99, the message was delivered by email within ten seconds. It was one of the very first public text to speech apps and at the time was quite revolutionary. The most popular one was "[Insert Name] can't get to the phone at the moment so, IT'S TIME... TO LEAVE... A MESSAGE," closely followed by "[Insert Name] Can't take your call as he's at the doctor's getting a CHECK-UP FROM THE NECK-UP." Hugh's background in manipulating spoken audio for video games meant that he had acquired the skill sets to enable him to build such a complex platform, one that could concatenate names and sentences together seamlessly to such a degree, that it sounded bespoke. You simply could not hear the edit points. Neither of us got massively rich off the back of it but we learned a lot about marketing and running a business and the capital we did raise, allowed us to launch our next venture together, a labour of love which was destined to grow into something much bigger and meaningful.

The phone call woke me from an afternoon nap in my studio. I don't usually take naps in the day, but I had had a particularly poor night's sleep, coupled with an immensely dull corporate script I was recording. As I peeled my face off the Auralex foam wall in my booth and placed the receiver to my ear, I heard my agent say:

"Peter, I have some good news!"

"Oh good," I thought.

My agent's voice always produced the same Pavlovian response. It invariably signalled the possibility of the potential next big thing. More often than not it was a routine booking but judging by the tone of her voice, this one sounded much more promising. One of Simon Cowell's producers had been on the blower from the Syco offices across town in the Barker Building, in the heart of affluent Kensington. Off the back of his hugely successful global franchise 'The X Factor', they now had the bit between their teeth and had developed a brand-new format which he had sold to ITV. I didn't know it then, of course, you never do, but this was a format that would go on to become *the* most successful and lucrative TV entertainment vehicle, the world had ever seen. It subsequently became clear that the reason that Ant and Dec couldn't do 'Gameshow Marathon' was that Cowell had just confirmed them as hosts on this new ITV/Fremantle/Syco show – that would become known in this country as – 'Britain's Got Talent'. The TV talent show genre is as old as the medium itself and is as simple as it gets. Cowell's genius, however, was to develop a unique talent show format for the modern age. Find the best, undiscovered entertainers in whichever country the show airs, and give them a huge, glittering showcase to compete in. Currently, there are almost sixty countries across the globe whose national broadcasters air the show. It's a TV entertainment phenomenon and one that was rightly recognised by Guinness World Records, as the world's most successful reality TV format. It has spawned and spun off countless stars. The initial audition for singing sensation and former mobile phone salesman

Paul Potts, who won the first season in the UK, has had over 121 million views on YouTube and his incredible story was made into a major motion picture called 'One Chance'.

As with 'Family Fortunes' and 'The X Factor', my physical presence in the studio for 'Britain's Got Talent' was not required. So, during the show's run, I would record and supply my voiceover packages from the purpose-built recording studio in the grounds of my home in Buckinghamshire. It's odd being on the cast of such a huge ratings hit, yet at the same time feeling slightly disconnected from it. So, every now and then, I would get into my car and head over to Fountain Studios in Wembley, where the show was made. I knew the studios well, as it's also where 'The X Factor' is made. My first stop was always the sound gallery where I would see my old pals, senior sound supervisor Robert Edwards and his trusty assistant Jane Scutt. Robert and Jane were responsible for me landing the voice work on 'The X Factor' and 'Britain's Got Talent'. It was their recommendation to the producers that sealed it, following the time we worked together on BBC's 'Test the Nation'. I would also stick my head around the door of the main production gallery and say hello, then head to the production office to shoot the breeze with whoever was there. Following that, it was into the studio to see the crew and watch the rehearsals for that evening's show.

It was in 2008, that I saw Susan Boyle sing live, for the very first time, it was a spellbinding performance. Boyle applied to audition for the third series of 'Britain's Got Talent' (as contestant number 43212) and was accepted after a preliminary audition in Glasgow. At her first appearance at the city's Clyde Auditorium, she said that she aspired to become a professional singer as successful as Elaine Paige. Everyone laughed politely. She should have taken heed of the wise words of the American philosopher, Ralph Waldo Emerson who once said: *"Beware what you set your heart upon. For it shall surely be yours."* As Boyle sang: 'I Dreamed a Dream' from 'Les Misérables', in the first round that night, she was watched by over ten million viewers. Immediately following her performance, the judge Amanda Holden referred to the theatre audience's initially cynical attitude on seeing Boyle shuffle onto the stage, by saying that we had all just had the subsequent: "biggest wake-up call ever." Overnight, ITV released the clip of her audition on YouTube and within seventy-two hours it had been viewed 2.5 million times. Within a week, 67 million people had watched it. On day nine, YouTube and other sites had clocked up over 104 million views. By the year's end, the clip was named as the most-watched clip of the year in the world, with over 120 million viewings. She was feted and courted by the world's media, from Brazil to Australia and from Japan to the United States of America. Although she was not eligible for the 2010 Grammy awards, host Stephen Colbert that year, paid tribute to her, telling a worldwide television audience that: "this year, the music industry was saved by a forty-eight-year-old Scottish woman in sensible shoes."

In her first year as a recording artist, Boyle, it is alleged, made £5 million. I am pleased to report that after a few initial wobbles, fame and fortune did not ultimately destroy her. Conservative estimates of her net wealth are in the region of £50 million. She is clearly having the last laugh. She still lives we are told, in an unremarkable, small family-sized home in Scotland – a modest four-bedroom ex-council house she purchased with her earnings in 2010. Although, to be fair she has probably had the bathroom and the kitchen re-modelled in marble and gold leaf.

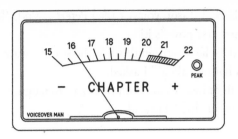

PAUL MCCARTNEY IS ON BOARD

├────────────────────┤

P eter Kay is a comedian I have never tired of watching. I have admired him for years. I like him for numerous reasons. Firstly, his comedy is rooted in the minutiae of everyday life. He can make a trip to the supermarket to do what he calls his 'big shop', sound funny. Millions of us agree. His 2010 UK stand up tour was officially inaugurated into the Guinness World Records Hall of Fame, as the most successful comedy tour of all time, playing to over 1.2 million people. The other reason I admire him is that he has stayed true to his roots and still lives in Bolton in the North West of England with his wife Susan and their children. Not for him the ersatz glitz and glamour of a showbiz lifestyle. More than this, however, it is precisely his ordinariness that is his real strength. He fiercely guards his privacy, rarely gives interviews and takes extended periods away from the limelight. We never tire of seeing him and consequently his longevity as an entertainer is assured, precisely because he is, like gold, that rarest of commodities.

He is also, I have since discovered, a huge fan of 'The X Factor' and the new 'Britain's Got Talent'. He told me this much, during a phone call in early February 2008.

"So, what's the real reason you've called Peter?" I said. "It's not to simply blow smoke up my arse now, is it?"

"No." He said. "I have written this TV show and I want you to be in it."

"Oh yeah. What's it called?" I asked.

There was a slight hesitation. Then he began to laugh.

"Are you ready for this?" He said.

"Yeah."

"It's called: Peter Kay's Britain's Got The Pop Factor... And Possibly a New Celebrity Jesus Christ Superstar, Strictly on Ice!"

There was dead silence. Then we both burst out laughing.

When I had regained my composure, I asked perhaps the most redundant question ever.

"So... err... what's it about?"

More laughter.

"Look, can you at least send me the script or a synopsis?" I pleaded.

"No. I can't I'm afraid. But, why don't you come to Manchester next week and we can discuss, and I can show you more? Then if you like what you see, we can record on the same day. How does that sound?"

"Deal," I said.

And so, the following week we duly met at a recording studio in the centre of Manchester. It remains one of the most sublimely funny afternoons of my professional career. I don't think either of us could have laughed any more than we did that day. The show, it turned out, was a very tongue in cheek parody of the burgeoning trend for reality talent shows on TV. The show with the impossibly long title, charted the journey – it's always a journey isn't it? – of fictional solo artist, Geraldine McQueen – played by Peter Kay. My role was, yes, you've guessed it, to give the show an authentic feel by providing the voiceover for the broadcast show sequences. I have to say that although I was flattered to be invited onto the cast of the show, I had deep reservations. Peter essentially wanted me to parody myself on a show for Channel 4, which was effectively taking a swipe at the two biggest reality shows on ITV. Alarm bells were ringing and something inside me was telling me that I might just possibly be writing my own death warrant. However, I have always taken the view that it is always better to ask for forgiveness than permission so, during a break, while we were waiting for yet another cup of tea, I disappeared to the loo to have a moment to think. A minute or two later, Peter followed, and we met in the corridor.

"Look, Peter," I said. "I am of course greatly flattered that you have asked me, but I do of course have reservations, for all the obvious reasons."

"Of course." He said. "I completely understand but honestly, you are the only man for the job."

"If I ask Cowell, he'll only say no, so I am tempted to agree to do it with one proviso."

"Oh? What's that?" He said.

'Well, I will record today if you can give me your assurance that this project will be a parody that is kind, warm and considered, not a hatchet job."

"You have my assurance." He said. "Paul McCartney is on board and so is Rustie Lee." He gave me one of his trademark winks. I was in. Who in their right mind wouldn't want to be on the same bill as Rustie Lee?

Back in the studio, the afternoon tea trolley had arrived, complete with an old fashioned, triple-tiered cake stand on which were the most amazing fondant fancies, fairy cakes, and Battenberg slices. Lashings of steaming, strong Lancashire tea were poured into large mugs to celebrate. We were on a roll. I headed to the booth and for the next hour shouted, "This is Peter Kay's Britain's Got The Pop Factor... And Possibly a New Celebrity Jesus Christ Superstar Strictly on Ice," until my eyeballs were bleeding like a ruddy Bond villain! When it was all over and I was about to leave, I reached into my pocket for my mobile phone to call a cab to take me back to Manchester Piccadilly station.

"What do you think you're doing?" He cried. "Don't be so daft. Come on, I'll give you a lift."

Outside, I jumped into the passenger seat of his Mercedes and we set off for the station, through the rain-soaked Manchester rush hour traffic. I thanked him for what had been a hugely daft day. Before I got out, he reiterated his promise to me that the show would be a good-hearted parody and that I wasn't to worry. I hoped he was right.

Harry Hill, who is another of my favourite comedians, had been in touch. My people were in conversation with his people, as they say in showbiz. His long-running hit, 'TV Burp' had been airing on ITV on Saturday night primetime since 2001. Inspired by hearing my work on 'The X Factor', 'Britain's Got Talent' and now; 'Peter Kay's Britain's Got The Pop Factor...

And Possibly a New Celebrity Jesus Christ Superstar Strictly on Ice', Harry wanted my voice on a comedy sequence for 'TV Burp'. Brittany Spears had been in the news that week. Reports, in some of the tabloid newspapers, claimed that she had been behaving oddly. No one should have been surprised. Coupled with the pressures of success, money and fame, she had recently given birth to her second child, filed for divorce from her husband, Kevin Federline and was mourning the death, from ovarian cancer, of her aunt with whom she had been very close. Then in February, she visited a drug rehab facility in Antigua, staying for one night. The following day she returned to Los Angeles and while in a Beverly Hills hair salon, shaved off all her hair with a pair of electric clippers. The TV Burp skit was centred-around this incident and public criticism of the nature of her recent mentoring of some of the acts on 'The X Factor'. It began with a series of bizarre images and videos of Brittany, stamped by bold 'X Factor' style graphics and accompanied by my voiceover saying things like "Away With The Fairies," "Not Very Friendly," "She Mimes When She Sings" and "Her Pants Are Too Tight." It sounds harsh when written like this in the cold light of day, but like Peter Kay, Harry has a way of presenting his material in such a family-friendly way, that it feels acceptable. After the show, Harry invited me to dinner at his club, The Athenaeum, just off Pall Mall. It's one of London's grandest clubs, though in no way could it be described as stuffy. We opted to sit at the member's table, which is a lovely club tradition as it affords an opportunity to meet other members who may be dining alone. I had one of the most bizarre evenings I have ever had, sitting between Harry Hill on one side and a High Court Judge on the other! It's not something that happens every day. Harry and I were to cross paths again, several years later on something so ambitious, ridiculous and surreal that not even he, with his overactive, fertile imagination could have seen coming.

'Blue Peter' was a BBC TV programme I used to rush home from school to watch. Valerie Singleton, John Noakes and Peter Purves were a brilliant presenting team. I was always envious when I saw a lucky viewer receive a much-coveted 'Blue Peter' badge, which was presented to viewers who had achieved some task or other. In the summer of 2008, my agent took a call from a BBC producer at BBCTV centre who was working on 'Blue Peter'. He wanted to know if I would be interested in doing a voiceover for a film that they had made about what goes on backstage at 'The X Factor'. Well, here was my chance. I couldn't resist. I told my agent that I would do it only if they sent me… yes, you've guessed it, the sought after 'Blue Peter' badge. The deal was struck, and I am very happy to say that at the age of fifty-two, I became the proud owner of a two square centimetre shield of white plastic with a print of a blue ship in full sail. I treasure it to this day. It very rarely leaves the house. I didn't know it then, but another childhood ambition was about to be realised, but I would have to wait another four years for that.

I have so far mentioned 'Guinness World of Records' several times, in connection with some of the shows I have worked on. By the end of 2008, I was to be involved with the brand in a much less oblique way. Former 'Blue Peter' presenter and wife of Charlie Brooker, Konnie Huq and Welsh heartthrob presenter Steve Jones, had been lined up to host a new show for Sky 1 called 'Guinness World Records Smashed'. A pilot had been produced with Fearne Cotton and Ben Shephard as co-hosts but as the show was green-lit, they were no longer jointly available. The studio format invited members of the public to try to set new world records in everything from leaping through burning hoops to somersaulting over cars. Celebrity guests, the audience, and the presenters also got involved with the record-breaking attempts. It was all pretty thrilling stuff. Unlike the totally live 'Cirque de Celebrite' however, this series was to be recorded so there wasn't quite the same frisson of danger if things went badly wrong. To add to the sense of excitement, the ten-part series was to be recorded at Pinewood Studios, on a stage right next to the mahoosive 007-BOND sound stage. I was looking forward to a tour of that if I could possibly swing it. On the first day of filming, I drove through the hallowed and very showbiz gates of Pinewood Studios in Iver, Bucks and navigated my way around the sprawling site to the parking lot, next to where the Guinness World Records production offices were based. I was hoping there would be a parking space. I needn't have worried. Right next to the front door, between Konnie Huq and Steve Jones' allocated parking spaces, was mine. I knew it was mine because the studios had printed a fabulous Pinewood branded sign with my name on it and attached it to a gleaming white post! You don't get that treatment at ITV. I arrived into the studio that morning with an inflated sense of my own importance, which was soon deflated when I saw how and where exactly I was going to be working for the next two weeks. Another bloody shed! This time, thankfully, it was inside the studio and just off to the side of the set out of sight of the cameras. On the front door, they had thoughtfully attached another sign, which read: 'Pete's Shed'! Ah well. That's showbiz, folks. Having your own little private space on a production is quite nice. I could disappear in there and read the paper and have a quiet snooze, while the director set up and rehearsed all the shots and blocked through the moves with Konnie and Steve on set.

On the sound stage next door to ours, a major motion picture was in production. It was called: 'The Wolfman'. It was directed by Joe Johnston and starred Benicio del Toro, Anthony Hopkins and Emily Blunt. During breaks, I would slope off and chat to the crew on their set. I even got a tour of the grand castle interior that had been constructed. The level of detail that the army of craft specialists had gone to was hugely impressive. Everything was so microscopically perfect, it was incredible. That's the difference I guess, between TV and film. Film gets the cream every time.

And I did get the opportunity to see the inside of the Albert R. Broccoli 007-BOND stage. I am disappointed to tell you, dear reader, that, James Bond was nowhere to be seen. Instead, when the gigantic aircraft hangar doors trundled open, all that was revealed was a vast empty space, 374 feet long and 158 feet wide. Impressive nonetheless especially when you discover that it was the home of 'The Spy Who Loved Me', 'Moonraker', 'For Your Eyes Only', 'Octopussy', 'A View To A Kill', 'Tomorrow Never Dies', 'The World is Not Enough', 'Die Another Day', 'Casino Royale', 'Quantum Of Solace', 'Skyfall', 'Spectre' and a thousand other big Hollywood movies. At almost 60,000 square feet it is the biggest movie sound stage in Europe and visible from space! Working at Pinewood was quite an experience and I loved every second of it. Its role in filmmaking history is inestimable.

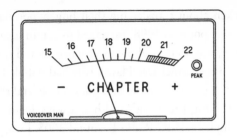

WHY DOES SANTA HAVE NO KIDS?

At some point in their careers, many radio DJ's and performers feel the need to try their hand at television. They will never tell you this, but most radio performers deep down, feel that they are the poor relation to their TV counterparts. Various talent agent friends tell me that getting their radio clients onto TV is all to do with, raising the artist's profile. Making money for the talent agent probably comes a close second. As Steve Wright subsequently found out, it can sometimes end in tears. The set of skills required are very different for both. Very few can do both well. One notable exception was Sir Terry Wogan, who was so horizontally laid back on both radio and TV; he made it look effortlessly easy. Mind you, he never rehearsed – something that threw the TV producers into a right old spin. Terry though had the auld Irish 'gift of the gab' that saved his and it has to be said, their bacon on many occasions. If an autocue would fail, he would just carry on regardless. He was mesmerising to watch and I've never met a TV presenter or radio host who didn't jealously admire his prodigious, easy talent.

Another radio personality to try his luck in front of the cameras was the Radio 1 breakfast DJ Chris Moyles. He and his radio sidekick Dave Vitty had often spoken about transferring their hugely popular radio show to television and at one point in 1998, managed to get an idea commissioned. The show, however, was seen by about twelve people and three dogs, on the now-defunct satellite channel UK Play. Chris had dabbled in TV over the years, appearing as a guest presenter and guest on several shows, from 'Top of the Pops' to 'The Big Breakfast', and had always acquitted himself very well. I had met Moyles at BBC Radio 1 around 2005. I was a guest on Scott Mills' show along with P.Diddy and Kylie Minogue. On that show, I had sung with Kylie on a country song live on air, accompanied by his producer on his battered, old acoustic guitar. Moyles had turned up at the studios unexpectedly after a long boozy lunch. During our meeting, he let slip that Simon Cowell was planning a spin-off show from 'The X Factor', called 'The X Factor: Battle Of The Stars'. The show went into production in 2006 and hit the nation's screens on Saturday night primetime on ITV, with me as the in-show voice. Moyles, it turns out was a decent enough singer and got all the way to the semi-final, when he was eventually voted off. Being back on TV though had rekindled his interest in performing in front of the cameras and so in February 2009, he called me up to tell me that a spin-off idea from his Radio 1 breakfast show had just been green-lit by Channel 4 and he wanted me to provide the voiceover elements. The show had the working title: 'Chris Moyles Quiz Night' and consisted of Moyles, alongside three celebrity guests, partaking in a traditional British pub-style quiz. The original series had the four of them competing to win a prized item that belonged to Moyles but it morphed with a twist into a quiz, with the loser singing karaoke-style at the end of the show. The opening show in March 2009 received poor viewing figures attracting just six percent of the total audience for the timeslot. However, the Channel commissioners thought it showed promise and it commissioned three further series. One of these aired between 26th February and 11th April 2010, and another between November and December 2010 and a final series between July and September 2011. After this final series, the show was cancelled. Chris and I share the same sense of humour and both of us like to push at the boundaries. On one show in series two, he came to me before the recording and discussed with me an idea he had where during the show, he and I would have a mock argument. I am always up for a bit of banter and as the show was being recorded, if it didn't work, the producers could always edit it out. Anyway, the moment arrived and Chris' guest, the opera singer Charlotte Church, who was in on the joke, asked Chris if he did any impressions.

"Yes I do," said Chris. "I can do a really great impression of Peter Dickson the voiceover man from our show."

He immediately launched into an impression of me and got a huge laugh from the studio audience.

"That sounds nothing like me!" Was my booming reply over the big studio PA system. An even bigger laugh!

"I think you'll find, it sounds *exactly* like you," retorted Chris.

My response was swift, "no, I am the *real* Peter Dickson."

Chris countered – "No! *This* is the real Peter Dickson."

"Oh, stop it, Chris!"

"No *I* am, so fuck you!"

I had the last word and the biggest laugh when I belted out at full volume:

"NO! FUCK YOU!!!"

Charlotte Church nearly fell off her seat. The altercation made it to the final cut and was broadcast. It caused a near meltdown on twitter, as it was the first time anyone had heard me swear on air. I am pleased to report that it actually felt rather good. It's the first and only time I have ever sworn on either TV or radio. I have a long way to go to catch up with Gordon Ramsay. Not that I'm keeping score but here it is anyway!

Peter Dickson: 1 — Gordon Ramsay: 1,345,326

On an evening In December 2011, at ITV's London Studios on London's Southbank, we recorded a 'Chris Moyles Quiz Night' Christmas special. The guests were Ollie Murrs, Louie Spence, who I hadn't seen since the toilet incident at 'Cirque de Celebrite' and James Cordon. The producer thought that since it was a Christmas show, they would allow me out of the sound booth and onto the set, to sit in a rather grand, high backed gilded chair, dressed as Santa Claus. They gave me one of those vintage looking Sure 55SH microphones that look quite cool. Somebody else on the production team also had the bright idea that it would be a good idea to put a bowl of fruit punch with a ladle and a silver tankard on a table by my side. I thought that it would just be fruit juice so imagine my surprise when I got on set, to discover that it was real alcoholic punch! Well, it was nearly Christmas, so why not? The show began and the cameras were rolling. I was feeling quite hot under the lights and a little thirsty so while the cameras were on Chris, I poured myself a liberal glass of booze and began to enthusiastically chuck it down my neck. What I hadn't appreciated was that my fake white beard was turning red as the wine seeped into it. All was going swimmingly, and I was just about managing to hit my cues until we reached a point about halfway into the show when Chris unexpectedly turned to his three guests and asked if they could remember any good Christmas cracker jokes that they had seen. Olly Murrs was up first.

"Yes," he said. "I have one. Why does Santa have no kids?"

The vision mixer in the production gallery cut to me briefly, looking bemused, then cut back to Chris.

"I don't know," said Chris. "Why does Santa have no kids?"

"Because… he only comes once a year!"

The audience exploded with laughter and the camera cut to me again. This was unscripted territory and I had no idea what I was going to say but I remember the following words tumbling from my mouth before I had even

Getting a lesson in 'cool' from P. Diddy – 2010 – BBC Radio 1, London.

Singing with Kylie Minogue on Scott Mills' Show – 2010 – BBC Radio 1, London.

had time to think that it was appropriate. The punch was weaving its magic inside my head. I was in big close up now. My cheeks and flowing beard all flushed with wine, six million people watching.

"Any more filthy jokes like that Murrs and I won't be emptying my sack on your floor on Christmas morning!" BOOM!

Cordon, Murrs, Spence and Moyles collapsed in a heap, laughing and the audience was in hysterics. Getting a laugh like that when you are not a comedian is quite something. As I rocked back in my chair, my beard almost flew off. It was quite a night and I'm delighted to say the fantastically rude exchange made the final cut and can still be seen on YouTube to this day. Chris was a natural TV performer; he understood the language of television, the demands of production and the constraints that presenters had to work under. This is actually quite rare, especially for a free spirit like Chris, but he is an intelligent bloke, a keen observer and a fast learner.

As 2009 drew to a close, I had the call again to head north to Scotland. After the recent brush with the country's first Minister, I wondered if I should perhaps go in disguise. I eschewed the idea and with careless abandon, boarded the 11.25am express from London Euston, bound for

Glasgow. We crossed the border without incident. I was about to embark on what, at first glance, looked like a doddle of a job but which turned out to be the most challenging two weeks of my career to date and one that nearly drove my fellow voice actors and me completely insane.

CBBC, the children's TV channel at the BBC had a year earlier, commissioned the most ambitious stop-motion animation project the Corporation had ever undertaken. Two vast, empty warehouses to the North of Glasgow were occupied by what at the time, was the biggest animation project in Europe. For the previous twelve months, an army of animators had risen each morning and gone to work, to physically move fruit, vegetables and various household objects one millimetre twelve times every second, to create the masterpiece we know today as: 'OOGLIES'. I had been cast alongside Tim Dann and Shelly Longworth to provide the voices for a diverse range of characters, ranging from a melon with a death complex, a lonely sprout, who none of the other vegetables liked, a cheeky carrot, a pair of bonkers conkers, a family of inquisitive mushrooms, a pair of dopy doughnut builders, a French maid scrubbing brush, two duelling toothbrushes and a cast of a thousand others! These were inanimate, household objects given life by a pair of stuck on eyes and the insane talents of a huge animation team. The initial commission was sixteen episodes of fifteen minutes each. Easy, I thought. Imagine my consternation when I walked into the studio in Glasgow on day one, to be told that there was no script. We had to make it up as we went along! Worse than this, we were forbidden from using recognisable English words or indeed words from any recognisable language. For the next fourteen days, Tim, Shelly and I took turns in the booth to view a short sketch on a tiny monitor stuck on the wall, which invariably ended with one or more of the characters being mashed, smashed, squished, squashed or blown up! We then had to provide a seamless sequence of emotive sounds and screams while the sketch was played to us again as we were being recorded. Again, on paper, this sounds easy but there were hundreds of sketches and over seventy characters and they all had to sound different. This was a monumental task and physically and mentally extremely draining. At the end of each days recording, we would head straight to the hotel bar for several sharpeners before dinner, just to calm down. By the end of day four, all three of us were beginning to hallucinate. The most inanimate of everyday objects, a telephone, a computer mouse, a bowl of sugar lumps, a bottle of wine began to appear alive to us. Small, beady eyes were every-where – watching us. Paranoia was setting in. It was as if our drinks had been spiked with acid – the weirdest sensation imaginable. Between 2009 and 2015 I returned, reluctantly to Glasgow several times to reprise this insanity, on two subsequent series of this BAFTA award-nominated series. I am proud of what we achieved but I hope to God it never returns!

Those who know me well will tell you that I only have a passing interest in sports, and not all sports at that. I enjoy watching international rugby and football and that's about it. Cricket, golf, tennis, swimming, cycling, you name it, hold about as much interest for me as watching an episode of 'Love Island'. One lovely sunny morning in the summer of 2010 how-ever, I found myself outside Manchester United's 'Theatre of Dreams', at Old Trafford in Manchester, where I was to be the live PA announcer on the bi-annual 'Soccer Aid' charity football match. As a boy growing up in Belfast in the 1960s, my friends and I had avidly followed the fortunes of Manchester United, principally because their star player, George Best had come from our home city. Seeing the incredible international success and pop star status that Best enjoyed, planted a nascent seed in my young mind. Although coming from seemingly very modest beginnings, Best had shown that it was indeed possible to break out of Northern Ireland, which felt very much like a provincial backwater and achieve greatness on an international stage. Wogan supplanted Best in my mind many years later, but those two examples serve to underline the potency of the role model in the minds of young people. It's something I've never forgotten and I'm extremely mindful of it when I am asked to speak at events where young people are present.

Anyway, there I was on that sunny Saturday morning in Manchester staring up at the towering structure of this cathedral to football, when a loud voice to my left rudely interrupted my reverie. It wasn't just any old voice; it was a voice I knew well. The voice of a man I had introduced on primetime TV on Saturday night for the past three years. It was none other than Mister DERMOT O'LEARY!

"Hello, mate!"

The vigorous slap on the back was given with the usual Celtic gusto he reserved for blokes. It was swiftly followed by that potentially awkward modern handshake, which looks to a casual observer that you are about to engage in an arm-wrestling competition. It wasn't over there though. Not by a long chalk. The arm-wrestling grip was followed by an abrupt pull forwards, a meeting of chests and several more, hearty slaps on the opposite shoulder. Dermot is a hugger, a man's-man and one of the nicest people you could hope to meet. He's also unexpectedly rather shy and reserved, an attribute that he hides well in public. His uber-confident, blokeish on-screen demeanour belies a thoughtful, intelligent and sensitive soul in private.

"What the hell are you doing here?" He cried, as his stylish stylist, Tom Stubbs joined us. Yes, Dermot has a stylist. Who knew?

"I'm fulfilling a childhood ambition," I said.

"Me too," then leaning in. "But… I'm an Arsenal supporter." He whispered conspiratorially. "I've always had a soft spot for the Reds. Are you on the old PA today then?"

He had guessed correctly. We made our way past security and into the ground. He disappeared off to his studio at the top of one of the stands and I headed pitch-side to the famous £3,500 red Recaro chairs in the Manchester United dugout. Alan Keegan, the team's resident stadium announcer was waiting for me and handed me a steaming mug of coffee and his trusty Sennheiser EW 300-G4 radio microphone – the mouthpiece through which he had entertained and informed 60,000 people at every home game for the previous ten years. My role was simple. The script called for me to introduce the teams onto the pitch. As this was a 'legends' versus 'celebrities' game, each player was introduced one at a time, to the deafening roar of an appreciative, family-oriented capacity crowd. At half time, the organisers had lined up a special treat for the home crowd. As the last player disappeared into the tunnel for the obligatory oranges and managerial team talk, I looked to my left and there he was. Standing there unseen and alone in the shadows, wearing the distinctive red shirt and carrying a new Nike match ball under his right arm. I was immediately transported back to Belfast in 1966 and an image of this same man, on a grainy black and white TV screen in the corner of my parent's living room. There he was – the same unmistakable profile. The blonde, comb-over hairstyle may have long gone but the lean, lanky stature that was familiar to millions, still in evidence. I knew what was coming. The 70,000 strong crowd, that was packed into Old Trafford that evening –didn't. Just before the big reveal, I introduced onto the touchline, former Arsenal and England goalkeeper David Seaman. Despite his Arsenal and Manchester City affiliations, he was warmly welcomed onto the pitch. Next, came the moment I was waiting for.

"Ladies and Gentlemen." I began. "Now, will you please welcome onto the pitch, a living legend. A man, who needs no further introduction here in the Theatre of Dreams. Please welcome… Sir Bobby Charlton."

Well, the words were hardly out of my mouth when place erupted. I have never heard a viscerally charged roar quite like it. The man who has been universally adored in this place for almost half a century, a true legend of the game, slipped from the shadowy safety of the players' tunnel and trotted youthfully down that famous Sir Matt Busby ramp onto the pitch, where he was joined by David Seaman and me. Even though the huge crowd was still roaring, I managed to hear Seaman say:

"OK Bobby, I will let you have the first one, you let me save the second and on the third, it's anyone's, OK?"

I looked across and saw Sir Bobby give him a friendly wink. Seaman ran off to the goal and I retired to the touchline to explain to the crowd that this was a penalty shoot-out between two of the finest English legends ever to play the game. It would be the best of three. Back on the penalty spot, Sir Bobby carefully placed the match ball on the ground, scanned the goal-mouth with half-closed eyes and with the same poker face that had struck fear into the hearts of the world's finest goalkeepers over an astonishing thirty-year playing career, took six long steps back. The crowd hushed with anticipation; you could have heard a pin drop. He glanced at the referee, the famous Pierluigi Collina who blew his whistle and with the crowd roaring, he began his run-up and swiftly despatched the ball towards the top left corner of the goal – a seemingly irresistible force, which promptly met the immovable object – David Seaman's size thirteen gloves. A huge cheer went up followed by an imperceptible wink from Seaman this time. The next ball that Charlton despatched was searingly fast, close to the ground and aimed with laser-like accuracy at the bottom right of the goal. Seaman, true to his promise dived left; the ball narrowly missed his outstretched right leg and slammed pleasingly into the back of the net.

I was on the PA in a flash.

"So, Ladies and Gentlemen, this is it. It's the best of three and with one save and one goal this will be the decider."

Only I knew that on this third attempt, both players would be out for themselves. All professional sportsmen hate to lose. Losing is contrary to everything in their DNA. So, as Sir Bobby stepped up for the third time that evening, even though he was a septuagenarian, I could tell that he was back in 1966. He meant business. He steadied his breathing, his gaze alternating from ball to goal and back again. The crowd, also sensing that the pride of each man was at stake, fell silent. But not for long, As Collina blew his whistle for the third time and Sir Bobby made his final run-up, the noise began, quickly building in waves and reaching ear-shattering intensity when the precisely aimed shot ricocheted inside the goal, slamming into and around the nylon netting, like a demented pinball. David Seaman was on the floor. Sir Bobby allowed himself the briefest of celebrations and with arms raised to acknowledge the richly deserved applause, he trotted over to the goal to shake hands with his opponent and then made his way back towards me on the touchline. I couldn't resist it. Without looking down, I flicked the switch on the side of my microphone.

"Some people are on the pitch. They think it's all over."

Then as Sir Bobby drew level with me, I looked him in the eye and said: "It is now."

He had a huge smile on his seventy-two-year-old face, and at that very moment, as he nodded appreciatively, the years rolled away for the both of us. We were both back at Wembley, in the summer of '66. It was a magical, personal career highlight and one I'll never forget.

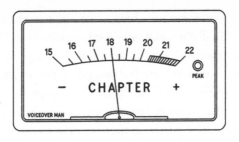

OH MY GOD! MY ARM'S FALLEN OFF!

I have never been particularly interested in video games. I suppose it's an age thing. When I was in my thirties they were just getting going and they were pretty rudimentary and by rudimentary, I mean crap. So, computer games as they were then known, kind of passed me by. Imagine my astonishment then, thirty years later to have participated in the production of over thirty AAA top gaming titles, including major movie franchise video game spin-offs!

In 2001 my game voice career kicked off with LEGO's 'Knight's Kingdom Creator' which was swiftly followed by a fairly big Eidos produced wartime themed epic, called 'Commandos 3: Destination Berlin'. Then came: 'Wings of War', 'Lords of the Realm, Sony's worldwide hit 'Hotshot Golf', 'Hidden and Dangerous 2: Sabre Squadron', 'Dragon Quest VIII: Journey of the Cursed King' from the excellent Square Enix, 'Black and White' from Electronic Arts, Sony's 'Folklore' and a host of other top titles. In 2004, I was cast in 'Fable' as the character 'Maze', which was the biggest game the world had ever seen. 2010 and 2011, however, were to be a bumper couple of years for my involvement with the gaming industry, playing major character parts in not one, not two but four big game titles. I was particularly pleased to be cast in the first game of a brand-new suite of titles, called 'Kinect Sports', developed by RARE and published worldwide for the Xbox 360 by Microsoft Game Studios. I was the narrator, encouraging and explaining the rules to a predominantly family-oriented market of game players, who had splashed out a hefty sum to be the first to play on this astonishing new tech. The game utilised unique, motion-sensing peripheral cameras which were able to map the joint points on the players in real-time and incorporate these movements into the actions of the respective player characters in the game. It was, I am told built with Israeli military technology and was pretty cutting-edge stuff. The kind of software code you probably could have ended up being shot by Mossad, for owning ten years earlier. I was pleased that for a short period of my career, I was considered quite cool by my two teenage sons, who up until this point had been largely indifferent or in some cases downright embarrassed by what I did for a living.

The Kinect Sport sessions went on for months and months. It was interminable. Thousands of introductions, explanations and unique phrases were recorded and incorporated into the finished game. I remember thinking to myself at the time that whoever played this game would be well and truly sick of my voice by the end. Kinect was followed by a bit of a cult classic, 'Xenoblade Chronicles' in which I played the rather grandly titled three hundred twenty-year old, Emperor Sorean.

"Oh." I hear you say. "Who on earth was he?" Well, he wasn't *on* earth for a start. He was the Emperor of the High Entia and the father of Melia and Kallian. You mean you didn't know? I'm shocked! This was a particularly tricky game to work on, as we were tasked with producing the English-speaking version of a game that had originated in Japan. During these recording sessions at SIDE UK's studios in London, the entire English and American cast had to listen to the recordings of the original Japanese voice actors in our headphones, while simultaneously sprouting the English translation that had been thoughtfully provided by the original game maker. The only problem with this is that spoken Japanese can at times sound rather aggressive to western ears and the tonality I was hearing in my headphones were those of what sounded like a very angry man. Now, I have never met him and I am sure he is a thoroughly nice bloke to go down the pub with for a pint of warm Sake, but Joji Nakata, my Japanese actor counterpart on the original game, very nearly did my ruddy head in with his harsh angry-sounding delivery. So much so that I had to ask the sound engineer to turn him down to a virtual whisper in my ears, because all of my lines were coming across equally angrily on the English version. Even on lines like:

"My darling Melia, I love you, I really do." The way I was reading them, sounded like I wanted to cut her head off with fifteen-inch Samurai sword and feed it to the ruddy pigs!

We got there in the end and the game, to this very day, has a considerable global cult following. I have often considered getting an Emperor Sorean mask and popping along to one of those international Comic-Con conventions and charging £10 for an autograph, £20 for a photo and £30 for the kudos of an Emperor Sorean voicemail message! Then again – maybe not. I'm not quite sure I could deal with the intense, nerdiness of it all. I would in all likelihood, end up punching some spotty teenager in the face while shouting something like; "Oh for God's sake man – get a ruddy life!"

'The Xenoblade Chronicles' was followed in swift succession by 'The Adventures of Tin Tin', in which I played both of the Thompson twins. The recording session for that game was hilarious, as I had to slightly differentiate their voices by giving one of them a slightly camp lisp. I would get about halfway through the line and then burst out laughing. I hope those who bought and played the game found it as funny as I did. It took bloody forever to record.

One of the biggest film franchises of all-time must surely be 'Harry Potter'. In early 2010, I was at home minding my own business, when the phone rang. I took the call. It was a particularly excited Hugh Edwards on the other end.

"What's Up?" I said.

"You won't believe this." He said. "I've been given the job of casting for a new 'Harry Potter' game for Warner Brothers and I want you to audition for it!"

Several weeks later, after having submitted my audition along with about half a million other actors, I received the good news from Hugh that I had secured not one, but three parts in this huge game, namely; Voldemort, Malfoy and a Death Eater! As I think I might have told you already, I love playing bad guys and zombies, so this game promised to be a lot of fun. I have to tell you that it didn't disappoint. I spent three glorious days in a studio in London grunting, hissing, moaning, dying and dying again. In fact, I died over a hundred times that week, took hits in varying intensities from spells cast from Ollivander branded wands and screamed like a bellicose Banshee, until I thought I'd never be able to speak again. At one point, I recall screaming "Oh no! My arm's fallen off." I hope it made the cut. Exhausting? Yes. Fun? Absolutely. So if you have ever played the game, or listened to it by proxy as a long-suffering parent, now you know that the guy who plays Voldermort, is the same guy who shouts "Come on Down" on the 'The Price is Right' and the same guy who introduces the contestants and global superstars on 'The X Factor' on TV and the same guy who when he was twelve years old, never in his wildest dreams believed that anything like that would ever happen to him. I am actually a little bit emotional when I write this because I have been so very fortunate in my career. I've met so many fantastically talented people, enjoyed so many wonderful opportunities and worked on some of the biggest entertainment productions. I never, ever take any of it for granted.

In 2010 a huge charity concert for Help the Heroes was staged at the home of English rugby, London's Twickenham Stadium, where I got to introduce all of the biggest stars in entertainment live on stage to an 82,000 strong capacity crowd. It was a memorable day and the closest I will ever get to a huge televised gig on the scale of 'Live Aid'. I had the pleasure of introducing Robbie Williams, who was joined on stage by Gary Barlow for the first time since their very public falling out. Also, on the bill; Bruce Forsyth, Enrique Iglesias, Jack Dee, James Blunt, Katherine Jenkins, Peter Kay, Michael McIntyre, Pixie Lott, Tom Jones and Plan B. It was quite a star-studded night and it went brilliantly. I was particularly pleased to catch up with Bruce, it would be our final meeting, though of course, you never know these things at the time. It was also great to see Peter Kay again. He walked over to my commentary position in the gloom of the wings, just to the left of the enormous stage, out of sight of the crowd.

"Hey! How's it goin?" He said.

"Pretty good Peter. Great to see you here!"

"Oh, I'm not stopping long me. I'm back up the road after this. Left the car running." He gave a chuckle and one of his trademark winks as he hitched up his trousers.

Peter Kay was never someone who was attracted by the bright lights of London. Unusually, for such a hugely successful figure in UK entertainment, he much preferred the home comforts and normality afforded to him back in Bolton – something that contributes to both his undoubted charm and success. He is very much a man of the people. He lent in a little closer, so I could hear him above the roar of the Twickenham crowd. Robbie had just unexpectedly joined Gary on stage and the fans were showing their appreciation of the unexpected reunion.

"Eeee! That Simon Cowell went berserk after the Jesus Christ on Ice thing aired." He said.

"Really? Why?" It was news to me.

"He hated it. Hated everything about it. Thought we were taking the piss, undermining his success. He sent me a really stinking email."

"Oh, dear. Sorry to hear that." I said. "He never mentioned it to me."

"Oh aye. He was particularly upset about your involvement and I felt a bit guilty about that as I had given you my word, when we met, that it was an affectionate parody but after the reviews came in and the praise for it was universal, he decided it was OK. Called me to apologise. Now't as queer as folk eh?"

The green light on my desk illuminated, indicating that Robbie and Gary had ended their set and that I was to standby. It was pretty obvious they had. The decibel level from the thunderous crowd in the stadium had reached eardrum-busting proportions and the entire stage structure began to rattle and vibrate, quite alarmingly.

"Sweet Jesus! How do I follow that?" Said Peter. Gesturing over at the centre of the stage where Gary and Robbie were taking their bows and milking the approbation of their adoring fans.

"You'll be fine," I said. "Everyone loves you. Even Simon Cowell!"

He threw his head back in laughter, winked at me and with his cheeky dimpled grin, took his position in the wings ready for my intro. I have never encountered a more casually relaxed performer than Peter Kay. He makes what he does look effortless, easy and natural. It's the mark of a true pro. His energy, persona and character are exactly the same on and off stage. And having watched many performers over the years, I think that's the key. I gave him the big build-up and announced his name over the huge PA system with all the stentorian gusto I could summon – he took his first few steps from beside me, to centre stage and the crowd responded with a huge roar before he had even uttered a single word. There aren't many people who command that level of respect and adoration, nor cause 82,000 people in one place to laugh after uttering just one word.

"Yarright?"

In 2010, I thought I'd done it all – I was wrong. There was plenty more ahead and one of the biggest gigs of my life was just around the corner. When I told you earlier that my interest in sport extends to watching the odd international football or rugby tournament, you will understand my lack of excitement when one afternoon in mid-2011, my agent dispatched me to Wembley Stadium to be the 'Voice of God' at a large personnel briefing for the forthcoming 2012 London Olympic Games. Thousands of members of the public had applied to be given garish purple tracksuits and pink Hi-Viz tabards to stand at railway stations, airports and outside games venues to assist the world's visitors in finding their way around our capital city. Over three long days, 70,000 of these unsung and unpaid heroes and heroines were given pep talks and mass briefings by the senior officials at LOCOG, the London organising committee of the Olympic Games. My job was to introduce them onto the stage and make a raft of other announcements on the big public address system at Wembley. By the end of day three, I was packing up to head home when a couple of cheery Australian blokes swung by my voiceover booth and introduced themselves as the Olympic Games beach volleyball managers.

"Jeez Mate." The sandy-haired, taller of the two began in the broadest Australian accent imaginable. "You were spoutin' some pretty funny shit these past three days."

"Really?" I said. "It's just typical airy British banter. It's nothing special."

"Nah, mate." Said the smaller one. "We was wettin' ourselves back there." The Australians have such a unique way with words.

"Well, that's very kind of you," I said. "I hope the Olympic volleyball works out for you guys. It looks like a lot of fun. I'll be sure to follow it on TV."

The taller of the two leant against the doorway, looked at his mate and then back at me.

"How's about you watch it from six feet away in the Olympic volleyball stadium on Horse Guards Parade?"

I rocked back in my chair. Not quite believing what I was hearing.

"I'm not sure I follow you," I said. "Are you offering to get me tickets?"

The shorter one interjected.

"Nah Mate. We want you to be the Olympic Games volleyball announcer!"

My first thought was that I couldn't wait to tell my pals. My second thought was, how on earth am I going to tell my wife! Beach volleyball, particularly *women's* beach volleyball has, in Britain at least, always had this 'nudge-nudge, wink-wink' connotation and to be fair it is pretty easy on the eye. My third thought was that we are only ten months away from games time, which was to open in the summer of the following year. Would I have enough time to prepare myself, get trained up and become familiar with the game and its undoubtedly exotic beach party culture? I put all doubts out of my mind and shook hands on the deal there and then and went to the pub to sink a few cold tinnies and chuck a few virtual prawns on the barbie with my new best friends from down under.

What a year 2012 was promising to be! Since the announcement that London had been selected to be the 2012 Olympic host city, the whole country had been swept along on a tide of elation and palpable anticipation. Globally, the expectation of the UK's hosting ability was rapidly building and I was now going to play a significant part right at the centre of the action, right in the middle of one of the hottest tickets in town, right in the heart of one of the greatest cities on earth. What a gig, what an honour... what on earth had I let myself in for? A few months before the Games were due to open, The London Organising Committee for the Olympic Games (LOCOG), contacted me and asked if I could record some announcements to be played in all the other Olympic venues across London, including the main stadium itself. So, while I was going to be physically confined to Horse Guards Parade, at least I could say that my voice was going to be heard more or less everywhere else.

By late spring in 2012, I had heard nothing further regarding the biggest sporting event on the planet. Not a phone call, email, letter or even pigeon. In my mind, I surmised that any day now a huge ring-bound, official-looking file would be delivered to my home by Daly Thompson, crashing through the letterbox, containing everything I ever wanted to know about the beautiful game of volleyball; the rules, the players and the countries that would be taking part. In June, I headed to East London to a LOCOG meeting but that was simply to collect my impressive looking laminated and hologram emblazoned AAA – *'Access All Areas'* Olympic Games pass. There was no discussion or briefing about the event itself, what was worse, my antipodean pals were nowhere to be seen. As June turned to July, a mild sense of panic began to set in. In desperation, I turned to YouTube and began to watch as many volleyball games as I could. Some of them were from the last Olympic Games, so at least I could begin to work out the format and protocol required in the formal setting of an Olympic event. Despite being quite good at extemporizing, I decided that I needed to write some words, to fall back on to entertain and inform the crowd, during those inevitable breaks in play and during the transition between matches. But what on earth could I say? Then it struck me. Here was a wonderful opportunity for some mischief! I realised that the crowd in the stadium would be made up of Londoners and Brits from all over the country and a significant proportion of foreign visitors. Here was my chance, I thought, to indulge in a spot of fakery. 'Fake news' had yet to be invented, my twist was 'fake history'. The Brits would love it and hopefully spot the fake stories and the tall tales, but the foreign visitors would be none the wiser and lap it all up in wide-eyed innocence.

Many years ago, the comedian Arthur Smith told me that he used to supplement his income during his early career in stand-up comedy, by taking unsuspecting American tourists on phoney historical walking tours of Edinburgh, during the city's annual cultural festival. Now, here was my chance to do the same but on an even grander scale. Two weeks before the games opened, I sat down and wrote about twenty-five different completely fictitious stories about Horse Guards Parade, The Mall, The Royal Family, The Prime Minister, Number 10 Downing Street, King Henry the Eighth, and a team of Olympic volleyball helpers and officials that I christened 'The Guardians of the Sand'. I neatly typed these up and put them in a laminated file I mischievously labelled 'VOLLEYBOLLOCKS'. It's childish, I know but we all have a duty to find amusement in life where and when we can.

On the opening day of the Olympic Games volleyball competition, I strode purposefully across a bright, sun-bathed Trafalgar Square clutching my prized 'VOLLEYBOLLOCKS' file under my arm, with my Olympic Games *'Access All Areas'* lanyard and pass around my neck. Its official, 3D security hologram glinting like a prism in the sunshine and blinding any Muggles who were foolish enough to step in my path. At the northern entrance to Whitehall, I was stopped by an armed Metropolitan police officer who on seeing my pass, gave me a cheery wave and opened the barrier to the western footpath that runs south from the square. His eye caught the title of my file as I passed, and I saw the bemused look on his face. On the eastern pavement of Whitehall, huge crowds and press photographers had begun to gather to witness the arrival of the many VIP's who had reserved seats for the opening of the Olympic Games volleyball. And there I was, in the middle of this impressive tableau walking on my own private and completely empty footpath, straight through the imposing gates that lead into the world-famous Horse Guards Parade ground. This space has been home for centuries to Trooping the Colour, under the watchful and not uncritical eye of many a Monarch, including the current one – Her Majesty Queen Elizabeth II. Once inside, I made my way anticlockwise underneath and around the vast dimly lit complex web of steel scaffolding and tarpaulin that had been built to support the 15,000 seats in what was then, the largest beach volleyball venue in Olympic history.

Emerging into the bright blinking sunshine on the western side, where the production and commentator positions were located, my breath was taken away by what greeted me. There in front of my eyes, an astonishingly beautiful cyclorama of some of London's most iconic buildings – illuminated by the golden light of an early morning summer sun. The golden hue of the Elizabeth Tower with its world-famous 'Big Ben' clock-face, The London Eye, rotating almost imperceptibly in the distance on the south side of the River Thames, the Admiralty building – home of the British Navy, the soot-black, brick walls of Number 10 Downing Street, the home of the British Prime Minister and the '60s majesty of the BT Tower among others, forming an incredible backdrop to a perfectly level rectangle of beautiful powdery soft sand, surrounded by dozens of rows of perfectly purple seats rising up to meet an azure blue sky. This was a modern-day amphitheatre, constructed in the ancient Olympic tradition – a stunning triumph of modern engineering. This seemingly permanent structure would be gone in four weeks. It was hard to imagine how. It was so vast and seemed so permanent.

On that first day, I was incredibly relieved to see that one of the Olympic volleyball live event directors was Phil Heyes. His counterpart was the top, live music video and studio multi-camera director, the fabulous James Russell. Phil is an old pal of mine and is a mighty fine live TV director. I had worked with him for several years on 'The X Factor' and we share the same overtly childish sense of humour. Also, on the team was a wiry, tousled haired Scotsman called Graeme Easton who, being an actual bona fide volleyball commentator of some repute, saved me from many a ghastly potential faux pas in the weeks to come. In every respect, this was a dream job for a live event announcer. Firstly, it was a never to be repeated experience and secondly, being at the front row just four metres from the beach volleyball action, made me the envy of most live sports event announcers in the country. Frankly, I couldn't believe my luck. But here I was, determined to make the best of it and boy, was I pleased to be here!

On day one, I opened the games in the morning to a capacity crowd. Because of the noise in the arena, I had to wear headphones to hear my cues from Phil and talk into a microphone that was attached to my headphones and which extended from my right ear to meet my mouth, at the end of a four-inch stalk. I was also able to select whether my microphone was live or not via a small on/off switch on a control panel in front of me. This feature I liked, but it also made me particularly nervous as switching it on was one thing but remembering to switch it off was another – particularly as the banter at the production table next to me was fierce and the language was often agricultural. The crew were continuously recounting rude jokes and making unflattering comments about people in the crowd and about some of the athletes. Most of them were unrepeatable never mind suitable for broadcast. My concern was that I might forget to switch off my microphone and my own comments might be broadcast to the entire arena. As it happened, there were no ugly mishaps, though I did once commit an error of protocol at one of the evening games by introducing the wrong team onto the sand. An error I had to embarrassingly correct much to the delight of the mostly drunk crowd and bizarrely, Prince Albert of Monaco, who for some unknown reason was standing behind me at the time!

There is a rule in beach volleyball that permits women players to wear long sleeves and long pants if the ambient temperature drops below 10°C. On one of the evening semi-finals, at around 8pm when the temperature had dropped considerably, I remember quite vividly opening my microphone to introduce the women from Austria, who were about to take on the women from the United Kingdom. First into the arena, as visiting athletes were Doris and Stefanie Schwaiger. Out they merrily trotted from the players' tunnel, over in the southwest corner of the arena and into the unforgiving glare of the bright arc lights. Their cheery waves and smiles were slowly met with a deafening wave of booing from a section of the crowd, many of whom were city brokers on a drunken lad's night out. The two sisters had exercised their right to cover up, as the chill of the night descended on London. Now, this is getting interesting I thought to myself, these boys most certainly were evidently not here for the sport. The Austrians put a brave face on it and continued to wave to the crowd, but I did feel sorry for them. I looked over at the players' tunnel and saw the home team girls Zara Dampney and Shauna Mullin warming up, just before they too bounced onto the sand on my booming introduction.

"Ladies and Gentlemen. Please welcome onto the field of play, the Great Britain women's team."

I knew what was coming before the crowd did. The hardy UK women had decided not to follow their Austrian competitors and had opted for the skimpiest bra and pants combo in Union Jack colours. I had barely said their names, before a deafening roar of, mostly male approval, clattered its way around the stadium. Beer was flying everywhere and shouts of 'Get In' could be heard from all corners. This was more like a beach party where there just happened to be an Olympic event occurring at the same time! At one point in that particular game during a time-out break, I flicked open my 'VOLLEYBOLLOCKS' file and began to read out something I had written in my study about four weeks ago when I was panicking about what to say in such circumstances. I began:

"Ladies and Gentlemen. May I have your attention, please? As you know, we are here in Horse Guards Parade in the heart of London. Over there, behind the east stand the official residence of our beloved Prime Minister, Mr David Cameron."

There was a little party-political booing from an otherwise silent crowd. I could sense they were wondering what was coming next. There was murmuring all around the stadium. The players looked across at my position as if to say, "what's he doing," I continued.

"Mr Cameron has sent me a message to relay to you. He is having a very early morning meeting tomorrow with the Japanese Prime Minister and so consequently, he is having an early night. He has, therefore, asked me if I could ask you to possibly keep the noise down." I switched off the microphone.

Well, you can imagine what happened next. There was a minuscule pause as my final word reverberated around the stadium, followed by what can only be described as an excoriating, braying sound, an outpouring of human approbation and outright derision that went on for a good minute. It was deafening. I looked across at Phil and Graeme who were on the floor and crying with laughter.

Phil was on the talkback and above the din, in my headphones, I heard him say, "Fuck me. You've done it now Captain!"

The next day, while preparing for the first evening game, Andy Burdin, the LOCOG volleyball manager came up to me. He didn't look best pleased. My fun and games last night, it seems, had struck a raw nerve inside Number 10 Downing Street. In a case of life imitating art, Cameron had been in bed when I made that announcement and was trying to get some rest. The next morning, he filed a complaint to the head of LOCOG, Lord Sebastian Coe asking him if he could tell me to desist from doing that again. Well, by now I think that you know me well enough to predict that this was like a red rag to a bull. I reassured Andy that Cameron would not be troubled again. Yeah, right! Later that night, in a 'time out', I began.

"Ladies and Gentlemen, may I have your attention, please? As you know, we are here in Horse Guards Parade in the heart of London. Over there, behind the south stand, just a stone's throw away is Buckingham Palace – the official residence of Her Majesty the Queen."

Again, there was murmuring all around the stadium. Phil looked across at me with open-mouthed consternation. Undeterred, I continued.

"Her Majesty's Equerry Sir Christopher Geidt GCB, GCVO, OBE, has sent me a message to relay to you. Tomorrow, Her Majesty will be having a morning audience with the new President of the Republic of Ghana The Honourable John Mahama. Consequently, Her Majesty is having an early night. Sir Christopher has, therefore, asked me if I could ask you lot to possibly keep the noise down."

Same result! Brilliant, I was on a roll. No one's job should ever be this much fun. I think after that, Cameron realised that he wasn't going to win this particular game and we never heard from him again. I suspect he did what most Londoners in the vicinity of Westminster did – either join the party or buy earplugs or in my case, both. LOCOG had accommodated us in Highbury, North London for the duration of the Games. The road outside, it seemed was the conduit for every single banshee screeching emergency vehicle in the capital. Added to the lack of sleep, was the increasing and worrisome strain on my vocal cords. I have always been careful with my voice. Those two small strands of mucous membrane in my throat are the only things that have kept my family and myself from the breadline, for the best part of forty years. I consider myself to now be virtually unemployable in any other capacity. The almost constant heavily projected talking on a microphone in the open air, in such a big rowdy venue was taking its toll on my voice much sooner than I had anticipated. My fellow announcers and commentators were all suffering the same fate and were ordered to take complete vocal rest, when not at the venue. I was gargling with honey and lemon and drinking over two and a half litres of water a day, to help my voice to recover and to stay hydrated. Drinking water is one of the best things that you can do for your voice. I am often asked about the best solution to prevent damage and increase vocal health and stamina. Most people expect me to recommend some exotic and expensive tincture made from Bee pollen and Guava oil, distilled in the Guatemalan jungle by artisanal craftsmen and look crestfallen when I say; "Adam's Ale." It may be boring but good old H_2O really is the oil in your vocal engine. So many avoidable vocal problems arise when those who speak for a living ignore their hydration. Of course, what goes in must come out. Under normal circumstances one is never far from bathroom facilities but remember, we were working in a completely temporary venue and the bright spark who had designed it had not taken into account that between the ending of one game and the start of the protocol sequence for the next one, the team had only three minutes and thirty seconds for a comfort break. The staff facilities for the women on the presentation team were located just behind the commentary position and were relatively easy to access. The men's room, however, was somewhat further away. Consequently, to prevent another 'Cirque de Celebrite' cola-tin incident, we had on many occasions to sprint to the loo. On one such break, Phil and I nearly didn't make it. We had to dive into the Ladies room screaming apologies as we clumsily barged into our individual cubicles accompanied by much swearing and the visceral sound of belts and zips being attacked with both hands followed by giggling and sighs of relief. People think my job is all glitz and glamour!

The following evening, I was on the late shift again and arrived at the

Time-out at the women's volleyball final – 2012 – London Olympic Games.

PETER DICKSON

7 famous voices – L-R: Tom Clarke-Hill, Marcus Bentley, Jon Briggs, Lewis MacLeod, Alan Dedicoat, Me, Julie Berry – 2017 – BBC Radio 2, London.

stadium at around 5pm, about an hour earlier than my shift time. I wanted to sit in the audience at the opposite end of the stadium to listen to the audio quality of the big PA system and hear my announcer counterpart, a guy called Adam Longworth. As the referee called 'time-out', I was more than a little surprised to hear Adam launch into one of my pre-scripted comedy routines about the 'Guardians of the Sand', referring to the young team of LOCOG helpers who were on hand to rake and smooth the sand on the court. He had evidently found my 'VOLLEYBOLLOCKS' script file and was reading all my material. As his shift ended and I arrived at the commentary position, he looked more than a bit sheepish. Later that night, I was asked by Phil to go into the crowd during the interval and lead a massive Brazilian-style conga dance around the entire upper level of the stadium. There was a real party atmosphere at night, as the after-work crowd arrived, many of them pre-loaded from time spent in the numerous pubs and bars in the West End, close to Horse Guards Parade. The six closed-circuit TV cameras captured the event in full HD on the massive LCD screens, as they followed me and about a hundred and fifty strangers snaking and shaking

Commentating on Beach Volleyball – 2012 – London Olympic Games.

With Phil Heyes and James Russell – 2012 – London Olympic Games.

PETER DICKSON

our way up and down the stairwells and corridors of the venue like we were at the Rio carnival. We might as well have been. Later that night, we were joined by two members of the USA basketball team – Carmelo Anthony and Kevin Durant – two of the tallest men I have ever met. That summer of 2012 in London is one I will never forget. The whole city was alive and turbo-charged. The air crackled with electricity. Every single building along the Thames was illuminated. Everyone was in a fantastically upbeat mood. The streets were alive to the sound of music, revelry and laughter. I wish we could have bottled it. It didn't take long though, for London to return to its usual ill-tempered self; as the games closed, the athletes and the visitors departed, and the venues closed their doors and turned off the lights for the last time. Within two weeks, the volleyball stadium was dismantled, put into sea-containers and loaded onto a ship bound for Brazil, where it would be utilised in four years at the next games. Whenever I am near that part of London today, I make a point of walking into the square to stand on the exact point where I stood in July 2012, where all that incredible magic occurred. There's now, not a shred of evidence that it was ever there. Tourists and visitors alike, now walk in the footsteps of sporting legends. Like a dream, it feels to me now as though it never really happened.

With US basketball legend Carmelo Anthony – 2012 – London Olympic Games.

Relaxing between games – 2012 – London Olympic Games.

PETER DICKSON

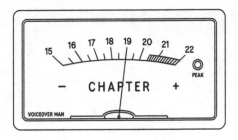

FOOTBALL FAUX PAS

M y mother's side of the family was mad keen on sport. My mother played hockey and my maternal grandfather was the president of the Irish Football Association. Aside from captaining the school swimming team age sixteen, nowadays I get breathless just playing draughts by an open window. My father was a keen rugby player in his youth and was an avid follower of English league football, in so far as the results were concerned. Every Saturday at 5pm, for as long as I can remember, he sat glued to the final score results on TV. In those days they spat out of a huge typewriter that appeared on the screen that clattered and shook like a weaver's bobbin as it disgorged the match results onto ticker-tape. He would sit there with his Meerschaum pipe in one hand and his pools coupon in the other religiously marking off his forecasts against the actual results, in the vain hope of winning that week's pools prize. He never did. In subsequent years, the final scores were read on radio by my pal James Alexander Gordon and on TV by Len Martin and laterally by my other former colleague at BBC Radio 2, Tim Gudgin. I used to marvel at the ability of these men to intonate the scores in such a way that a losing score began on a downward inflection and a winning score would begin on a rising

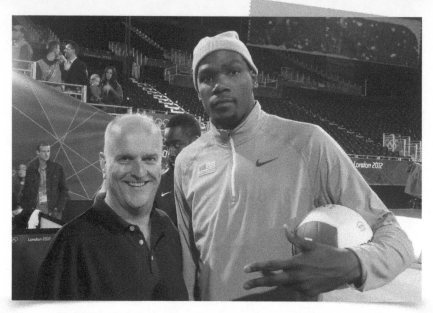

With US basketball giant Kevin Durant – 2012 – London Olympic Games.

Leading a giant conga around the stadium – 2012 – London Olympic Games.

inflection. This occasion on both radio and TV became an appointment to listen and view, for football fans up and down the country and continues to this very day. The only other broadcast that comes close in terms of its stylised, hypnotic vocal cadence is the nightly shipping forecast on BBC Radio 4, that not only warns seafarers of impending storms but also sends many a landlubber to sleep. Both the shipping forecast and 'Final Score' are the stuff of broadcasting legend and incredibly have been in the hands of just three men since 1958.

Since 2010, I had been assisting a well-known and well-loved charity called 'Comic Relief' and in 2012, they came up with a wheeze to ask various personalities to unexpectedly pop up on radio and TV, to promote the cause. Fund-raising for 'Comic Relief' was a bi-annual event. Every other year, the charity harnessed the power of sport to raise funds under the banner 'Sport Relief'. Various charity football matches were planned that year and the proposal that came in via my agent was both exciting and at the same time, terrifying. I was invited to read the football results on 'Final Score' on BBC1 at 5pm next Saturday. What an honour to be able to join that exclusive band of three, if only for one day. I brushed any doubts aside and duly turned up at the new BBC Sport studios at Media City, in Salford Manchester on the following Saturday. I was shown to my dressing room and as the door closed behind me the room began to feel claustrophobic and terribly warm and airless. I was in the condemned man's cell. Was I having a panic attack? It was hard to tell, but it certainly felt like it. Had I bitten off more than I could chew? Why do I agree to do these things? I seriously considered backing out. As I sat there staring at the walls, I reflected on the fact that so little of what I do these days is properly live. It was 4.30pm and with thirty minutes to me going properly live, now was not the time for a crisis of confidence. The producer popped his head around the door and with a cheery smile led me through a set of double soundproof doors into the BBC Sport studio, where Gabby Logan was live on air, interviewing a couple of Football pundits under the bright lights of the BBC's new virtual 'Grandstand' set. As we skirted past, behind the cameras and tiptoed over the myriad of audio and camera cables that crisscrossed the studio floor, she spotted me out of the corner of her eye and flashed me a smile and a knowing wink. The producer guided me to an area behind the set, which had been set up for me. There was an office chair and a desk, on which there was a TV monitor and a Coles 4104 commentator's lip microphone. I stared down at the arrangement and couldn't help noticing that there was no script. Pre-empting my next question, the producer moved closer and whispered in my ear that as the results were coming in live, they would appear on the monitor in front of me at the same time that the viewing public saw them. I hadn't considered that this would be a sight-read, but when I thought about it, it was kind of obvious. Fair enough, I thought. I'll just take my time and not rush things. The seconds on the big digital clock up on the wall of the studio ticked remorselessly down to 5 o'clock and I heard Gabby on the other side of the studio say those immortal words:

"It's 5 o'clock and time for: FINAL SCORE."

The VT introduction began to play, and I could hear that familiar tune that has echoed down the years, through a million homes up and down the land, booming around the studio. I received that familiar jolt of adrenalin all performers get just before they do their thing. Psychologists call it 'the fight or flight response'. Pilots call it 'V1' – the point of no return. We were now committed; the stick had been pulled and the wheels were off the deck. I considered hiding under the desk, running out of the door or pretending to faint but none of these was an option.

I heard the floor manager say, "fifteen seconds, counting down... 10, 9, 8..."

I looked at the monitor in front of me expecting it to flicker into life at any second. Nothing.

"7, 6, 5..."

I began to panic. With five seconds to go there was still no picture on my monitor. I gesticulated wildly as a cameraman, whizzed around a corner of the set and pointed his shoulder-mounted camera in my direction. Jesus! I was going to be in-vision! No one had pre-warned me! Seeing my consternation, one of the production team glanced at the screen and hurriedly reached in to press a hidden switch on the side. Christ Almighty! It hadn't even been powered on! The big LCD screen flashed instantly into life. Thank God!

"4, 3, 2, 1 and Cue Gabby!"

The music ended and I saw myself appear on the monitor in front of me with Gabby's introduction accompanying my somewhat terrified and now familiar, 'rabbit caught in the headlights' expression.

Gabby continued. "And this week the results from all of today's matches

In the studio with Terry Gilliam – 2017 – Redwood Studios, London.

are read on behalf of Sport Relief by the voice of 'The X Factor', Mr Peter Dickson."

We were off!

"Hello Gabby, thanks for having me and what an honour to be here on behalf of a fantastic charity that I know is close to both our hearts."

"Yes, indeed Peter. Thanks for being with us. It's all yours."

The screen flickered and cut to the first batch of results.

I began. "Here are the results from today's Premiership matches."

I looked up at the screen and saw the first line of results. It read:

'Manchester United 1 – 2 Arsenal 19'

This is going to be a breeze, I thought so with growing confidence I proudly announced,

"Manchester United 1, Arsenal 19."

From the other side of the set, I could hear Gabby laughing followed by assorted snorting and suppressed guffaws. I looked again at the screen and quickly realised I had mistakenly read the Pools forecast number instead of the Gunner's goal tally! Holy crap, I'd only just started, and I'd cocked it up already! My grandfather, had he been alive to witness it, would have been mortified and would have quite possibly, disowned and disinherited me and quite rightly too. In my cosy, usual, relaxed world of pre-record, it would have been an easy matter to wind things back, start again, perform another take and sort it out in the edit. But this was as live as it gets, and millions of the nation's football fans were hanging on my every word and quite possibly hanging off the arms of their sofas in hysterics. I can only assume what the reaction of the Arsenal fans must have been. I was quite possibly responsible for several cardiac arrests that day. There was nothing else I could do have done but simply carry on as if nothing had happened. About seven minutes later, without any further mishap, I reached the end, collapsed in a heap on the desk and was eventually led, dripping, out of the studio on a walk of shame, past Gabby and her guest pundits. She was taking great delight in correcting my earlier error to an amused and bemused nation. Needless to say, I haven't been asked back.

Looking back, 2012 was a pretty busy and fun-packed year, filled with lots of new and exciting opportunities. The Olympics and Final Score were quickly followed by a second series of 'Guinness World Records Smashed' with Welsh heartthrob Steve Jones and Charlie Brooker's wife Konnie Huq at Pinewood and the tenth series of 'The X Factor', which was won by James Arthur.

Two other big events in that year requested my 'Voice of God', live stadium announcer services. One of them was at London's O2 Arena and the other, in an altogether more upmarket venue. The O2 Arena is a venue that I absolutely despise. It was built for the Millennium celebrations and was ordered by the then Prime Minister, Tony Blair, who cajoled Her Majesty the Queen to join him at the O2 Arena for a night of forced jollity on 31st December 1999. The evening culminated in Her Majesty being unexpectedly and awkwardly coerced into joining hands with Blair and his party of acolytes to sing an overly vigorous, shoulder-ripping version of 'Auld Lang Syne'. The whole awkward event was played out live on TV. I remember seeing The Queen's expression at the time. It quite clearly read, 'I am never, ever coming back here again for as long as I live, so help me God'. As far as I know, she never has. I wish I could say the same. The place is a windswept hole. The acoustics are terrible, the drinks are poor and overpriced and it's uncomfortable, difficult to get to and even harder to get home from. Trust me, the best view of the O2 is in the rear-view mirror of a westbound Uber.

Sport Relief had asked me to make a short speech to a packed O2 Arena in September 2012 and to introduce the various acts on stage. When I got to the venue, it became apparent that the plan was for me to get up on stage and be in vision and not in my customary position in the stygian gloom backstage. The stage, by the way, was not in its usual position at one end of the arena; it was smack bang in the centre – boxing ring style. When the moment for me to perform arrived, a sound tech assistant handed me a Sennheiser radio microphone and a pair of headphones.

"Oh no thanks, I won't need those," I said. "I'll be fine."

"Take them with you just in case. Here, put them around your neck."

I did as he said and on a cue from the show director, the lights in the O2 dimmed and four large one thousand-watt spotlights, one in each corner, il-luminated the centre stage and bathed it in bright, incandescent white light. My play-on music began, and I bounded enthusiastically up the short flight of stairs and into the limelight with a deafening cheer from the capacity crowd. As I got to the centre, I looked up to address the good folks at the O2 but wasn't quite prepared for the fact that I couldn't see a single one of them. The huge spotlights were so bright, that all I could see was a kind of grey mist. I raised the microphone to my mouth and belted out the opening phrase used by every stage host that ever was.

"Good evening Ladies and Gentlemen!"

And that was where things began to unravel. Badly.

The massive Bose 'Showmatch' 360° loudspeaker arrays, that served the arena, were positioned high up in the cavernous roof of the venue and sus-pended from a huge circular steel truss. The distance between them and me was over thirty metres. Higher still in the upper tier seating, thirty-two large Bose 'Showmatch' directional speaker arrays ensured everyone up there could hear every word. Unfortunately for me, the sound of my voice, punching its way out of these unbelievably powerful speakers, travelling at 343 metres per second slammed into the back walls of the venue and returned to my eardrums almost a third of a second after I had uttered that initial welcome. It might not seem like much, but that infinitesimally small delay created utter chaos inside my head. There was a kangaroo loose in the upper paddock and it was running amok. I challenge anyone to do it, to sound normal while speaking under such circumstances. It's impossible. You begin to slur words, you sound like you have had one too many or that

With Chris Tarrant at the 'Centerpoint Charity Cricket' – 2016 – Lords, London.

worse, you are having a stroke. Luckily for me, I had taken the advice of the audio technician and had those DT-100 headphones still around my neck. I quickly whipped them over my head and onto my ears. Problem solved. Inside my head, all was now calm and normal. The kangaroo was back in his box with the lid shut and my voice was now back in sync with my brain. However, I was now struggling to regain control of my breathing, following the initial adrenaline jolt from the shock of the audio delay. It seemed like an eternity but in reality, it was only a few seconds and I'm pretty sure nobody had noticed so I soldiered on. I welcomed everyone to the event and read out a list of celebrities present who were supporting the charity, ending with the name 'Katie Price' and giving it a bit of projection with a rising inflection. I paused at this point for the audience to applaud and show their appreciation. It started gently and almost imperceptibly but quite quickly it spread around the arena like a bush fire. Christ! They were booing. They were booing Katie Price. My embarrassment quickly turned to anger. What had she done to deserve this? When did we as a nation consider it acceptable to publicly boo and deride someone who had freely given of his or her time at a charity concert? I had to rescue the situation somehow, but how? Many stand-up comedians have since told me that the best thing to say is the first thing that pops into your head. The first thing that popped into my head that evening was... "Alright you lot, shut the fuck up!" I quickly decided against that and instead opted for the infinitely more creative... "No! She really is here!" This caused a fair bit of confusion among the crowd and what psychologists call cognitive dissonance. It had a magically instant calming effect. I took immediate advantage of the lull and introduced Michael McIntyre onto the stage to thunderous applause and as I passed him on the way down the stairs and into the gloom, he looked at me and shouted, "nice one mate."

This slightly awkward stage moment though, pales into insignificance beside another potentially disastrous faux pas in front of a huge crowd at The News International Christmas party at their massive Wapping print works, later that year. I had struck up a friendship with the showbiz editor Rav Singh who had invited me to the bash as his guest. Inevitably though, there is no such thing as a free lunch or indeed a free drink. As he thrust the second of many Harvey Wallbangers that I consumed that night into my sweaty hand, he asked me if I would do the honours and introduce the star guests on stage. No problem, I was only too happy to oblige. As the evening wore on and the alcohol began to weave its magic inside my head, I realised, several hours later that I had forgotten that I had some work to do. Rav was back.

"OK, mate. Let's get the stars of the show on now."

I usually write these things down on a card rather than commit them to memory but that evening, as it was just one band to introduce, I thought that this wouldn't present me with too much of a problem. Now, before you say anything, I know I had broken the golden rule of no booze before work, but this was a favour and, in any case, what could possibly go wrong? So, emboldened with Dutch Wallbanger courage I dashed up (though in truth, I probably stumbled up) onto the stage and brought the huge crowd to silence.

"Ladies and Gentlemen." I began, with as much gusto and faux importance as I could muster.

"Ladies and Gentlemen, it is now time to introduce our headline act this evening. Tonight, Mr Murdoch has pulled out all the stops for you." There was thunderous applause. Rupert Murdoch, the billionaire media magnate was in the crowd, surrounded by a posse of sycophants.

"As you can see, no expense has been spared on this fantastic Christmas party and now it's time… it's time – for the stars of the show. Get ready to raise the roof for…"

As I said those words, I realised with a growing sense of panic, that I had forgotten the name of the band I was now supposed to be introducing. While filling for time, I looked stage left and there, smiling at me in eager anticipation were Shane Filan, Markus Feehily, Nicky Byrne, Brian McFadden and Kian Egan. My problem was that while I recognised all of them individually, for the life of me I couldn't recall if they were collectively called Boyzone or Westlife!

I began to mentally run down the names of that other band managed by Louis Walsh. Ronan Keating, Shane Lynch, Mikey Graham, Stephen Gately and Keith Duffy to see if that would jog my dumbass memory. Nothing. Zip. Nada. It was hopeless. I couldn't go across and ask them what they were called, that would be horrendous. The crowd was looking at me now. I am not a gambling man but there was only one thing for it. I couldn't call a friend or ask the audience. It was 50/50, red or black. Rien ne vas plus. In a matter of seconds, we would soon know the answer and either I would be back at the bar beside Rav, with another Harvey Wallbanger in my hand or in a fast car home or quite possibly an ambulance. I squeezed my buttocks, closed my eyes and clenched my teeth before letting rip and bellowing out with as much confidence as I could muster:

"WESTLIFE!"

The crowd went wild and as Shane Filan and his mates bounced onto the stage, I turned to my left and with huge relief saw smiles all round and a cheeky wink of acknowledgement from Kian as I departed the spotlight. From that day on, when doing stage introductions, I always write things down. In the heat of the moment, it is all too easy to become distracted and lose concentration, even for a split second. I now leave nothing to chance. If you've been paying attention up to this point, you will know dear reader, that this is a complete lie. I still don't do it.

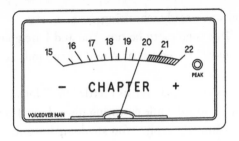

YES, YOUR MAJESTY, HAMMOND IS A PRICK

s you already know, I am a keen ambassador for the great work Comic Relief and Sport Relief carry out around the world. They often call upon me to give voice to their many and varied projects and I am always happy to oblige. One such fundraising idea was to orchestrate an international global 'Sport Relief Mile' challenge, where individuals would run a sponsored mile. There were forty of these events across the planet organised by the Foreign and Commonwealth Office and the British Council, but by far the biggest was in London on the Mall in front of Buckingham Palace, the residence of Her Majesty The Queen. I was asked to be the official voice of the event and to appear on camera on the BBC worldwide broadcast alongside Richard Hammond, who was to host the show. On the big day itself, I arrived at the designated call time and made my way through the gathering crowds on the Mall, to the extremely smart temporary studios that had been built on the lawn just in front of the palace. I remember looking up as I arrived and noticing the Royal Standard, gently fluttering in the summer breeze high above the palace façade. As most Londoners know, this is the outward sign that the Queen is in residence. We all had to be on best behaviour. A cheery floor manager led me to the studio where Hammond was already rehearsing.

"Hello mate. This is going to be fun. You and I are going to have to do the run too you know!" He said as he waved a hand indicating that I should join him on the sofa.

"Well, that's news to me," I said, as I settled in. "Not sure I have the right footwear, old boy," I added while gesturing toward my desert boots.

"No excuses." Came the reply. "You are doing it – and that's that!"

I hadn't run anywhere, not even for a bus in years, so this was going to be interesting. My immediate concern about the prospect of going for a run was interrupted by the floor manager.

"Peter, they want some level from you in the gallery."

He handed me a Coles 4101 microphone and indicated that they were ready in sound. I grabbed it from him and looking at Richard, shuffled forwards to the edge of the sofa, took a deep diaphragmatic breath and with all the self-importance I could muster bellowed out:

"Ladies and Gentlemen, Richard Hammond is a PRICK!!!"

The reaction was instant but not exactly from the quarter I had expected it. From outside the studio, through the semi soundproof walls, I heard the most almighty roar followed by laughter. Lots of laughter – mainly from middle-aged men. Hammond was laughing too, until he too slowly realised that my unguarded comment had left the confines of the studio and had been broadcast over the huge public address system, to the crowds along the full mile of the Mall and around the Victoria Memorial, Canada Gate, Australia Gate, South and West Africa Gate and the Memorial Gardens. We both looked at each other and at the floor manager who was now standing in front of us looking ashen-faced. I looked out the window and swore I saw a curtain twitching at a first-floor window to the right of that famous balcony on the palace. In my mind's eye, I could picture Her Majesty and Prince Phillip slowly nodding in agreement with my unexpected, though accurate terse summation of the character of the man who was sitting next to me. Luckily, he saw the funny side of it. Hammond that is, not Prince Phillip. All those years of being on the receiving end of abuse and barbed banter from Clarkson and May had blunted his sensibility to such matters. There were a few raised eyebrows from some of the dignitaries in the VIP section of the crowd, but I am pleased to say that for its entire career-ending potential, the incident seems to have only enhanced mine. The matter wasn't over for Hammond however, he made damned sure I received a good beasting on the mile run down the Mall and demanded a free voicemail message recording from me for himself, as punishment.

I have always been reluctant to take holidays as the fear of missing out on work always wins the day. But as we know, all work and no play can make Jack a dull boy. Therefore, I have in the past often forced myself to take time off to rest and recharge. It's actually a good thing and I have come to realise its importance. A few years back, I was beginning to feel the strain of constant work and the pressure of deadlines in the studio, so I booked a week-long holiday for myself and the family in a gorgeous villa, near the beach on Portugal's Algarve coast. All was well until three days into this trip, my agent called with the news that ABC's 'Good Morning America' wanted me to voice a couple of promos and introduce their host Katie Kouric, who was in London for a commemorative royal event. Luckily, I had brought my laptop, my trusty Sennheiser MKH 416 microphone and various other bits of kit with me. So, I agreed to do the job. As soon as I ended the call from my agent and while I waited for the scripts to arrive by email, I walked through the villa looking for the best place to record. Much to my utter dismay, every room had a marble floor and minimal soft furnishings. Not enough to absorb the sound reflections that would ruin a recording. The smallest room in the villa was the downstairs loo and while that too was all marble, I at least had some chance of containing it. And so, at 2 o'clock in the ruddy morning, while the family slept and I was a slave to American Eastern Time, I found myself sitting on the loo seat, with my MacBook Pro perched precariously on the sink in front of me. I was in my pyjamas, completely draped in duvets and blankets holding a torch in one hand and a microphone in the other and shouting, "Good Morning America – now, here's your host Katie Couric" – over and over again. A three-man production team at ABC's studios at 77, West 66th street in New York, who were recording me over a high-speed broadband connection and unaware of my dire circumstances, eventually gave their tacit approval on take fourteen! The temperature under the duvet was at least 30°C and when I was almost at the point of passing out due to lack of oxygen, I heard a voice at the back of a studio in New York say:

"We have it. Thanks, Peter."

I was never more pleased for a session to end. I threw the duvet and suffocating blankets off, wiped the sweat from my eyes and thought as I took a cold shower, if anyone ever suggests that what I do is easy, I wish they could have seen me that night!

Of all the many fantastic things I have ever done and experiences I have had in this bonkers voiceover business that I work in, I think that being part of the Olympic Games must be pretty well, up there but a close second must surely come the time I gave voice to a children's TV puppet that had remained completely speechless for sixty-five years. For those of a certain age in the UK, mention 'Sooty and Sweep' and the very names conjure up many happy childhood hours, spent in front of a TV set on a Saturday morning. Sooty came to life way back in 1948 and made his first TV appearance in 1952 on the BBC's 'Talent Night' show. Harry Corbett who was Sooty's owner and puppeteer, won the show and secured a contract to be a regular guest on the BBC's Saturday Special between 1952 and 1955. In 1976, Matthew Corbett, Harry's son took over Sooty's career and he enjoyed a new wave of popularity on British television. Harry Corbett and Sooty were awarded the OBE for services to entertainment. At the ceremony at Buckingham Palace, Sooty squirted his water pistol at The Duke of Edinburgh. Corbett was a braver man than most. The Duke is not known for tolerating fools, but he too has an anarchic sense of humour, so it seems he actually enjoyed this particular jape. More than that, I am pretty sure that privately made his day!

In 2014, Richard Cadell, who had by then taken over as Sooty's handler, called me to ask if I would like to be the first and probably only actor to give the legendary puppet a voice. Would I? Hell yes! It was a very short scene in one of the shows, where Sooty performs a magic spell, which ends up with him shouting in my loud booming voice, the one I reserve for 'The X Factor'. During the scene, the volume of his voice causes plates and glasses to smash and pictures on the walls to crash to the floor. It may only have been ninety seconds long and passed many people by but for me, that was a total career highlight.

My pro bono work for Comic relief was rewarded that year with a trip to South Africa to witness first-hand the wonderful difference that the charity's fundraising and grant-giving is making to people in that country. Kevin Cahill, the CEO personally invited me to join him along with Alexander Armstrong – the host of 'Pointless', Cilla Snowball – the CEO of one of the UK's biggest advertising agencies AMVBBDO, Tristia Harrison – the CEO of UK mobile and broadband provider TalkTalk and TV producer and agent Peter Bennett-Jones, the man behind hit TV classics such as The Vicar of Dibley and Mr Bean. Before this point, none of us had met before and only had one thing in common apart from our showbiz connections – the desire to raise money through Comic Relief to help disadvantaged and vulnerable people in the UK and across the world. As we boarded the flight to Johannesburg at Heathrow that day, not one of us apart from Kevin who had made the trip several times previously had anticipated what lay ahead nor how the entire experience would radically change our lives and in more ways than we at the time could ever have imagined. We were to visit a handful of projects; a football initiative supported by Nike and Comic Relief in Soweto, a housing project also in Soweto and a community of displaced migrants from Zimbabwe, Lesotho and Botswana who were occupying a disused and abandoned warehouse in downtown Johannesburg and who, following threats of eviction were receiving pro bono legal support from a firm of city lawyers.

As we drove into the centre of the city that day, I couldn't help but notice how many private homes were surrounded by high brick walls topped with metre upon metre of galvanised razor wire. This was a city that clearly had a problem and we were about to come face to face with it, whatever *it* was. Our first day was pretty harrowing, but not in the sense that any of us felt personally threatened. We were invited to watch a football match and training session at the brand-new Nike football training centre in the heart of Soweto township. This was a facility, where 1,200 teams and over 20,000 young people play football together each year. To say that this place blew my mind, would be an understatement. We have nothing like it in the UK. There are two full-size artificial pitches, two junior turf pitches, state of the art lighting, a luxuriously appointed architect-designed modern clubhouse, a player's lounge, a gym, physiotherapy rooms and first aid centre, catering facilities, a viewing deck and multiple changing rooms. It soon became apparent what all this investment was all about. The charity and Nike were using the football facilities as a magnet to get young people from the township into sport and once there, professionals would engage them in sex education and in particular educate them about HIV and AIDS. This was a massive problem not just in Soweto but also throughout South Africa and education was seen as the way to save lives, which were tragically being lost. We were invited into one of several small tents that were set up along the touchline, where sexually active teenagers could if they wished, be tested for the virus before a match and then return for the result after the game. I will never forget being present in one of these tents when a young eighteen-year-old lad came in. The doctor invited him to take a seat and gently broke the news to him that he was HIV positive. I had to look away, as it felt so intrusive. The good news, if indeed there is any good news, is that this young man and others in his position were offered counselling and retroviral drugs to stop the advance of the infection. Others who tested negative were enrolled in an education programme and given condoms to use. It was a difficult day, but it was encouraging to see that donations of UK money to the charity were being put to very good use. I do not doubt that many lives have been and continue to be saved, through this admirable intervention.

As difficult a day as it may have been, nothing was to prepare us for was to confront us the following morning. As our minibus snaked its way into the heart of the city of Johannesburg – past shopping malls, prosperous-looking businesses and pretty private estates whose perimeter walls were draped in Bougainvillea, I noticed that the walls supporting the razor wire were getting higher and the locals were looking less welcoming. Half an hour from our hotel, as we began to slow down and turn into the maze of streets in the downtown district, my heart sank as we stopped outside what looked like a derelict building in a street that no one in their right mind would walk down in the daytime, never mind after dark. There was litter everywhere, weeds grew unchecked between the cracks in the mostly broken pavement and as the door of the minibus opened, we were assailed with the visceral stench of rotting urine and human excrement. Alexander Armstrong, who was sitting beside me turned to me and said:

"Well, here we are. Home sweet home. Let's go and meet the neighbours."

It was his typical gallows humour but both Cilla and Tristia looked horrified. Accompanying us on our visit were two former members of the South African Special Forces brigade, the Recces. These two 'man mountains', with forearms thicker than my two thighs put together, exited the van first and met with a man at the entrance to the building. A building I hasten to add that had no door and no windows but that was the least of its worries.

They weren't the only things missing, as we were about to find out. We huddled together on the pavement, our conspicuously white faces seeking the shade from the looming brick façade of the vast warehouse, under a blazing, midday African sun. Each of us acutely aware that our presence in this place was already attracting unwelcome attention and each of us, now mouth breathing to prevent us from physically retching from the stench. Kevin introduced the man who had come out to meet us, he was a community leader and his validation of our visit and his continuous presence, would be the only thing that would ensure our security and quite possibly our lives, for the next ninety minutes. Another vehicle pulled up at the kerb and two young sharp-suited black men wearing expensive-looking Ray-Ban aviators jumped out. These two, it transpired, were the city lawyers who were being funded by Comic Relief to act on behalf of the inhabitants of the building we were about to enter. Inside, we were told were two hundred and fifty souls who had come to Johannesburg, crossing huge distances on foot from neighbouring countries, to seek work. Their journey's end was here, squatting in a most undignified way in this utter hellhole. Let me put it this way, if someone ever needed to give the earth an enema, this is where they'd put the tube. Under South African law, it is illegal for a landlord or a building owner to physically evict a person or persons from their accommodation, whether their occupation of it in the first instance, was lawful or not. The evictor needs to have in place alternative accommodation. The owner of this building was attempting to evict without an alternative being proposed. Comic Relief was here to ensure that when the departure of these people from this place did eventually come, it was carried out in an orderly and dignified manner, with alternative accommodation arrangements in place, before their eviction. Human rights, it seems, were not high up on the list of priorities in this country.

The briefing was over. Our hearts sank as the moment had come. We were going in. Cilla Snowball grabbed my hand as we slipped into the dark, fetid atmosphere of the entrance hall. My eyes had not yet fully adjusted from the bright sunlit street, but my nose was having no such difficulty. The stench of human excrement, rotting urine, and the reek of unwashed bodies was overpowering. The cacophony of voices of men, women and children and transistor radios playing at full volume, emanating from upstairs was deafening. If you had asked a leading Hollywood set designer to create a

With Tristia Harrison, Kevin Cahill CBE, Dame Cilla Snowball DBE, Peter Bennett-Jones CBE, Alexander Armstrong – 2014 – Johannesburg.

vision of a boiling, satanic, Dickensian slum he could not have designed anything better than this. It was hell on earth. My pulse was racing, all of my senses – alert to the potential imminent threat that could come out of the shadows at any moment. As I looked across at Alexander Armstrong, I could tell we were both thinking the same thing – what in God's name were we doing here? With the help of the building's captain and our two man-mountain guards we moved quickly across the dimly lit hall and began to ascend a steep flight of cold stone stairs to the first floor.

"KEEP TO THE LEFT!" came the barked instruction from man-mountain number one.

"KEEP CLOSE TO THE WALL, SINGLE FILE AND STAY CLOSE!" was the command barked from the back of the party by man-mountain number two.

We obediently complied, without question. By now, my eyes were adjusting to the gloom and what I saw next completely horrified me. A little girl, who could have been no more than five years old, came running down the narrow stone steps past us. We were a good three stories up now and there was no handrail. It had been removed some time ago. One slip and she would have hurtled into a dark basement and certain death. The noise from the upper floors was now horrendous. On the fourth floor, we turned off the staircase and into the body of the building – a vast floor space that had been carved up into small rooms and alleyways, using any materials that had come to hand. Cardboard, rusty corrugated iron sheeting, discarded wooden pallets and barbed wire – cobbled together to give individuals and families some semblance of shelter, privacy and security. An old advertising hoarding had also been employed. I couldn't help being struck by the irony of a faded image of a pretty, young American model advertising Chanel Number 5 perfume. It seemed so horribly incongruous. Exposed makeshift cables that were connected to the mains electrical supply across the street outside – crisscrossed dangerously at head height. The air crackled and hummed with electricity as we snaked and twisted our way around the myriad of dark alleyways, lit by the occasional bulb strung overhead. Here and there a door would open, dark eyes watching our every move, shadows everywhere, a young man in a doorway. A sudden glint of metal as he sharpened a huge machete – a palpable sense of danger in this highly charged atmosphere. At one point we paused and were shown into a room if indeed I could call it that, in which there was a soiled mattress on the floor and some ragtag clothing and meagre possessions placed on filthy upturned cardboard boxes. On the bed was a young, heavily pregnant woman nursing a young child. With a look of deep concern, she looked up as we entered. Our guide explained our presence and she relaxed a little. It was a heart-breaking scene. I could not imagine spending even one night in that place, never mind three years as this poor woman had. I asked her if she felt threatened living here and having asked, felt immediately stupid. She nodded; her gaze fell back to the floor. I reflected on my own life; on the peace and security we all enjoyed and took for granted. I wish I could have done more but alleviating desperation on this scale requires huge joined-up thinking and effort. I had to comfort myself with the knowledge that funds raised by Comic Relief were at least going to ensure that her future and that of her children and indeed everyone in this dreadful place would not be quite as bleak, as it otherwise might have been. When we returned to the hotel later that day we headed to the bar for a stiff drink and to talk about what we had just witnessed. We all agreed that it was a sobering reminder of the contrast and disparity of our lives compared to those poor unfortunate souls in downtown Johannesburg.

As the wheels of the big British Airways Boeing 747-400 touched down at Heathrow, I was never so glad to return to the UK and as I turned the key in the lock of my house, I made a promise to myself that I would begin to lend my support to a homeless charity in the UK and never, ever complain about the circumstances of my life again. For all its faults and shortcomings, the UK is one of the best places to live on this planet and my visit to South Africa was a real personal wake up call. The whole trip left such an impression on us all, that when we bump into each other again, we shudder at the memory of that week and count our blessings. As for Kevin Cahill, he is credited with changing the lives of millions of people across the planet. He was awarded a CBE in the Queen's New Year honours. As journalist Simon Briggs noted in the Daily Telegraph in 2016:

"Very few men have achieved so much while remaining so unknown to the general public."

His moniker: 'The Billion Dollar Man' is a fitting tribute to a man who after more than twenty-six years at the helm of Comic Relief, retired in 2016. He should have received a Knighthood.

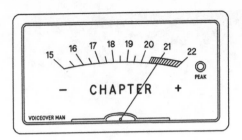

THE DUKE OF KENT FELL
ASLEEP ON TOP OF ME

O n the 26th March 2014, the big, plush velvet curtain over the proscenium arch at the London Palladium rose on the opening night of a brand-new West End musical. This was no ordinary production. With a budget of £7 million, it was one of the most expensive ever mounted in London. It's title, in glittering, bright lights above those famous doors on Argyll Street was: 'I Can't Sing!' Written by Harry Hill and Steve Brown, the show was in homage to the TV entertainment behemoth 'The X Factor'. Starring in the title role was a little-known actress at the time, Cynthia Erivo. She has now left these shores for Hollywood and has appeared in a raft of huge movies and was a 2020 Oscar nominee for her role in the $17M blockbuster called 'Harriet'.

Two years earlier, Harry Hill had invited me to his home in London to show me the storyboard he had created for the show. In the original story, a young girl who lives with her grandfather in a dilapidated caravan under a West London flyover enters 'The X Factor' talent show and goes on to win it. The story that Hill described to me that day, contained all the much-loved clichés, memes and tropes that have become the hallmark of the series but with the expected Harry Hill surrealist twists and turns, including a scene

With Alan Dedicoat, we can't stand each other! – 2018 – Soho, London.

where Cowell is consumed by an alien! I told him that it was quite possibly the most bonkers idea I'd ever heard and that he had little more than an ice cream's chance in hell of ever getting Cowell to buy into it. I underestimated Hill's determination. He had by his own admission spent £250 of his own money on a storyboard artist and he wanted to see a return on his investment! He contacted the ITV boss Peter Fincham, who helped him arrange a meeting with Cowell. To everyone's utter amazement, Cowell tentatively bought into the project and agreed to attend a workshop several months later, where an assembled cast of musical theatre actors would play out several of the show's key scenes and songs. Harry had written me into the project as the narrator. Outside the RADA Studios rehearsal room, Cowell ordered his driver to keep the engine of his gleaming black Rolls Royce Wraith running, and to request a seat for him close to the exit, in case the show was boring, and the songs were crap. He stayed. In the audience, that day were the owners of all the big West End London theatres. Following the workshop, which was great fun and got many laughs, the impresarios, began a bidding war to be the first to host the show. Andrew Lloyd Webber's 'Really Useful Company' won the bid and so, the show was bound for the biggest theatre in London, The mighty London Palladium.

Following the opening night, the after-party at a venue in a converted church on the Marylebone Road was a truly star-studded affair. I had a lovely conversation with Lord Andrew Lloyd Webber who told me that he laughed out loud when he first heard my voice in the show. That was nice of him. Ronnie Corbett was also there, and I was pleased to have been able to chat with him too. He died a few years later, another one of our comedy greats gone forever. In retrospect, Cowell is on record as saying that he wished he had toured the production first in smaller regional theatres, built an audience and then moved it to London. The show was a resounding success with critics and audiences who saw it, during its all too brief six-week run but with huge rent and spiralling costs, 'I Can't Sing!' was not able to gain the traction it needed to sustain a long, profitable run. It closed with catastrophic losses and a cast and company in shock and dismay at its untimely demise. It still remains as one of the best musicals staged in the West End in years but one that hardly anyone saw. I was and I am still proud to this day at being able to play my small part in it.

They say that you should never meet your heroes as they ultimately disappoint. In 2016 and 2017 I was to meet three of mine. Terry Gilliam, Terry Jones and John Cleese. I have been a Monty Python fan all of my life. I have watched every TV show, bought every album, seen every movie and watched every live show. Heck, I can even recite word for word many of their sketches. My professional association with them came courtesy of a guy called Jeff Simpson who I knew from my time at BBC Radio 1 when Jeff was the press officer for the national pop station. Jeff had since gone on to be a producer and had produced a fantastic animated feature based on the autobiography of Graham Chapman, one of the Python six called: 'A Liar's Autobiography'. He had asked me to play a very small part in it. This was recorded at Redwood Studios in London by a hugely talented and long-serving sound designer called Andre Jacquemin. Andre had recorded everything the Pythons had ever done, dating back to their very first album 'Monty Python's Flying Circus' in 1970, which was recorded in his father's greenhouse and eighteen further albums since. He was the only person the Pythons trusted to handle their audio and to many, he is considered the seventh Python. Redwood Studios back then, was located on the first floor of a rather nondescript terraced building on Great Chapel Street in Soho. I can't begin to tell you what a thrill it was for me to record in the same room as the Pythons. The walls of that studio were adorned with Python memorabilia, including a life-sized cardboard cut-out of the late Graham Chapman. There was a short length of thick rope, which hung on a hook on the wall. I asked Andre why it was there. He told me he had used it many times on the movie 'The Life of Brian', twisting and turning it in front of a Sennheiser MKH 41s shotgun microphone, to create the sound of straining ropes during that infamous crucifixion scene. He'd also employed it on the movie 'Time Bandits', simulating the sound of a ship pitching and yawing in full sail. The magic of the movies never fails to amaze me.

Well, I must have passed the test following that initial visit to Redwood because a year later, a producer called James Peak called me via Andre asking if I would be interested in playing a few character parts in a BBC Radio 4 series called 'John Cleese Presents'. Interested? I would have crawled up the hard shoulder of the M1 in my underpants to be in it. The series was an excuse for Cleese to read extracts from his nascent autobiography 'So, Anyway...' with the various character parts along the way read by a small cast of actors. I was to play his psychotherapist Professor Langoustine and an irate Scottish man called Mr MacLeod, who calls in to harass Cleese from time to time. I had christened him Mr MacLeod that day as Cleese was searching for a name and I thought why not name him after my best mate Lewis MacLeod. On the day of the recording, I made my way to Redwood Studios with some trepidation. What if he was ghastly to work with? What if he turned out to be totally unlike the John Cleese I had imagined him to be? I needn't have worried. The day got off to a cracking start in the Control room over coffee, where the great man leapt onto his high horse and regaled us with his robust views on everything from Donald Trump to the state of comedy today and how nowadays, very few things made him laugh. I thought that last observation was quite sad, yet I understood where he was coming from. Here was a septuagenarian king of comedy, a professional mirth-maker, who has probably not only written but also heard every joke that ever was. We finished our coffee and headed into the booth. Two Neumann U87 microphones had been set up and positioned side by side next to a pair of script stands. We did a couple of run through reads for sense and timing – and so that Andre could set the recording levels. A quick thumbs up from Andre on the other side of the glass and we were good to go. I cleared my throat, took a deep breath and began.

Prof Langoustine: "So, Mr Cleaze, what brings you here today?"

Cleese: "It's Cleese! Rhymes with Niece!"

Prof Langoustine: "Ah, I see. So, Mr Cleaze, what can I do for you?"

Cleese: "Well, I am experiencing those panic attacks again Professor."

Prof Langoustine: "I see. And tell me as an actor on stage and TV did you suffer from zee... Stage Fright?"

I remember giving the word *'fright'* a really hard, Germanic glottal stop and thought that I had perhaps overcooked it and that he would stop and ask me to go again. I waited for the call to stop. It didn't come. Neither did his next line. Instead, out of the corner of my right eye, I saw the slightest heaving at first, which was followed by a deep nasal in-breath followed by an ear-shattering wheeze of a belly laugh. I looked around, his face was contorted and red and he was now doubling up, with his hands on his knees. Well, that was it for me. A wonderful thing had just happened. I had made John Cleese laugh. What a feeling. I am sure you are reading this and thinking get a life, but this was a real career highlight, a personal top moment and one I will treasure forever.

Following my work on 'John Cleese Presents', Andre called me again in late 2015 to work on a film that another Python; Terry Jones had made called 'Boom Bust Boom'. It was to be his very last movie out of a total of twenty-five, spanning almost forty-five years. I was very sad to hear of his death following a long illness, on the 21st January 2020. On hearing the news, Cleese took to Twitter to express his sadness:

"It feels strange to me that a man of so many talents and such endless enthusiasm should have faded so gently away... Of his many achievements, for me, the greatest gift he gave us all was his direction of 'Life of Brian'. Perfection, two down four to go."

Having spent time already with Michael Palin on my BBC Radio 2 show, at the Python O2 reunion concert and in the Merion hotel in Dublin in 2016, the only other Python I had yet to encounter was Terry Gilliam. Terry was in the process of finally finishing his magnum opus – 'The Man Who Killed Don Quixote'. It was a movie that nearly finished *him* off, having unsuccessfully attempted to make it many times over twenty-nine years. Gilliam is one of the nicest men you could hope to meet. He has an infectious, almost boyish enthusiasm for life and to get to work with him directly on the ADR for this movie was a total blast. In one scene, I play one of a pair of giants who are engaged in a battle with Adam Driver. Gilliam himself voiced the other giant. Being directed by him was a dream come true and as I stood there in the booth on that day in early March 2018, I couldn't help but think that I really did have the best job in the world!

Alongside my film ADR work and my work on commercials, entertainment television, gaming and narration, another sector began to loom large; live corporate awards and events. To date, I have done hundreds of these, during the awards season I practically live in the Great Room at London's Grosvenor House Hotel, on Park Lane. My former BBC Radio 2 colleague and good pal Alan 'Dedders' Dedicoat and I, voice a lot of live events, though I know he does more of them than I do. Principally, because he likes to get out of the house and he's cheaper! We have twice been booked to voice at the same events. One was the Glass and Glazing Federation's annual awards, where they actually built us a double-glazed soundproof booth, the size of a phone box right in the room surrounded by eight hundred diners. The other was the 'National Rail Awards', where we were surrounded by; a

With Joe Cipriano, the voice of 'The Emmys' – 2018 – One Voice Conference, London.

With Producer James Peak and John Cleese – 2017 – Redwood Studios, London.

thousand train drivers, signalmen and train managers. Hilarious! Announcing at these live dinners and events in front of up to two thousand people looks relatively straightforward, but it requires immense concentration. It may be the 'National Double Glazing Awards' but to the people in the hired dinner jackets and posh frocks, who have paid upwards of £100 each to be there, it is their 'Oscars' night and as such, I have to treat each and every one with the utmost respect and professionalism. I don't amend my performance as others do, depending on how prestigious the event might be. On some occasions, of course, things do go wrong and when they do, the wheels can fall off pretty spectacularly. On two big events, I have had to rescue potentially disastrous outcomes and on one, I almost caused a riot when I got it badly wrong.

At the 'Recruitment in Advertising Awards' in the Great Room at The Grosvenor House Hotel one year, the host, Omid Djalili was struggling to get the one thousand five hundred very drunk recruitment executives on his side. During the main course, he came running up to my commentary position on the balcony and pleaded with me to do something. After a few minutes of chin-scratching, we came up with the idea that he would start a mock argument with me that would end with me calling him a 'fat bastard'.

At Monty Python HQ with John Cleese – 2017 – Soho, London.

The joke, if it could be called that, referenced something that a Government minister had said in public that day and was now creating a social media firestorm.

"Are you sure this is going to work, Omid?" I asked.

"Of course." He said. 'Trust me."

"Well, OK if you think it won't backfire?"

"Look." He said. "It's a risk but I bet you we can pull it off."

Sometimes desperate situations call for desperate measures and this was a pretty desperate situation and so, at the agreed point during the awards, he began to chuck insults at me from the stage down below. I protested, rather lamely at first and then the argument began to get heated. You could hear the sharp intake of breath from the one thousand or so people room down below.

Omid: "Why don't you shut your arse and give your mouth a chance."

Then, after the briefest of pauses.

Me: "Oh shut up! You fat bastard!"

Well, that brought the house down and generated immediate sympathy for poor Omid on stage, following which he had the audience eating out of

With best pal Lewis MacLeod – 2018 – Portsmouth.

his hand for the rest of the night. I too was thrown clear, as the next morning the organiser called me up to say that our little contrived argument was the talk of the event and that it made his night. Just in case anyone from the English Defence League is reading this and thinking of booking me for their next 'racist of the year' awards, don't bother.

At another event I was co-hosting at the magnificent Great Room in the Grosvenor House Hotel on London's glittering Park Lane, the organisers had booked Barry Humphries to appear as Dame Edna Everage. The ambitions plan was for me to go on stage and make a mock apology to the one thousand or so diners who had packed in that night, for the 'Travel Weekly Travel Awards'. I was to apologise that the Secretary of State for Transport couldn't make it but that we had, at the last minute, sourced a replacement. Then there would be the big reveal. In the Great Room, two rather grand staircases descend from the reception above. The show director thought it would be a good idea if I announced Dame Edna from the stage and she made her grand entrance, accompanied by fireworks and semi-naked male dancers with oiled torsos down one of the staircases and made her way through the tables and onto the stage to join me. On paper and in rehearsals it worked well. On the night, however, as Dame Edna reached the bottom of the stairs and began to make her way over to the stage, which was thirty metres away, she was mobbed by over a hundred drunk travel agents. It took ten minutes to get her to within a metre of the stage; such was the melee and scramble for selfies. Barry's wife, who was in the audience, was going apoplectic and screaming at me to do something. So, I jumped off the stage, pushed my way through the crowd, while giving a running commentary on the microphone and grabbed Barry by his sequinned shoulder and shoved him up the steps. It was a night none of us will ever forget, not least of all for Barry's opening remark.

"Do you know," he said. "I had a coffee enema last night. I slept like a baby, but my backside was up all night with one eye open, staring at the ceiling!"

Very occasionally though, the wheels of some live events do fall off pretty dramatically. At the annual 'Scottish Retailer Awards' in Glasgow a few years ago, I was booked to be the on-stage host. The evening had started full of promise. There was no autocue, so I was reading off a pre-prepared script on a lectern on stage. During the main course, unknown to me one of the event organisers had gone up to the lectern and left me a handwritten note, alerting me to a change in the upcoming awards script. When I got back on stage, I was aware there was a note but as I had already begun the next raft of presentation, I could neither fully read it nor make the necessary changes further on. We were off! I tried to locate the page that the note referred to, but my efforts were in vain, everything was moving too quickly, and I needed to focus. These things move forwards like an express train and require one hundred percent concentration. It goes like this: read the nominees, introduce the award presenter, reveal the winner, wrangle everyone on stage for the ubiquitous 'grip and grin' and then shepherd everyone off the stage and then rinse and repeat. I decided that I would have to wing it. Ten minutes later, I turned to the dreaded page forty-three. And there, in pencil, were some scribbled notes that I had neither the time nor eyesight to read and so, I steamed proudly on.

"And the winner of the Scottish Convenience Store of the year is… SPAR!"

A huge cheer went up from the SPAR table. The rest of the room responded with a smattering of polite but sustained applause. I looked out across the room and smiled as the kilt-wearing managing director of SPAR Scotland heaved his not inconsiderable frame out of his seat and with his entire grocery team, began to make his way through the tightly packed tables towards the stage to collect his award. It was then, that my eye was drawn to a woman at the front of the stage who was waving her napkin in the air and gesticulating at me, with a look of sheer panic on her face. I leant down to hear what she had to say. Above the din of the room and the sound of ample backs being slapped as Mr SPAR and his pals lumbered closer, I heard her say; "you announced the wrong winner. You should have said NISA!" I am sorry to report that the ground didn't swallow me up, as I wished at that moment it had. Neither did a trap door open in the floor, nor a shepherd's crook yank me unceremoniously off the stage nor a huge boxing glove on the end of a concertina punch me in the face. Any one of those comedic options would have been preferable to what happened next. There was nothing else I could do. I looked across at my stage assistant, who was holding the award on which the word NISA, not SPAR was clearly inscribed. I looked out at the audience and at the approaching posse being led by the ruddy-faced, fat-fingered grocer of the year, who was heaving his ample frame and sporran between the tightly packed chairs and tables towards me. There was nothing else for it. I held my hands up in the air, palms forward.

"Ladies and Gentlemen," I said. "Ladies and Gentlemen, I am most terribly sorry. I have made the most unforgivable error."

The room fell silent. The ruddy-faced SPAR boys who had almost reached the steps to the stage at this point, stopped dead in their tracks, gasping for air after their unexpected exertion. Everyone was looking at me and wondering what I was going to say next. This was my very own OSCARS 2017 'La La Land' moment. How on earth was this going to play out? I had no idea but what I did know was that it wasn't going to be pretty or indeed crown me in any semblance of glory. I am also ashamed to say that at this very point I desperately tried to remember if my agent had received and banked my fee in advance but hey, that's show business!

"Ladies and Gentlemen – I'm most terribly sorry. I'm afraid I announced the wrong winner's name. The winner of the Scottish Convenience Store of the year is… NISA!"

There was a beat of a pause, followed by a deafening uproar in the room. The SPAR boys looked at first confused then very, very angry. None of them was sure what to do or indeed which way to turn. If they had decided to go back to their table at that point, they would have met the NISA boys head-on, who were coming the other way. All hell would have broken out. What am I talking about? It already had! The NISA contingent was already on their feet and punching the air and whooping like cheerleaders. After an extremely awkward presentation, I returned to the podium. I couldn't think of anything appropriate to say. So, I simply blurted out:

"Now… I realise that this is incredibly disappointing to you chaps at SPAR but as compensation, I am happy to… err… record for each of you a personalised mobile voicemail greeting at… err… no charge… err… whatsoever. My treat."

The words were out of my mouth before I realised how crass, cheap and wholly inappropriate that sounded. It was greeted with the utter silence it so richly deserved. A woman who was sitting two tables away gently lowered her head into her napkin. The event organiser, a portly woman in a black dress, was trying to placate the head of the Glasgow Chamber of Commerce. In retrospect, I, of course, should have said:

"And as a penance for my unacceptable and wholly unprofessional and unforgivable error, I shall, of course, be donating my entire fee from tonight to a charity of your choice."

But I didn't. Instead, when it was all over, I limped back to my dimly lit room in the Grand Central Hotel and wept gently into a tumbler, containing a miniature of single malt Scotch whisky. I sneaked out of the hotel the next morning before breakfast, to avoid being seen and I caught the first train back to London. It will come as no surprise to learn that the following year, the good grocery retailers of bonnie Scotland enjoyed the excellent company and presenting skills of the infinitely more talented Gyles Brandreth who no doubt, covered himself in glory like he always does.

Mishaps at events are quite common. There are just so many moving parts. I have hosted the annual Royal Airforce Benevolent fund awards for some years now. At the very first one I did for them, I was welcomed onto the stage to polite applause and as I launched into my opening remarks, there was a massive power cut. The room was plunged into darkness. The medals on the chest of Sir Andrew Pulford, the Chief of the Air Staff, twinkled from the front row, illuminated by the faint light from the emergency exit sign. Beyond that, it was inky black. Producing my mobile phone and switching on the built-in torch, I held it above my script and gamely carried on as though nothing had happened. I got a round of applause for that. Appreciation I guess, from a military audience for fortitude in the face of adversity!

More often than not, it is the job of the Voice of God or live event announcer to cover up the mistakes of others. On one event, I was the Voice of God at a ceremony to induct over four hundred newly qualified motor mechanics into employment at a well-known German car manufacturer. By 6.30pm, the room was set, and each individual's framed and signed certificate of competence was placed on their chairs at the table. During the ceremony, I was to announce their names, one at a time, as they took their framed certificate up to the stage for a grip and grin photo opportunity with the Chairman of the company, who had flown in from Munich that afternoon. Before the doors opened to allow the eight hundred or so guests in, the event organiser instructed the lighting director to dim the lights to make the space more inviting and atmospheric. All the engineers, together with their wives and partners filed into the room. Before too long, the air was filled with excited chatter and... the sound of breaking glass – as the buttocks of four hundred engineers lowered into their seats, reducing their expensively produced awards to a pile of broken wood, paper, glass and blood. I had to laugh. And as I did, I quietly amended my script to remind myself to tell them that their new certificates would be posted out to them the following week. It was one of those moments that someone with an eye for detail should have foreseen – but didn't.

One of the nice things about working pro bono for charities, which I do a lot, is that occasionally they invite me to lovely events, where I am not required to work. One such event is the annual Cirencester Polo Club Centrepoint charity invitational, set in the stunning grounds of Cirencester Park, The Earl and Countess of Bathurst's magnificent estate in Gloucestershire. It's such a quintessentially English scene. Pristine white marquees, flags fluttering in a gentle summer breeze and smartly dressed, well-heeled country folk sipping champagne and treading in at halftime. It really is a different world. At one such event, I was introduced to the two polo-playing Princes, William and Harry. This I stress was in happier times, when they were speaking to each other. Prince Harry's team won that day and as he stepped up to receive the trophy and a magnum of Champagne, a woman on my right shouted out – "Well done Hewitt!" It took all my strength to contain a loud guffaw. We got talking and have remained firm friends ever since. So much so, I was invited to her wedding – to a senior Royal Airforce officer! My hope is that one day they will find themselves on the guest list of a Buckingham Palace garden party. Can you imagine the carnage?

Childline is another wonderful charity that I am only too happy to support. I once made a successful bid at an auction they ran, for a year-long membership to a rather exclusive film club held each month in a private cinema, in the very posh Mayfair Hotel in London. Barbara, my wife and I looked forward to these occasions as it was an opportunity to see all the big movies, pre-release. I remember quite clearly the first time we went, as it was, to say the least, a uniquely different experience from a trip to our local multiplex. On arrival at the hotel, we were checked in and escorted down a dimly lit marble staircase to the cinema's private bar where we enjoyed a pre-show cocktail. We must have somehow lost track of the time because we suddenly realised that most of the guests had gone into the cinema and had begun to take their seats for the show. We finished our drinks and joined the back of the queue and entered the jaw-droppingly lovely auditorium. To our immediate left, rising in rows almost to the ceiling, was the deep maroon, plush velvet seating. It was packed, hardly a seat left in the house – not surprising as this was the first private screening of the brand-new movie: 'Les Miserables'. As my eyes adjusted to the gloom and I began to scan the rows for a couple of spare seats, I was astonished to see an empty pair, right in the centre and about three-quarters of the way back – the sweet spot for sound and vision! I couldn't believe my luck! We pushed on up the stairs and as we arrived at the row, we excused ourselves as we shuffled awkwardly past those who were already seated, until we arrived at the vacant seats and sat down. I turned to my right to check that Barbara had settled in OK and as I did, was mortified to see the eighty-year-old face of the Queen's first cousin His Royal Highness, Prince Edward, the Duke of Kent – staring back at me. It was now abundantly clear why these two seats had been left empty! People around us were trying hard not to look but it was clear that everyone was. Luckily, at that point, the theatre house lights dimmed and afforded us a modicum of relief from what was an inadvertent breach of royal protocol. About two hours into the movie, Barbara gave me a nudge in the ribs with her elbow. I turned around and leant in closer to hear what she had to say.

"Don't look now," she whispered. "But he's fallen on top of me!"

I paused for a few seconds and slowly moved my gaze to her opposite shoulder, on which gently lay the balding pate of the Duke of Kent. His eyes were firmly closed and his chest, somnolently rising and falling in the arms of Morpheus.

"I think he's asleep," she continued.

As soon as she said it, we both saw one eye open and he slowly raised his head to the traditional upright position. I couldn't help but discern a slight knowing expression on his face, which made me chuckle. As the credits rolled on the almost three-hour-long film and the house lights faded up, the Duke got to his feet and turned to his companion and said in quite a loud voice: "Well, I didn't understand a word of that!" Outside on the street, we saw him approach a waiting black London cab. "Where to Guv'nor?" Said the cabbie through the nearside window. The reply? "St James' Palace please." And with that, he got in and sped off into the Mayfair night.

Gok Wan, is someone who I would never in my wildest dreams have expected to be working with, but I did, and I am so glad because the night in question will go down as one of my favourite live events of all time. Every year, Centrepoint hosts a massive pub quiz in a different venue. In 2016, The Box Nightclub in London's Soho was chosen. The Box is perhaps one of the most infamous clubs in London. On Thursday, Friday and Saturday nights, the rooms upstairs, it is rumoured throbbed to the sound of electro-beat and the slap of flesh on flesh. Downstairs in the tightly packed main room, which used to house Porn Baron Paul Raymond's Revue Bar, naked dancers would appear from the ceiling, lowered into the crowd on plush velvet ropes. The Centrepoint Pub Quiz that year was extraordinary. There was no stage to speak of, so Gok and I were forced to stand on tables and bar counters to present the show. The room was packed with celebrities from the world of British entertainment and some of the richest benefactors in Britain, who paid small fortunes to have these celebrities, sit at their table. Unknown to us both, the owner of The Box had decided to spice things up a little and arranged for one of his dancers to be lowered, naked, in a bathtub of bubbles into the centre of the room, right beside Gok and myself. What a night!

The Northern Ball was a staple on my event calendar for years. Held at the Old Trafford Cricket Ground in Manchester, it was the gathering and

Co-hosting a national award dinner with Huw Edwards
2019 – Grosvenor House, London.

With Seyi Obakin OBE. CEO Centrepoint and Princes William and Harry
2012 – Cirencester Park Polo Club, Gloucestershire.

social highlight of the year for travel agents north of the Watford Gap. There are certain professions that like to party. Hairdressers and travel agents are two that really know how to paint the town. The Northern Ball has to be one of the rowdiest, most drunken events that I have ever attended. The night always started with a modicum of civility and decorum, even though most of them appeared to have arrived fully pre-loaded. As the night wore on and the alcohol began to weave its inexorable magic, some of the Lycra mini-skirted, orange-faced women took to standing on the tables to show off their dance moves. Though I don't ever recall seeing on 'Strictly Come Dancing' or indeed on 'Dancing with the Stars', a routine that involved hitching up your dress and yanking your pants to one side! That night a £2000 LCD stage video monitor was smashed to smithereens following a misplaced kick by a stiletto heel, over two buckets of vomit had to be re-moved from the dance floor and judging by the stench of urine, I don't think many of them made it as far as the bathroom.

By far the grandest event, at which I have been the official announcer, was the Queen's Birthday Party, held at the Royal Albert Hall in London, on 21st April 2018 to celebrate the ninety-second birthday of the Monarch.

Organised by the Royal Commonwealth Society, the event coincided with the end of the 2018 Commonwealth Heads of Government Meeting, which had taken place during the previous week. The concert was presented by radio and television presenter Zoë Ball and featured contemporary artists, as well as those from the worlds of classical music and jazz, all of whom were from countries that belong to the Commonwealth of Nations. Artists included Tom Jones, Kylie Minogue, Sting, Shaggy, Shawn Mendes, Anne-Marie, The George Formby Society and Ladysmith Black Mambazo. The Queen was joined by other members of the Royal family in the Royal Box. The concert was also broadcast on BBC One and BBC Radio 2 in the UK and the Nine Network in Australia.

My previous outing to this most regal of venues, was for the 'World Latin Dance Championships' when I was at the very start of my career and I had to put up with not only having no dressing room but having to perform my commentary in the quick change area backstage. So, this time, as the seasoned professional that I now was, I was expecting my welcome to be somewhat grander. I needn't have got my hopes up. This time it was arguably worse. There was still no dressing room. I was provided with a

Hosting the Stock Exchange Small Cap Awards – 2018 – London.

fold-up plastic chair next to a stack of packing cases and a single Anglepoise lamp backstage, right next to the stage entrance. Still, at least I would have a grandstand seat right next to the performers as they made their entrances and exits. The concert went well, even though the audience were in place an hour before it started because of the tight security surrounding an extended Royal family and as many heads of state of Commonwealth countries as you could shake a stick at. The end of the show had a surprise twist and one I hadn't been expecting. I was shuffling my script together and as I turned around to find a wastepaper bin to put it in, my eye was met by the hem of an elaborately embroidered ball gown about ten inches from my chair. I looked up and there, standing next to Prince Charles was Her Majesty The Queen. My startled appearance must have amused her and before I almost fell off my chair, she smiled at me and gave me what I thought was an almost imperceptible wink with her left eye. Seconds later, out on stage, I heard Zoe Ball introducing the birthday girl, where she received the traditional hip-hip-hooray and three cheers, led by Charles and the audience. Her place backstage was taken seconds later by Prince Harry and his then-fiancée Meghan Markle. Observing them both from the unlit gloom of my commentary position, they looked to be very much in love. I couldn't help but wonder what the future held for them both. Now we all know, that the fairytale was more Hans Christian Anderson than Disney.

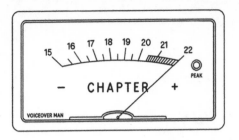

IT'S ALL GRAVY, BABY

I n the summer of 2018, my old pal and fellow Johannesburg survivor Alexander Armstrong invited me to be a contestant on his long-running BBC TV teatime quiz show 'Celebrity Pointless'. It's one of those shows that up until that point I had never really watched. I had caught the odd glimpse of it here and there but to be perfectly honest it had largely passed me by. Xander, however, is quite a persuasive chap, he is so polite and well mannered, it's hard to say no to him. In the run-up to Christmas the year before, he had asked me and Stephen Fry to perform seasonal readings at his uber posh Knightsbridge church carol concert. An evening that ended with him, my wife, Kirstie Allsop, Rob Brydon and me downing Limoncello shots in a Mayfair Italian restaurant followed by brandy and cigars, late into the night in 5 Hertford Street, which must surely be London's poshest and most ridiculously exclusive club.

As you have probably guessed by now, I agreed to appear on 'Pointless', so I stuck the date in my diary and promptly forgot about it. Two days before the recording at Elstree Studios in Hertfordshire, I thought that perhaps I should at least familiarise myself with the rules of the game. I sat through an episode I had recorded, watching it with a mild sense of rising

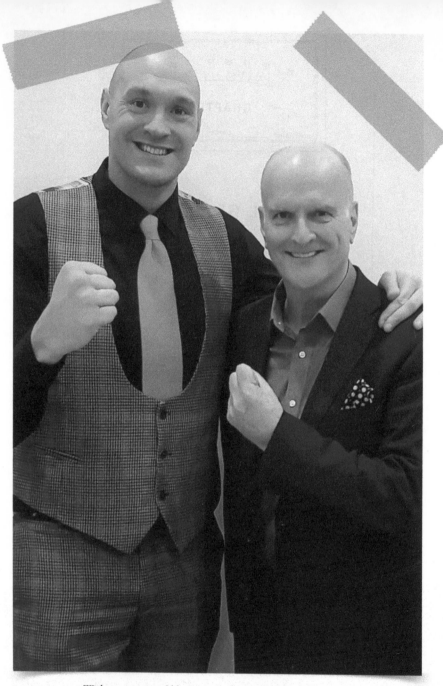

*With two-time world heavyweight boxing champion, Tyson Fury
2018 – Dressing room, Excel London.*

panic. I hadn't the foggiest idea what the show was about. From what I could tell, contestants had to guess the least likely answer to a question to gain maximum points. But that was my only understanding. I took some comfort in the fact that on this 'celebrity' voiceover special edition; I would be partnered up with Jon Briggs, the one-time voice of the Apple virtual AI assistant 'Siri'. I could always ask him if I didn't know the answer! The day arrived and I was shown into my dressing room at the studios, feeling very apprehensive. No, I tell a lie. I was crapping myself. I headed out into the corridor to find Jon's dressing room.

"Do you know how this game works mate?" I said.

"No." was his monosyllabic reply. "Do you?"

"No," I said.

"Great, then we will both look like complete dicks!"

Fantastic, we were both about to publicly humiliated on national television.

When the time came, we were marched like condemned prisoners from our holding pen onto the studio floor, where a small but appreciative audience of pensioners awaited, like the judge and jury in a murder trial. My instinct was screaming at me to bolt out of the door and run until I reached the main road but by that time, the door had been firmly bolted.

Xander and Richard, the hosts, appeared on the studio floor to rapturous applause and before we knew it, we were off. Round after round, although dazed and confused like a couple of pensioners grappling with the internet, Jon and I seemed to inexplicably keep on winning, despite one awkward moment when I confused an archive recording of the voice Mahatma Gandhi for that of George Bernard Shaw! That brought the house down, for all the wrong reasons. In these touchy, uber-sensitive, politically correct times – I wondered in my head whether my answer might have come over as being ever so slightly casually racist. The rest of the show is a bit of a blur but my lasting memory of it is of Jon and I at the very end, being the last men standing on the shiny winners' podium – each of us being presented with our winning and I have to say, now highly coveted Perspex 'Pointless' trophies.

Looking back on my career so far has been quite an illuminating process. I can honestly say that I have enjoyed every single mad second of it. I have met the most wonderful and not so wonderful people, laughed lots and learned so much about not only myself but about others. I have indeed been more fortunate than I could ever have imagined. My father was right when he said, pick a job you love, and you will never do a day's work in your entire life. I didn't understand him at the time, but I sure do now. Thanks, Dad. If he were alive today, I think he would be quietly pleased with the way I turned out.

In Chapter twelve, I briefly mentioned Hugh Edwards, who is a video games voice and casting director. For several years, we had been running 'bricks and mortar' courses for actors who wanted to get into the gaming sector. After much discussion and it has to be said copious amounts of white wine, we decided to launch a global online school for voice talent. A place, where both the seasoned pro and the complete beginner could come, to exchange ideas and learn new skills. And so, the oddly named 'Gravy for the Brain' was born. To date, I am pleased to say we have trained and provided mentorship and guidance to almost 54,000 actors around the world and set home recording studios up for quite a few, including the stage and screen actor, Hugh Bonneville.

Our company – *'gravyforthebrain.com'* is now the planet's biggest voice acting training academy with a global presence and is growing exponentially with each passing year. After over forty-three years as a voice actor and Hugh's twenty-plus years as a director, we have between us a wealth of experience that we felt we had a duty to pass on to those coming behind us. We now have offices and territory controllers in South America, the USA, Canada, Arabia, Scandinavia, Spain, France, Australia and New Zealand with more countries coming online, as each year passes. It feels good to have finally reinvented my purpose one more time. Helping others get to where they want to be continues to be a real undiluted and unexpected pleasure. It has not come about however without its problems. Some of the old school, more seasoned VO pros have sadly taken a dim view of our enterprise. The chief accusation it seems is that we have opened an otherwise firmly closed door and in so doing we have enabled and encouraged many newcomers to our profession, affording them a foothold in an industry where the route to entry had been pretty opaque. Well, balls to them I say, it's not an exclusive club. No one is guaranteed a living. 'Times they are a-changin', my friends," nothing stays the same. We might as well have them inside the tent, pissing out as outside pissing in. Our industry is changing as rapidly as any other. The digital revolution heralded not only a sea change in the way we work but it lowered the barriers to entry to those who before, would simply never have got a look in. Those who hire voices can do so with the click of a mouse, from the comfort of their office. '*Gravyforthebrain.com*' has undoubtedly raised the standard of voiceover professionals globally and has opened the door to a fantastic career to many, who would otherwise never have had the chance. How do I know this? Because I receive the most wonderful testimonials and daily messages of thanks, from people all over the world. Here are just a few:

"I've really enjoyed signing up to 'gravyforthebrain.com', I've been an actor and voiceover for a long time and when I started there was very little training or advice out there. I can see how much there is to learn and I'm really enjoying keeping up and getting up to date! It can feel very lonely at times working as a voiceover and the support on there is brilliant! Thank you!"

"I've been a member with 'gravyforthebrain.com' for the past eighteen months and I can honestly say it's been fundamental to the success of my voiceover business. Their regular webinars have helped me upgrade my studio to a pro standard, which has ultimately reflected in the number of jobs I have picked up in the time I've been with them. Hugh & Peter have built a unique resource for voiceover talent across the world that stands against scammers and low-payers, by educating EVERYONE involved in the industry on all sides. Thank you, gentlemen."

"I've been in the business for a long time. So have the folks at 'gravyforthebrain.com'. Their input has been on point in getting my marketing up to standard. While they are straightforward in their assessments, they always soften it with genuine care and a sense of humour. I have found them engaging, informative, and correct. I just started my new marketing effort late last week and I've already booked two very good jobs. I recommend them highly. In fact, I recommended them to a friend over the weekend."

"Simply the most comprehensive one-stop-shop for voiceover talent on the web. No matter where you are in your professional journey, 'gravyforthebrain.com' will help you start, stay current and remain relevant. The staff is outstanding, and the focus is on continuous improvement and education – in both business and performance. If you're serious about your voiceover career, check them out."

Clueless with Jon Briggs on 'Pointless Celebrities' – 2018 – Elstree Studios, London.

Comments like these and our five-star rating on Google reaffirm my belief that we have done and continue to do the right thing for the industry. Alongside the virtual offering, we also run numerous 'One Voice Conference' events and awards around the world bringing together those in our industry to socialise have fun and learn together. If you are even remotely interested in voiceover, I would like to think that one day you might join us. Join us anyway; you'll have a right laugh!

Well folks, there you have it. I hope that it has given you some insight into my world. I have spent the last forty-three years locked in acoustically isolated, padded rooms shouting about pizzas, cars, gas boilers and three-piece suites, playing zombies and wizards and fighter pilots and working with and alongside some of the planet's biggest stars. And yes – I've had the most unimaginable fun. I have been the voice of over 200 TV series, many of them multi-award-winning, the promo voice for over 60 TV channels, acted on over 30 of the world's top-selling AAA game titles and I've voiced over 30,000 TV and radio commercials. Perhaps surprisingly, very little of what I have done survives, much of it having been broadcast, is now far away in the ether – halfway to Mars – and will eventually clatter around the cosmos forever. God help the inhabitants on Planet Zarg at the outer reaches of our universe when 'The X Factor' eventually reaches them in the 25ᵗʰ Century. Lord only knows what they will make of it!

My agent has just called. Tomorrow at precisely 10am, I will be in a post-production studio in Soho, giving voice to a cat for an anthropomorphic pet food commercial. Well, we started this journey with me barking like a bitch on heat for Pedigree Chum, so this seems like a good place to place to leave it. Wish me luck and keep your ears open. You'll be hearing from me soon. Woof, Woof! Or should that be – Miaow, Miaow?

Posing as HM Queen for an E4 TV Promo – 2018 – Goldsmiths Hall, London.

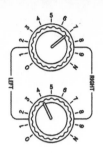

A MESSAGE FROM
THE AUTHOR

⊢————————————⊣

Thank you very much for buying this book. If you enjoyed
reading it, please consider leaving a review on Amazon.
It would mean the world to me. Very many thanks.

Find out more about the author: *peterdickson.co.uk*

Twitter — *@peterdickson*
Instagram — *@peterdickson*

To learn more about the art of voiceover join — *gravyforthebrain.com*

Peter is represented by Hobsons — *hobsons-international.com*